One Hundred Days of Healing

Other books by Caroline Pover

One Month in Tohoku:
An Englishwoman's memoir on life after the Japanese tsunami
(Winner of Best Memoir, The Next Generation Indie Book Awards)

Being A Broad in Japan:
Everything a Western woman needs to survive and thrive

Guide to International Schools in Japan
(English and Japanese editions)

Ask Caroline
(student and teacher editions)

Love with a Western woman: A guide for Japanese men
(English and Japanese editions)

Covid Vaccine Adverse Reaction Survival Guide

Caroline also produces a collection of sweary planners, notebooks, and stickers under "The Sweary Planner"

A WORKBOOK FOR
SICKNESS,

SEPARATION & SORROW

One Hundred Days of Healing

Caroline Pover

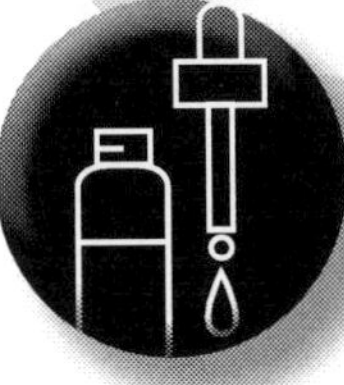

One Hundred Days of Healing: A Workbook for Sickness, Separation & Sorrow

Creator, designer, typesetter: Caroline Pover with thanks to Dexter Fry for guidance
Proofreader: Cindy Fujimoto
Cover design and icons: Simon May – May Media Graphic Design

First edition.

ISBN 978-1-8380727-9-7

For Michelle

Who is this for?

This workbook is for anyone who wants to dedicate some time to healing.

This could be time spent healing after the end of a relationship, a bereavement, or any kind of trauma. All of these events – expected or not – require significant adjustments in life. They often involve grieving the life or the person that existed before. Perhaps that person you grieve is yourself, and who **you** were before. This book is for you.

It is for anyone who is dealing with a serious illness, or perhaps recovering from major surgery. Maybe your recovery means that you are unable to work, exercise, or enjoy your usual hobbies. Maybe you are temporarily struggling to fulfil your usual responsibilities and are finding it frustrating to be forced into convalescence. Maybe you are finding it difficult to give yourself time to heal and are keen to get on with life again. Maybe you have countless healthcare appointments and treatments to manage. This book is for you too.

This book is especially for anyone dealing with a long-term, complicated, and perhaps permanent illness. It is intended to specifically help you manage the appointments, treatments, research, and emotional impact that accompany a chronic condition, especially in the early days.

We live in a world that expects us to "get back to normal" as soon as we can after a life-changing event. We are expected to get divorced, bury a loved one, have an operation, or deal with a chronic condition as quickly as possible and then return to what life was like before. For many people, life can never be the same as before. If you have lived through anything like what I've mentioned here, and now feel utterly lost, then this book is for you.

It is for anyone who is feeling depressed or anxious, or finding it difficult to live with their emotions, regardless of whether the cause is identifiable or not. Your feelings are valid and show that you are human. You don't need a reason for them.

You don't need any **big** life-changing event to be your reason for using this workbook. We have all had times in our lives when we haven't been getting enough sleep, when our diet hasn't been especially healthy, when we have spent too much time in front of our phones, and have lost sight of the love that exists in our lives. If all you want to do is keep your life in balance, then this workbook is for you as well.

This book is designed to be appropriate for children as well as adults, although younger children may need support in understanding some of the vocabulary. I hope that by teaching kids about the many different words they can use to define their emotions, they will grow to become adults for whom the "hard" emotions are easier to sit with.

This book won't "fix" anything. It won't bring a loved one back, it won't make everything OK again, and it won't make the pain disappear.

But I do hope it will be your friend as you dedicate yourself to healing.

Ways you could use this workbook

Firstly, and most importantly, don't feel like you have to work your way through this book every single day for one hundred days. If you just want to commit to one hundred days of healing within a year, or not within any timeframe at all, then just do that. If you **are** the kind of person who likes to focus on something every day, then by all means, go for it!

Use coloured pens or pencils if you like – you don't have to use black pen or a pencil. Or just use an ordinary pen. Use a lip liner if it does the job. Write, note, doodle, anywhere you like. There's plenty of space.

Each double-page spread is divided into several sections. Here are some ideas for how you could use them if you need a bit of inspiration to get you going.

Today's Loving Moments is intended to help us stop and identify them, even when we're having a really tough day – perhaps especially when we're having a really tough day. Whether we spent a few moments stroking the dog, or we spotted an elderly couple holding hands, or perhaps we tended to the single cactus we have managed to keep going – all of these things are sending love out into the world. These loving moments in our days don't have to be about someone loving **us**, or us loving someone else – this is just a section where you can think about love and what it means on that day, to you.

How I Feel Today is a way to help identify emotions that can so easily feel overwhelming, especially if there are a lot of emotions happening all at once. Sometimes it's really difficult to identify exactly what we're feeling, so hopefully this list will help – there's also space to put other emotions. You could circle, highlight, or cross out words in this section, and it might be interesting to see if the same words crop up over and over again.

how I feel today ...
accepting afraid amazed angry annoyed
anxious bereft blessed bitter calm cautious
cheerful comforted confused contented
defeated defiant delighted desperate
determined disappointed disgusted

The **Healing Appointments**, **Resources**, **Expenses**, and **Tests & Results** section might help you organise some practicalities without letting them take over your day – it can be so easy to allow healthcare management to dominate life. Perhaps this section can be a good place to note down interesting books or websites that might be useful for you to come back to later, rather than having to immediately go to your phone and get stuck browsing. Perhaps this section might prompt you to book a massage that you have been meaning to get.

The **Activity** section could be a way to keep track of everything physical, social, and restful, as well as monitoring screen time if that's something you think isn't helping you. Sometimes it can be easy to get to a week without having had any human interaction – hopefully this will help.

There are so many different ways to use the **Food & Drink** section! You could use it restrospectively, so you can see what you've already eaten, and perhaps use that information to see if your nutrition is impacting your healing. Or you could use it as a meal planner, to organise that day, or plan ahead for a week. You could write in it, or if you're feeling artistic, then draw pictures of your food. There is space to write specific nutritional elements all around it, so if you like to make sure you're getting enough of a specific vitamin, then you could monitor that. And if you're fasting, then you could just add the times for when you'll be eating the delicious food you've planned. You could even annotate this section with the special place you had a meal at, or the people you shared that meal with.

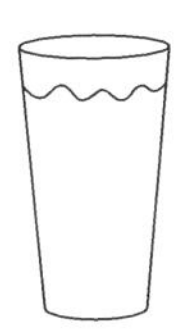

The **Lotions & Potions** section could be used not just for keeping track of remedies you might be taking to help you through this healing time, or that might be a part of your daily routine anyway, but also for taking notes on other products that you might want to explore later. It might be handy to keep track of what you've taken, if you don't already have something to follow.

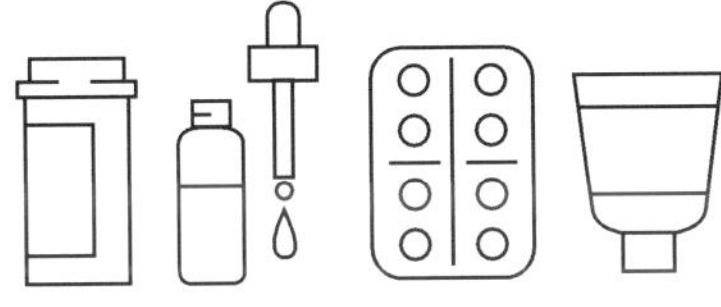

In the **Connections with Nature** section, you could write notes on places you have been, or plan to visit, that are focused on the world outdoors. You could use this section just to spend some time sketching something in nature. Maybe you want to try to do more hiking, and this workbook might be your inspiration. Being with nature doesn't have to be anything big though – even something as simple as spending a few minutes watching the clouds go by could be something that brings your thoughts to nature for a while.

Sometimes when we're trying to focus on healing, or when we're dealing with a challenging time, intrusive thoughts can take over our minds and distract us. The **Wondering & Wandering Thoughts** bubble-cloud is intended to be space for when thoughts feel like they're running away. If you find yourself trying to understand "Why?" rather a lot, then this could be a good place to just get those questions out, and perhaps come back to them another time, or just leave them on paper rather than in your mind.

There's also a daily planner running down the side of every page, which you could use to organise your day or keep track of things like sleep. Perhaps, if you're taking time away from a normal routine in order to deal with this particular life challenge, you might use the planner to try to retain some level of routine. Maybe you want to set aside specific time each day just to focus on you and your healing.

These are just some ideas for how to use ***One Hundred Days of Healing***. There is no right or wrong way. We are all different and there are so many different ways to prioritise our healing. I just hope that this helps you as you prioritise yours.

With love,
Caroline
xxx

One Hundred Days

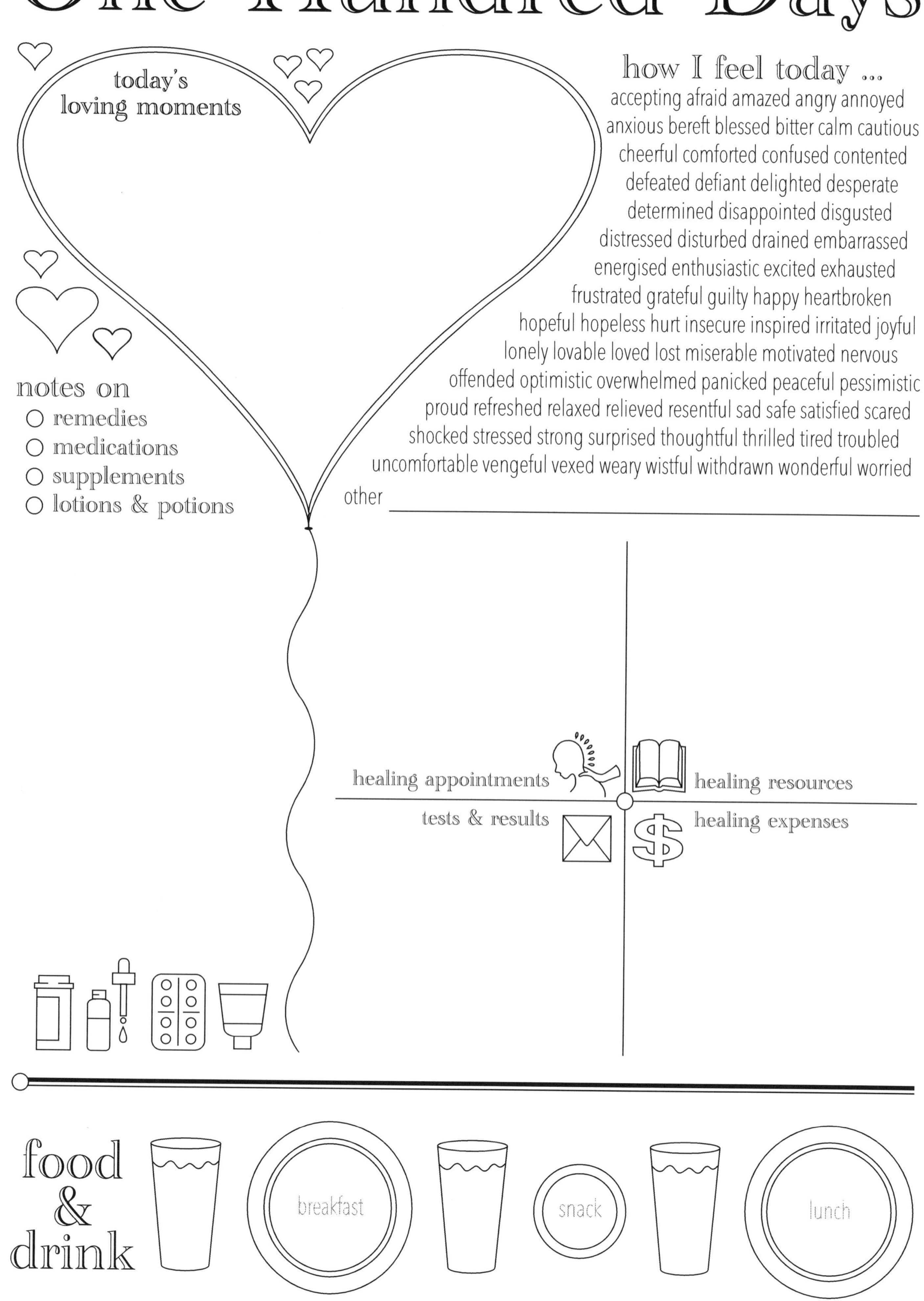

# of Healing

physical activity

social activity

screen time

resting time

connections with nature

wondering & wandering thoughts

snack

dinner

day 1

midnight

1am

2am

3am

4am

5am

6am

7am

8am

9am

10am

11am

midday

1pm

2pm

3pm

4pm

5pm

6pm

7pm

8pm

9pm

10pm

11pm

midnight

date:

One Hundred Days

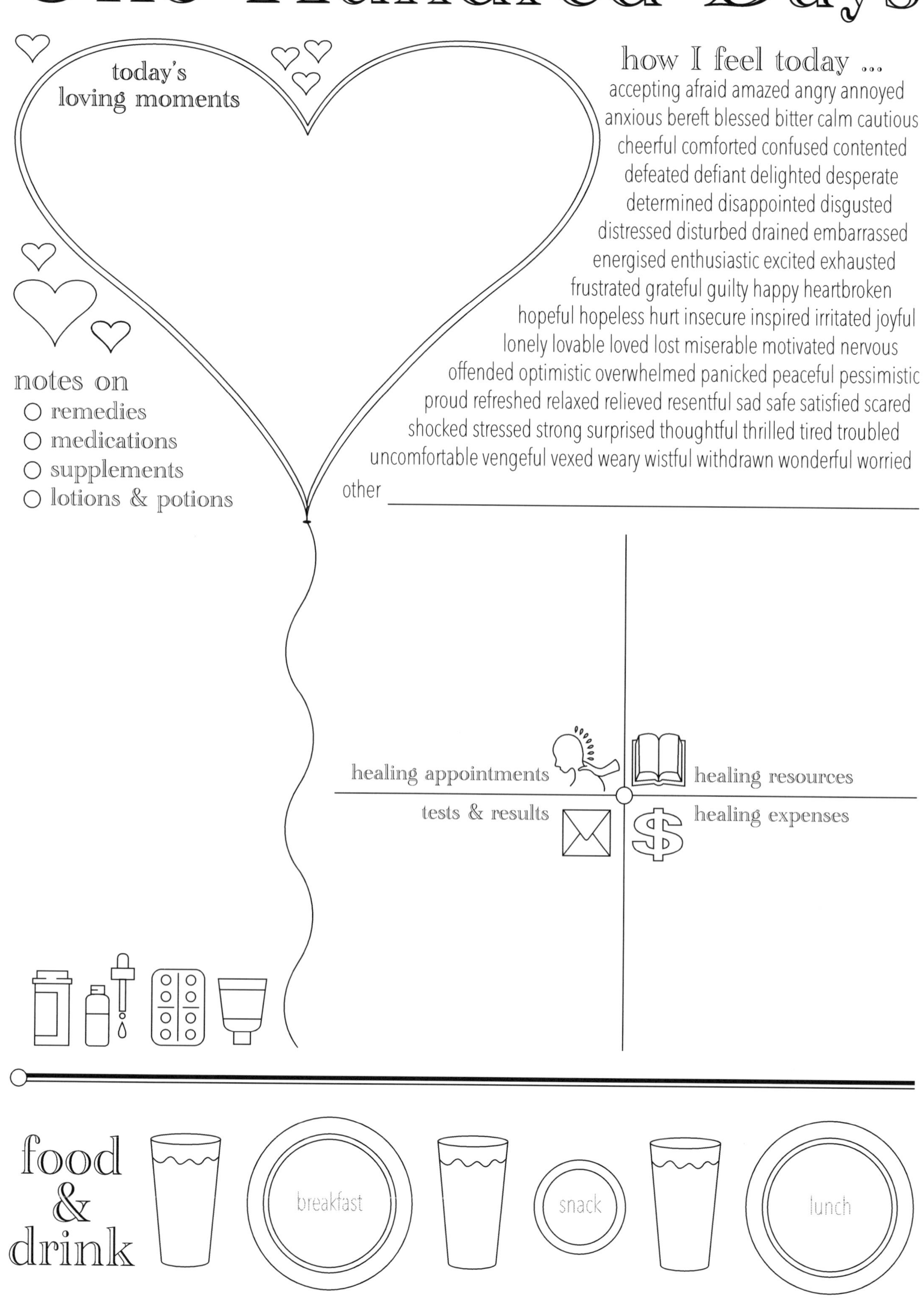

# of Healing

physical activity

social activity

screen time

resting time

connections with nature

wondering & wandering thoughts

snack

dinner

day 2

midnight

1am

2am

3am

4am

5am

6am

7am

8am

9am

10am

11am

midday

1pm

2pm

3pm

4pm

5pm

6pm

7pm

8pm

9pm

10pm

11pm

midnight

date:

One Hundred Days

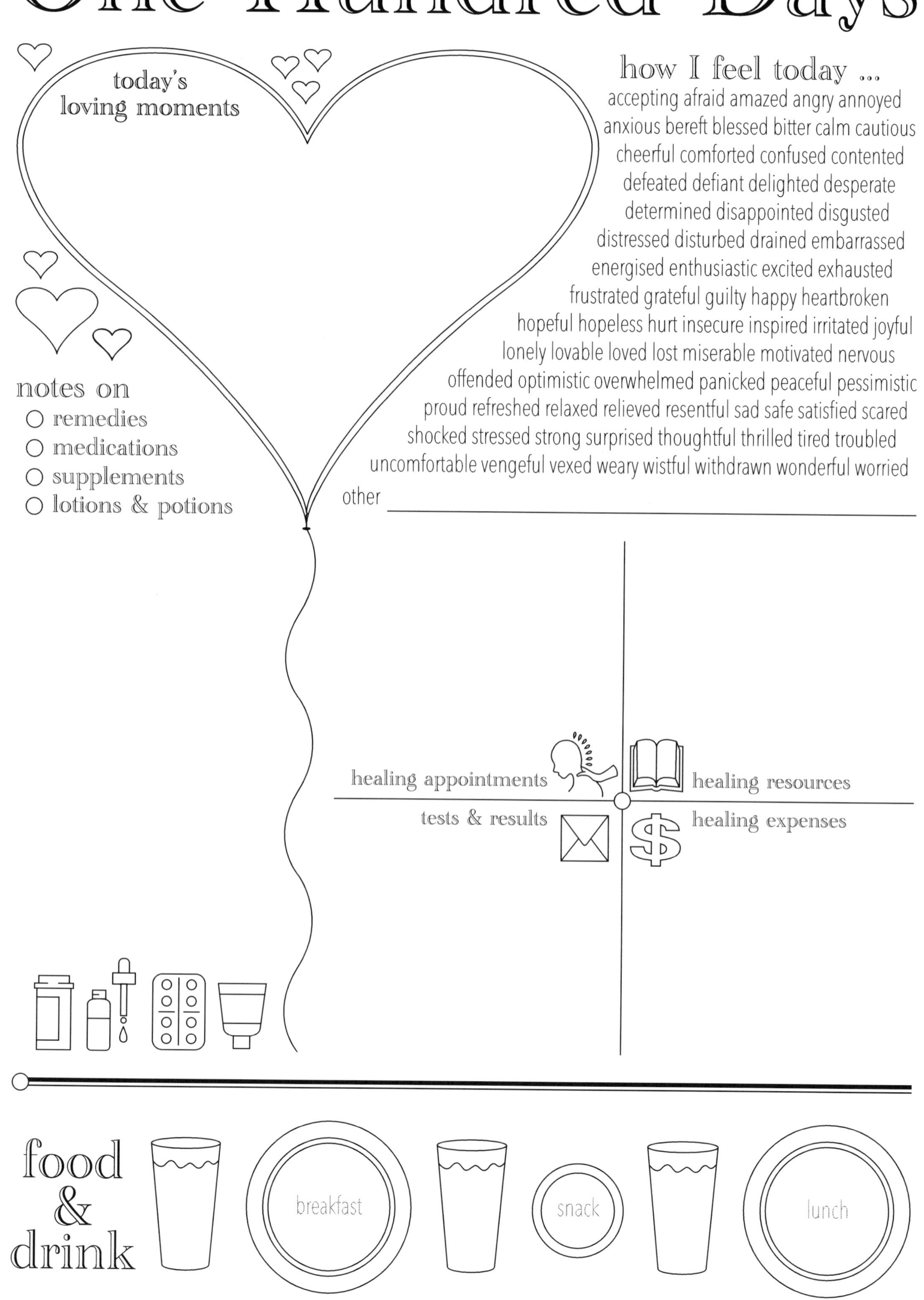

food & drink

breakfast

snack

lunch

# of Healing

physical activity

social activity

screen time

resting time

connections with nature

wondering & wandering thoughts

snack

dinner

day 3

midnight

1am

2am

3am

4am

5am

6am

7am

8am

9am

10am

11am

midday

1pm

2pm

3pm

4pm

5pm

6pm

7pm

8pm

9pm

10pm

11pm

midnight

date:

One Hundred Days

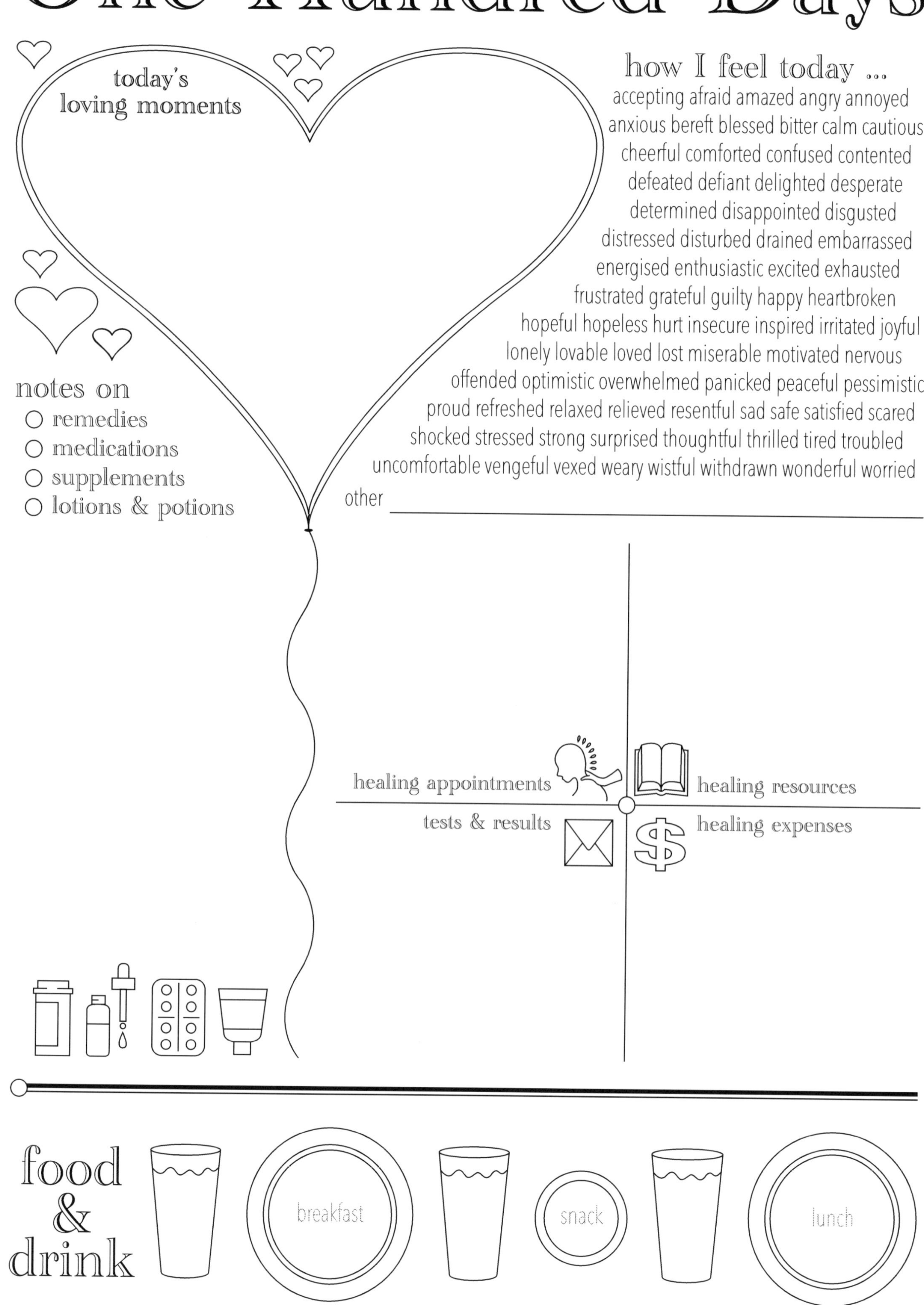

# of Healing

physical activity

social activity

screen time

resting time

connections with nature

wondering & wandering thoughts

day 4

midnight

1am

2am

3am

4am

5am

6am

7am

8am

9am

10am

11am

midday

1pm

2pm

3pm

4pm

5pm

6pm

7pm

8pm

9pm

10pm

11pm

midnight

date:

One Hundred Days

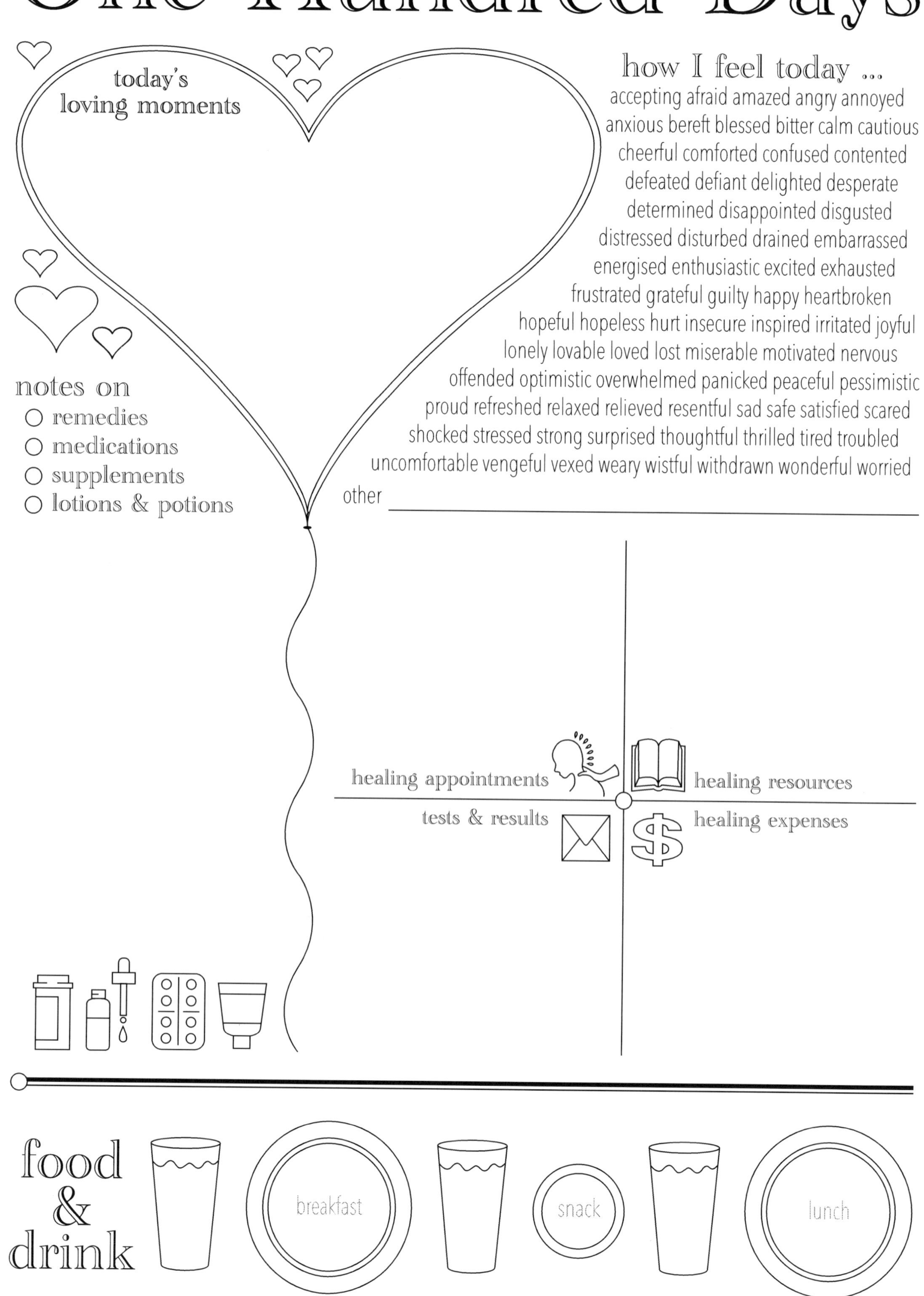

# of Healing

physical activity

social activity

screen time

resting time

connections with nature

wondering & wandering thoughts

snack

dinner

day 5

midnight

1am

2am

3am

4am

5am

6am

7am

8am

9am

10am

11am

midday

1pm

2pm

3pm

4pm

5pm

6pm

7pm

8pm

9pm

10pm

11pm

midnight

date:

One Hundred Days

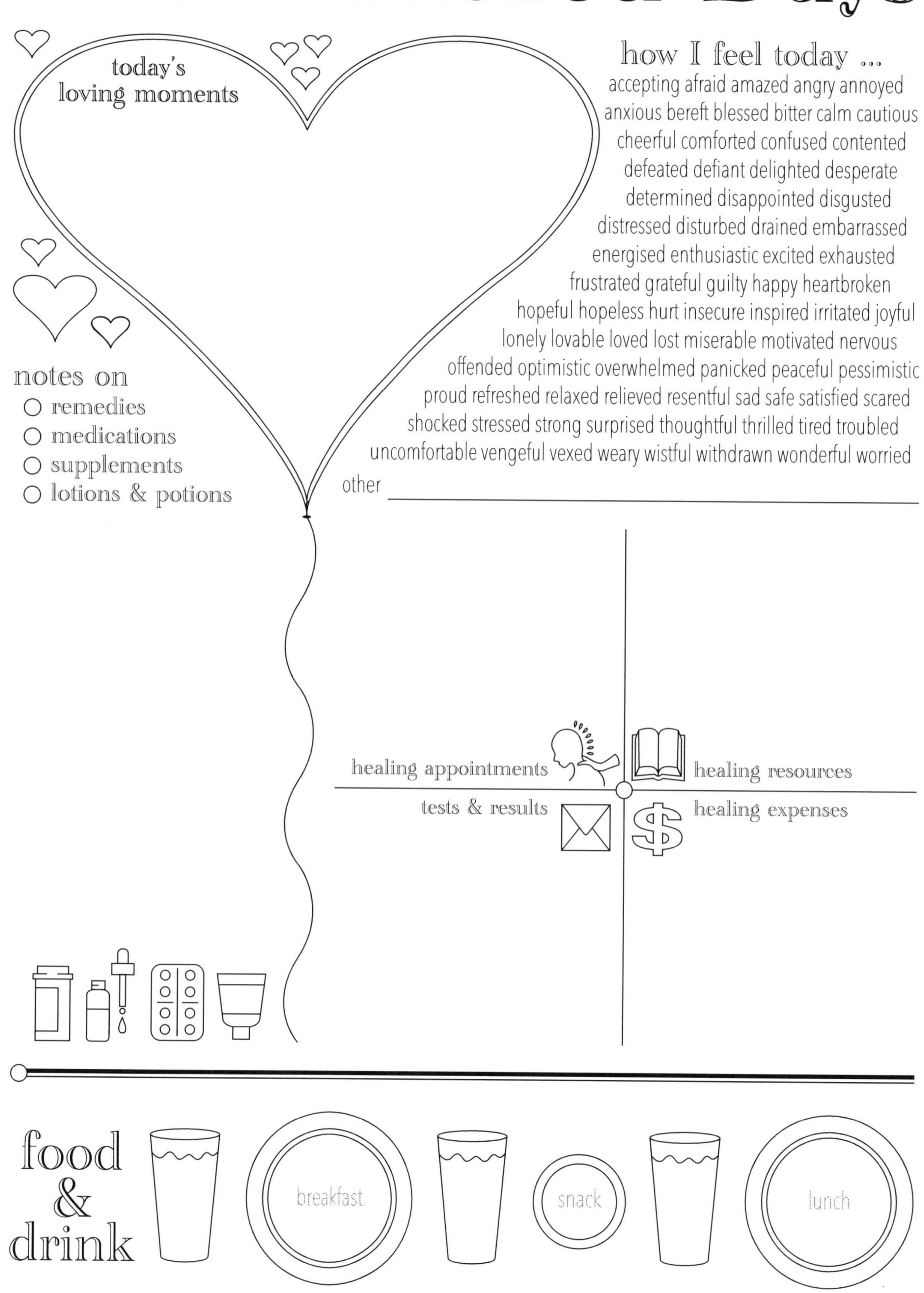

food & drink

breakfast

snack

lunch

# of Healing

physical activity

social activity

screen time

resting time

connections with nature

wondering & wandering thoughts

snack

dinner

day 6

midnight

1am

2am

3am

4am

5am

6am

7am

8am

9am

10am

11am

midday

1pm

2pm

3pm

4pm

5pm

6pm

7pm

8pm

9pm

10pm

11pm

midnight

date:

One Hundred Days

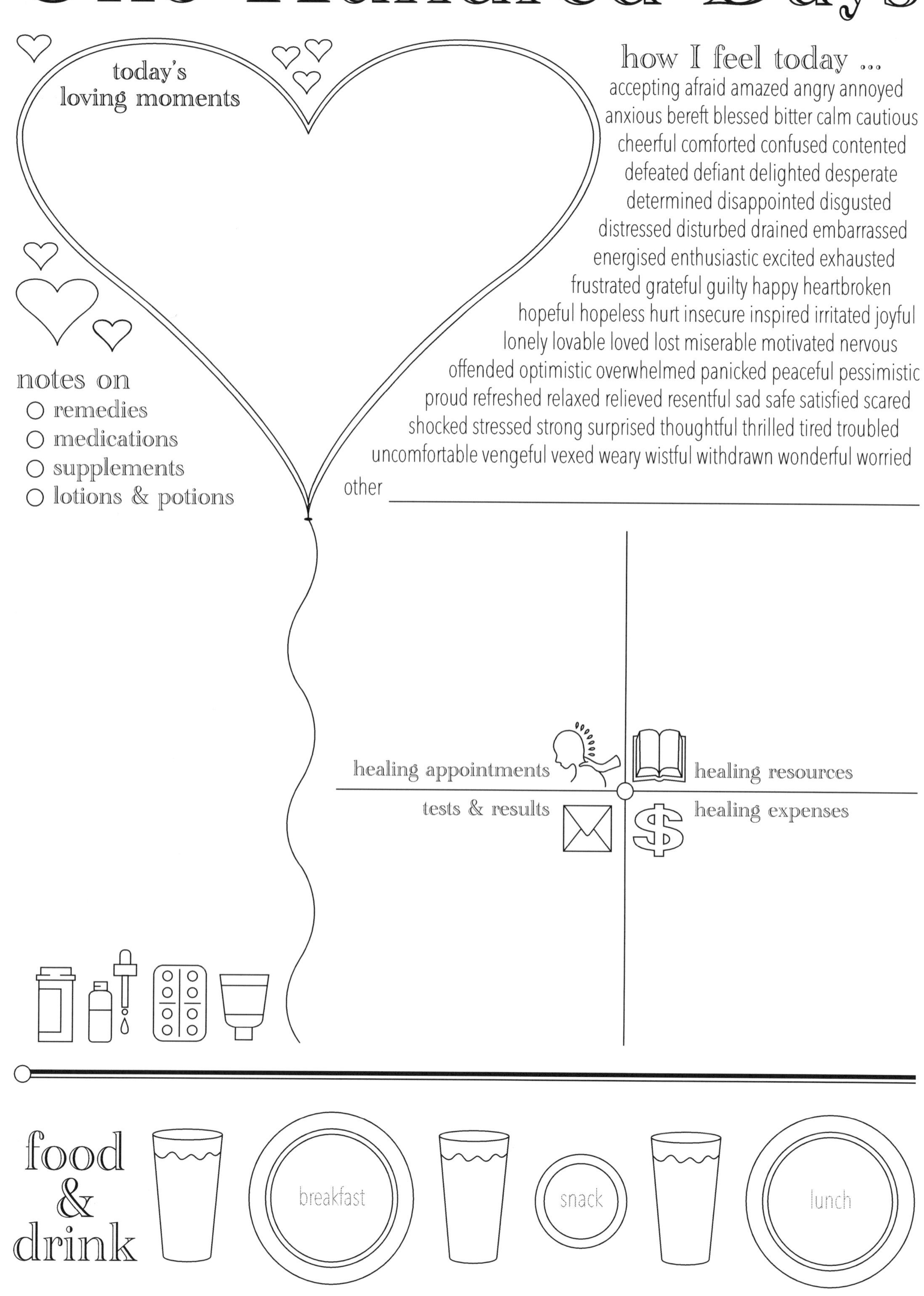

food & drink

breakfast

snack

lunch

# of Healing

physical activity

social activity

screen time

resting time

connections with nature

wondering & wandering thoughts

snack

dinner

day 7

midnight

1am

2am

3am

4am

5am

6am

7am

8am

9am

10am

11am

midday

1pm

2pm

3pm

4pm

5pm

6pm

7pm

8pm

9pm

10pm

11pm

midnight

date:

One Hundred Days

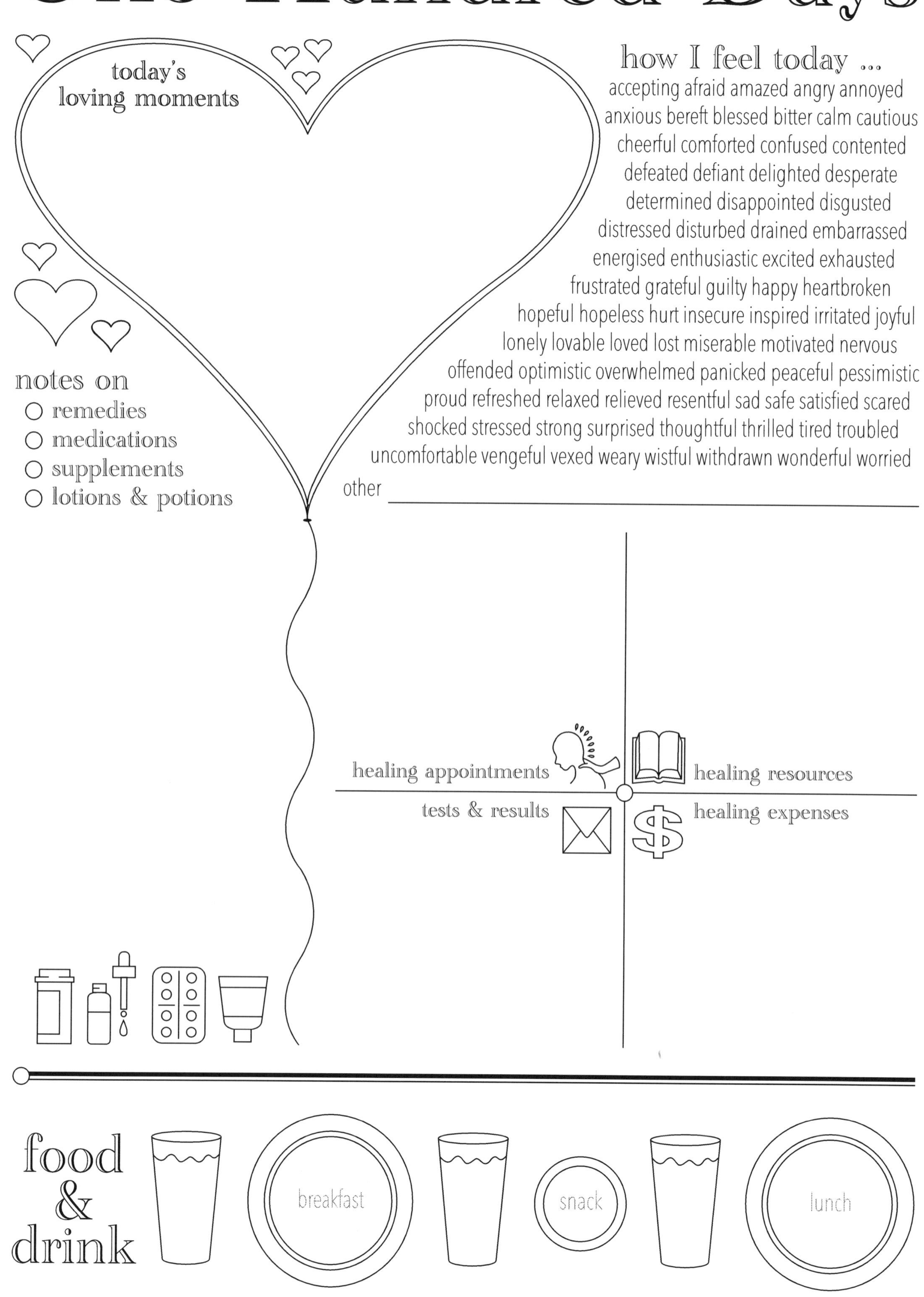

# of Healing

physical activity

social activity

screen time

resting time

connections with nature

wondering & wandering thoughts

snack

dinner

day 8

midnight

1am

2am

3am

4am

5am

6am

7am

8am

9am

10am

11am

midday

1pm

2pm

3pm

4pm

5pm

6pm

7pm

8pm

9pm

10pm

11pm

midnight

date:

One Hundred Days

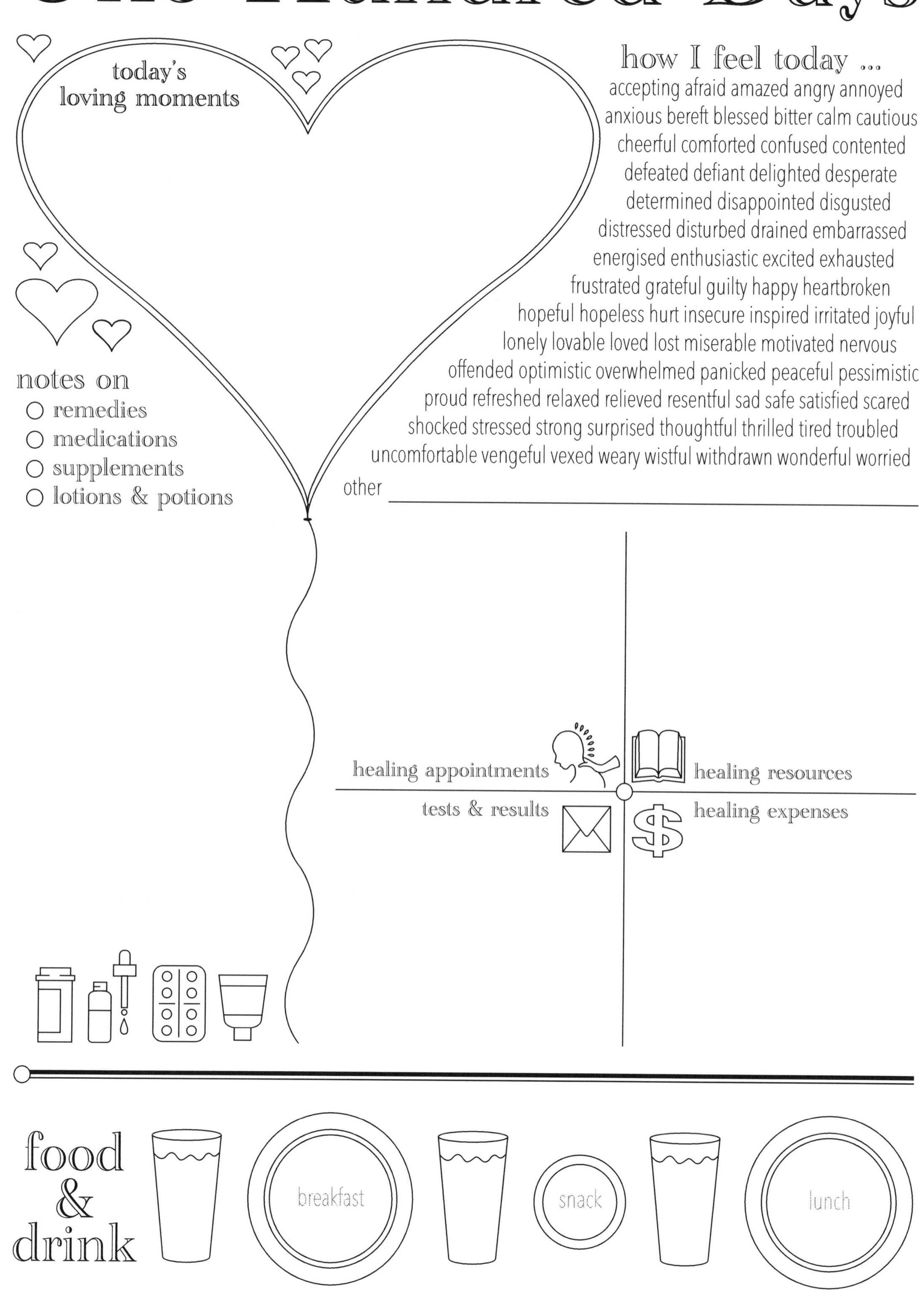

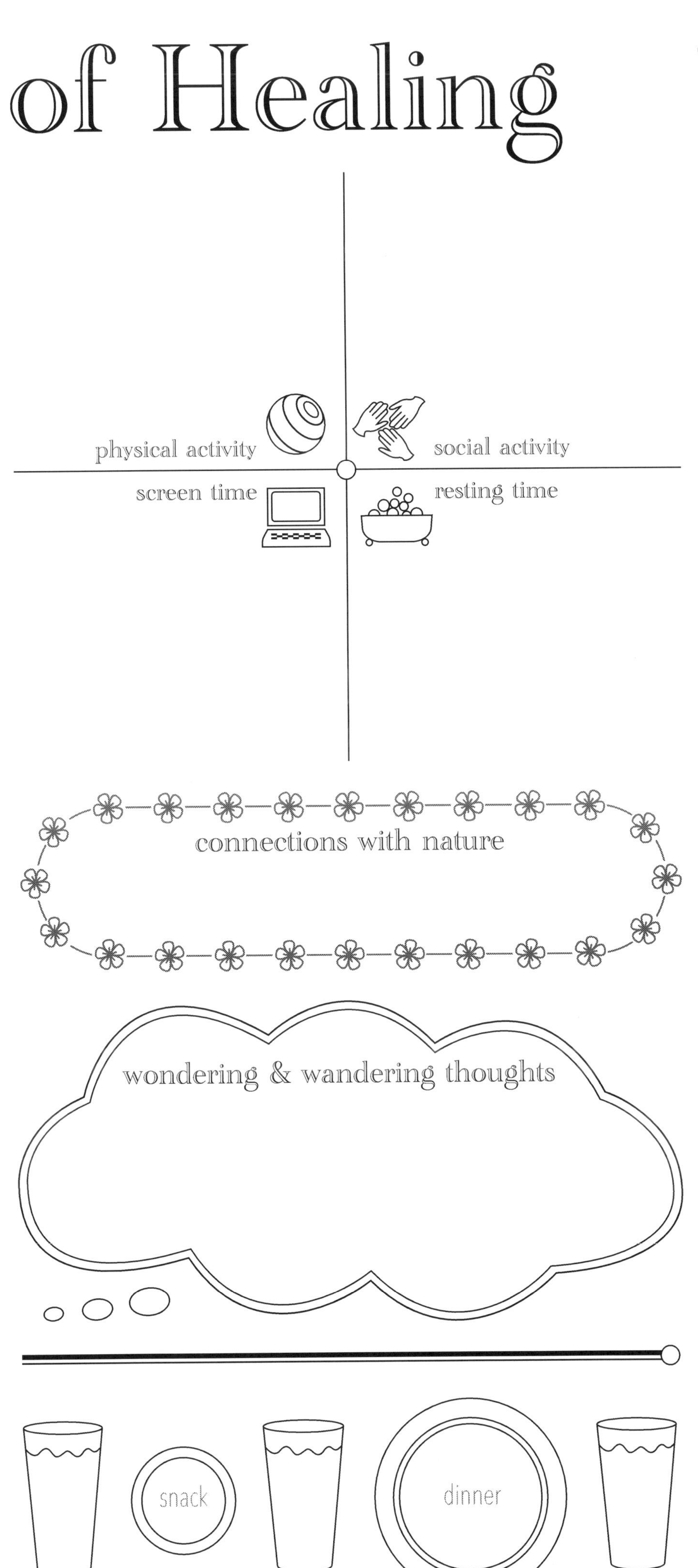

day 9

midnight

1am

2am

3am

4am

5am

6am

7am

8am

9am

10am

11am

midday

1pm

2pm

3pm

4pm

5pm

6pm

7pm

8pm

9pm

10pm

11pm

midnight

date:

One Hundred Days

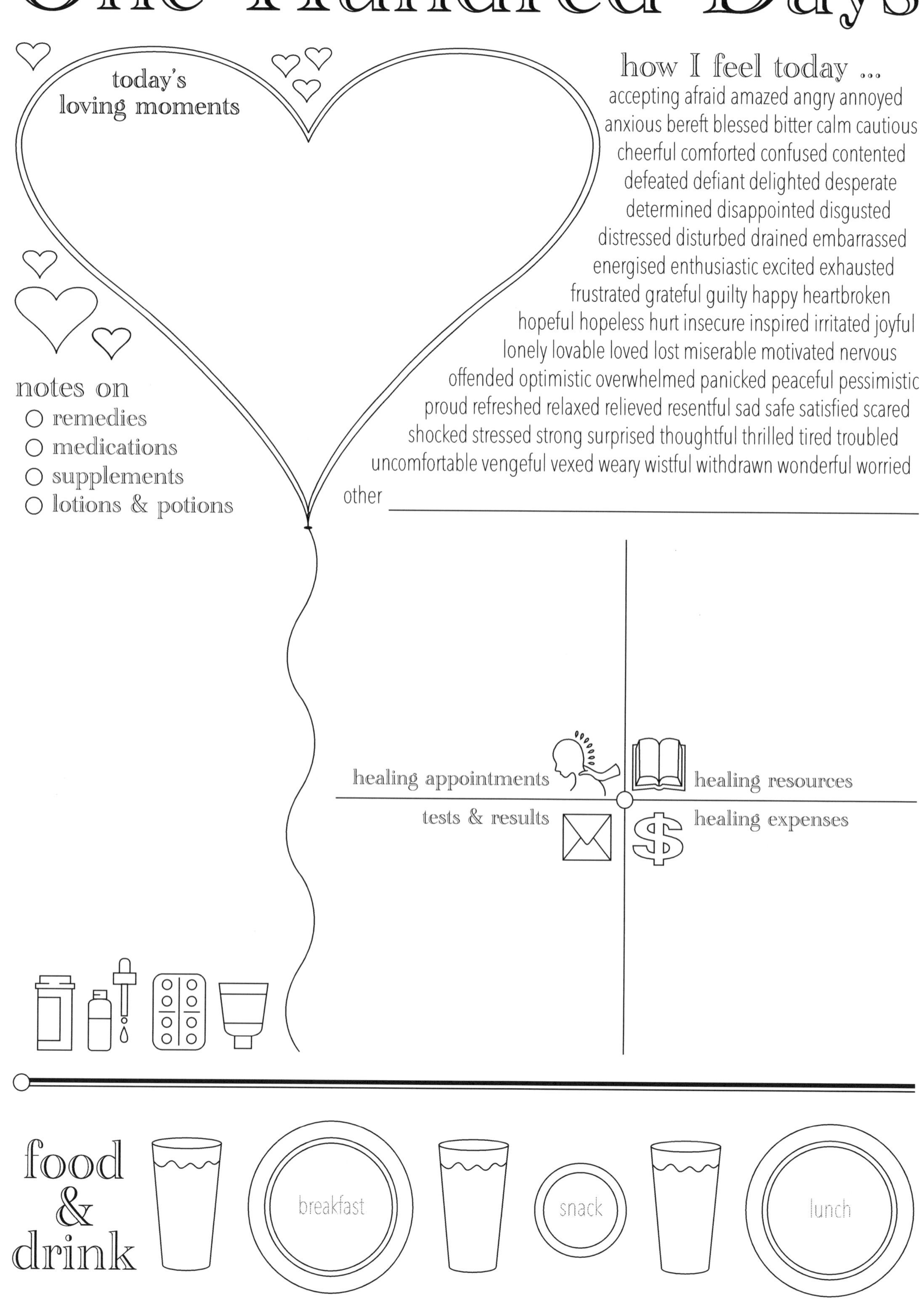

# of Healing

physical activity

social activity

screen time

resting time

connections with nature

wondering & wandering thoughts

snack

dinner

day 10

midnight

1am

2am

3am

4am

5am

6am

7am

8am

9am

10am

11am

midday

1pm

2pm

3pm

4pm

5pm

6pm

7pm

8pm

9pm

10pm

11pm

midnight

date:

One Hundred Days

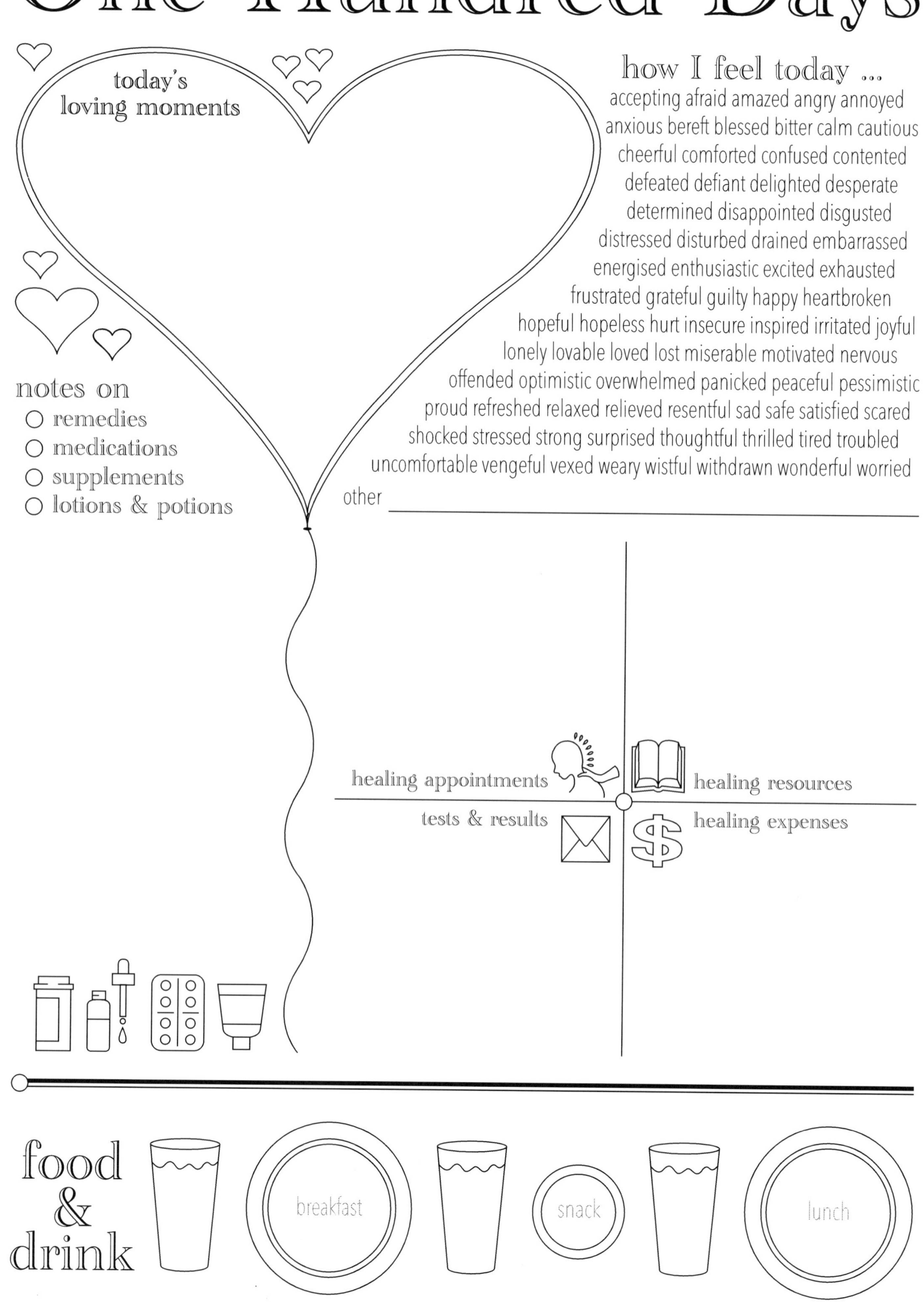

# of Healing

day 11

midnight

1am

2am

3am

4am

5am

6am

7am

8am

9am

10am

11am

midday

1pm

2pm

3pm

4pm

5pm

6pm

7pm

8pm

9pm

10pm

11pm

midnight

date:

One Hundred Days

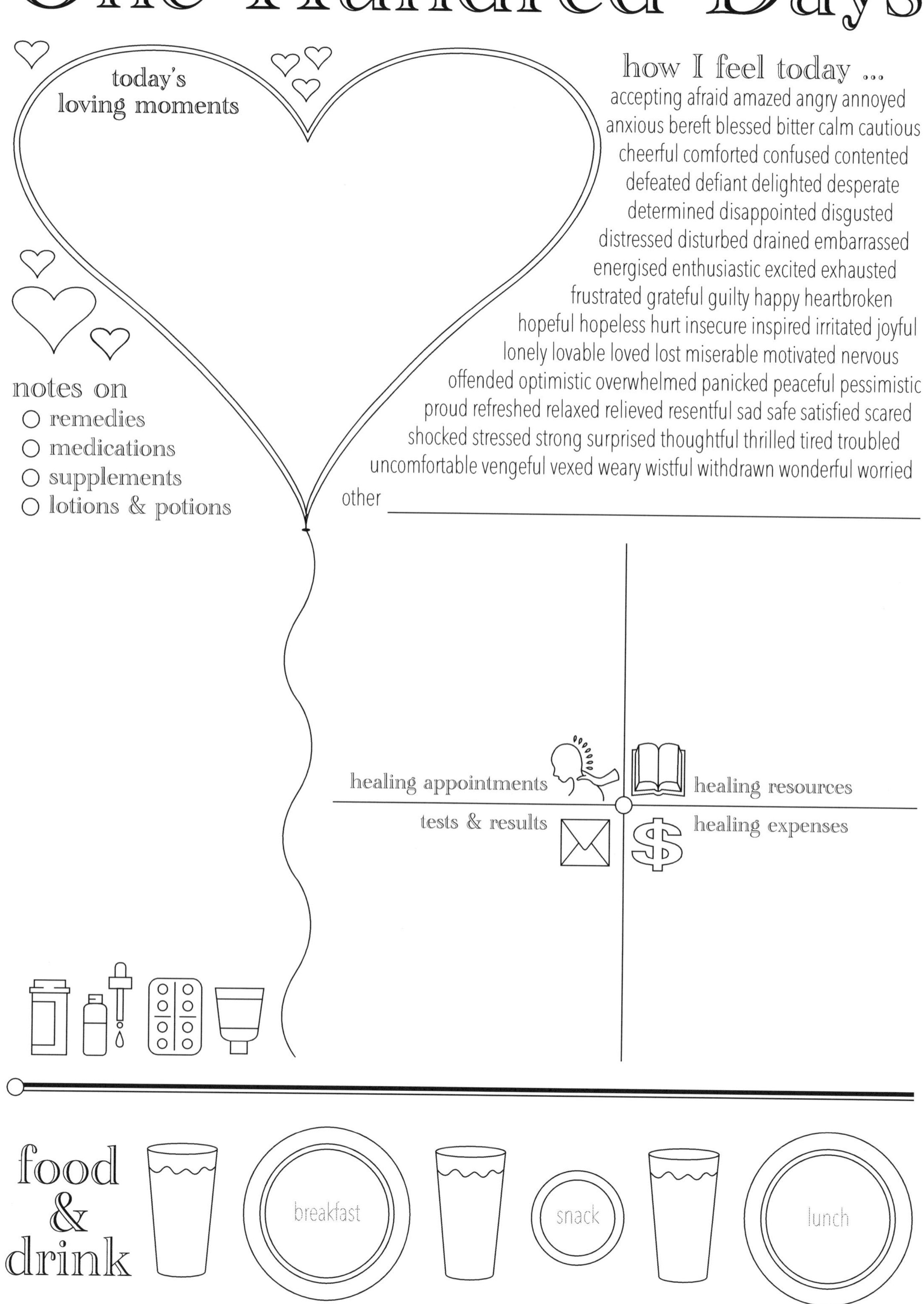

# of Healing

physical activity

social activity

screen time

resting time

connections with nature

wondering & wandering thoughts

snack

dinner

day 12

midnight

1am

2am

3am

4am

5am

6am

7am

8am

9am

10am

11am

midday

1pm

2pm

3pm

4pm

5pm

6pm

7pm

8pm

9pm

10pm

11pm

midnight

date:

One Hundred Days

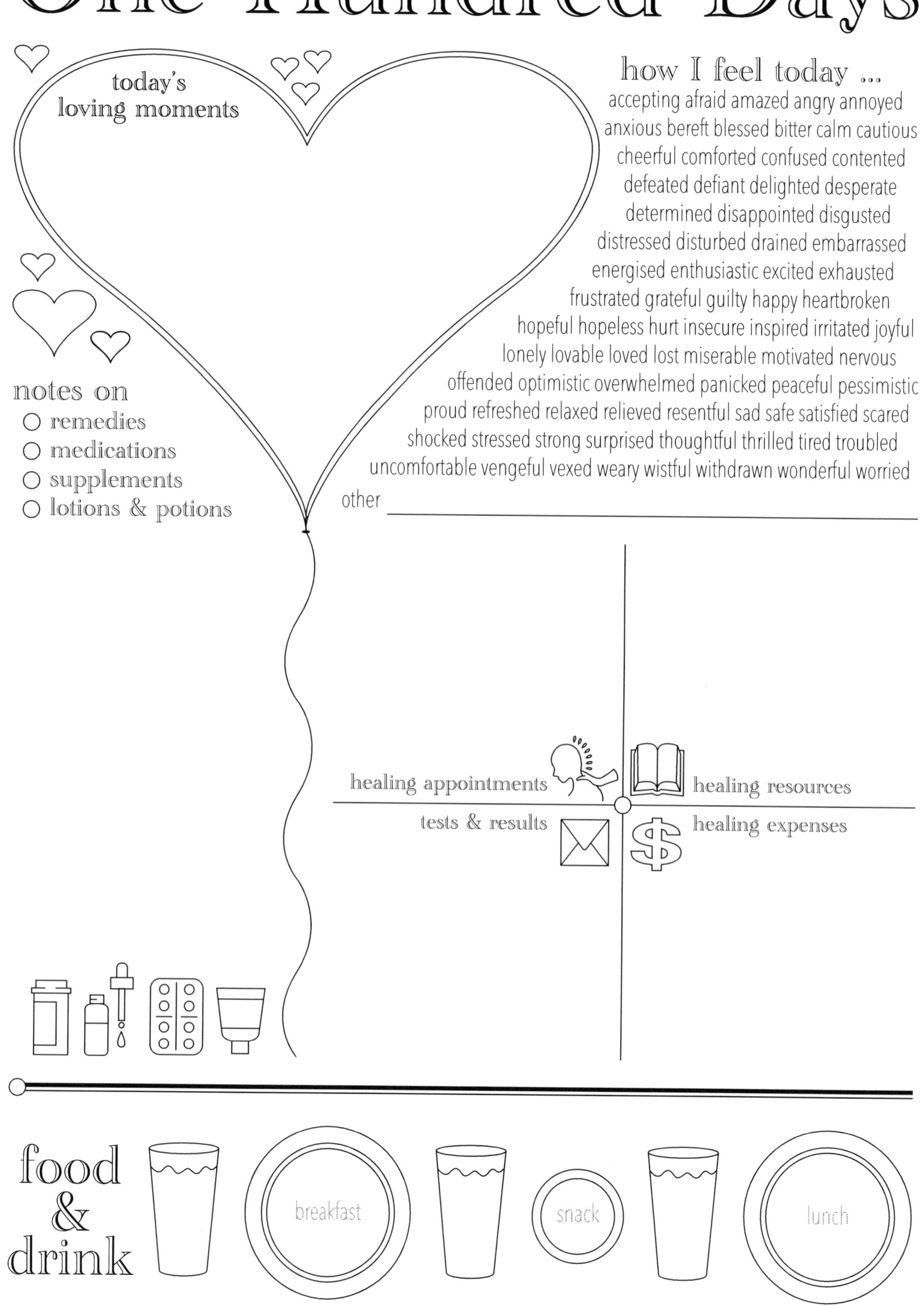

# of Healing

day 13

midnight
1am
2am
3am
4am
5am
6am
7am
8am
9am
10am
11am
midday
1pm
2pm
3pm
4pm
5pm
6pm
7pm
8pm
9pm
10pm
11pm
midnight

date:

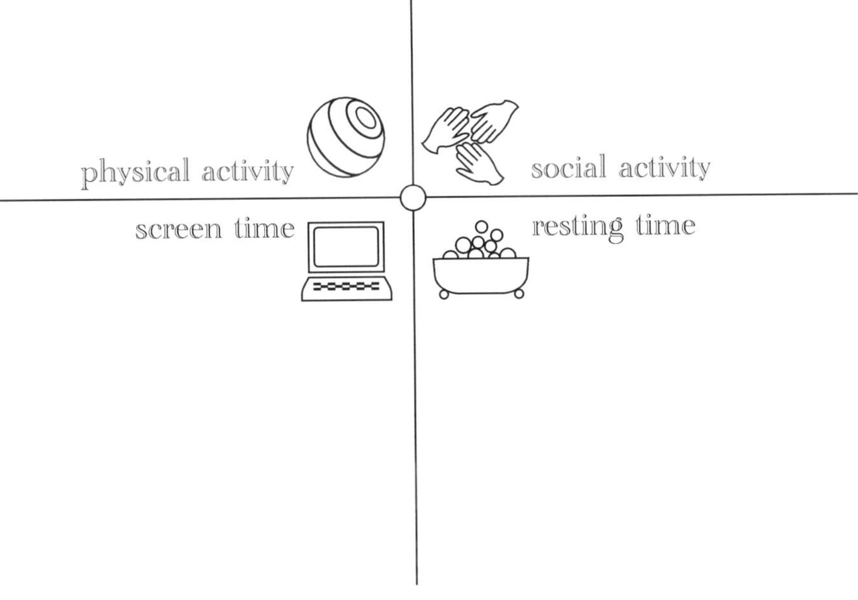

connections with nature

One Hundred Days

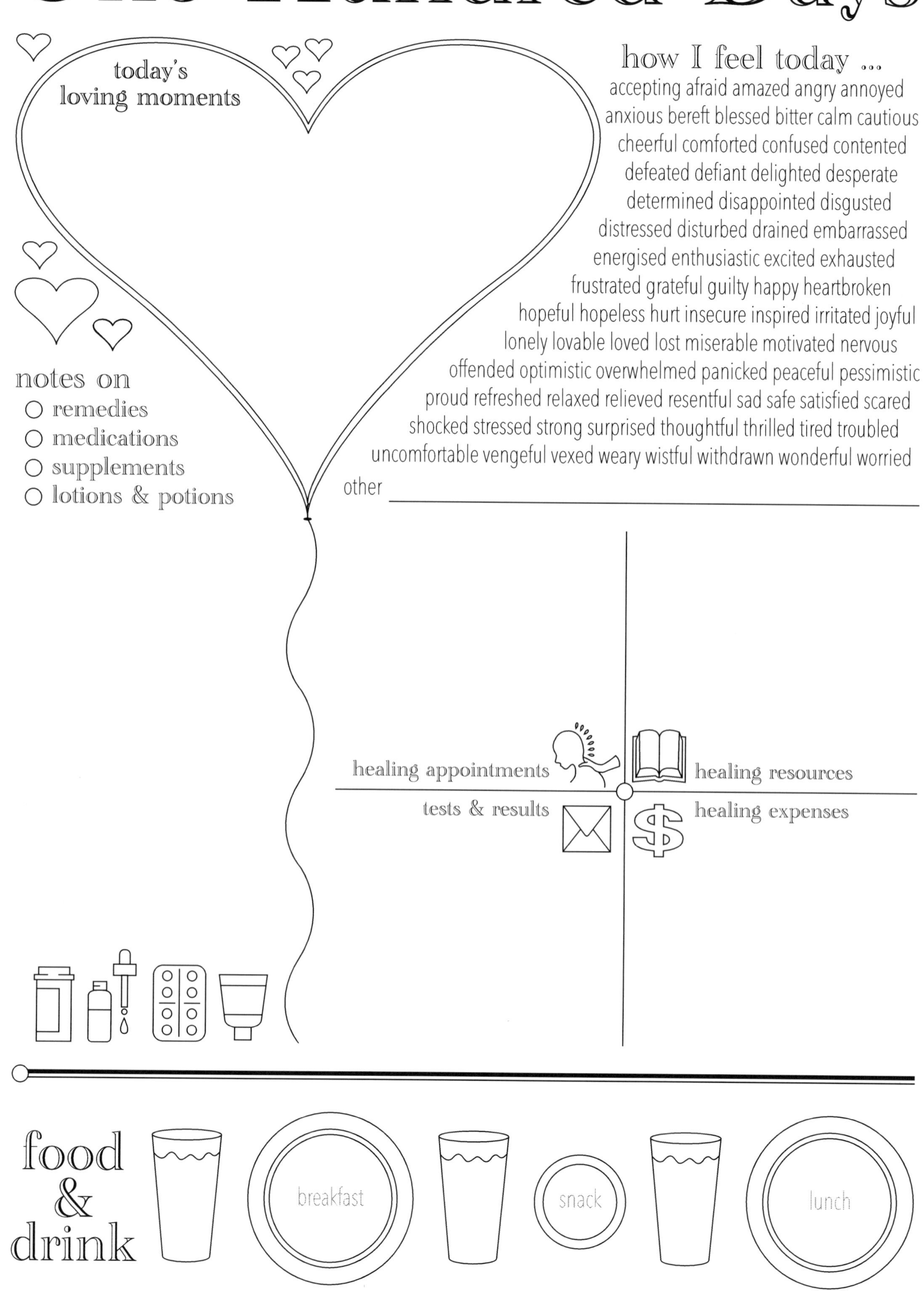

of Healing

day 14

physical activity

social activity

screen time

resting time

connections with nature

wondering & wandering thoughts

snack

dinner

midnight

1am

2am

3am

4am

5am

6am

7am

8am

9am

10am

11am

midday

1pm

2pm

3pm

4pm

5pm

6pm

7pm

8pm

9pm

10pm

11pm

midnight

date:

One Hundred Days

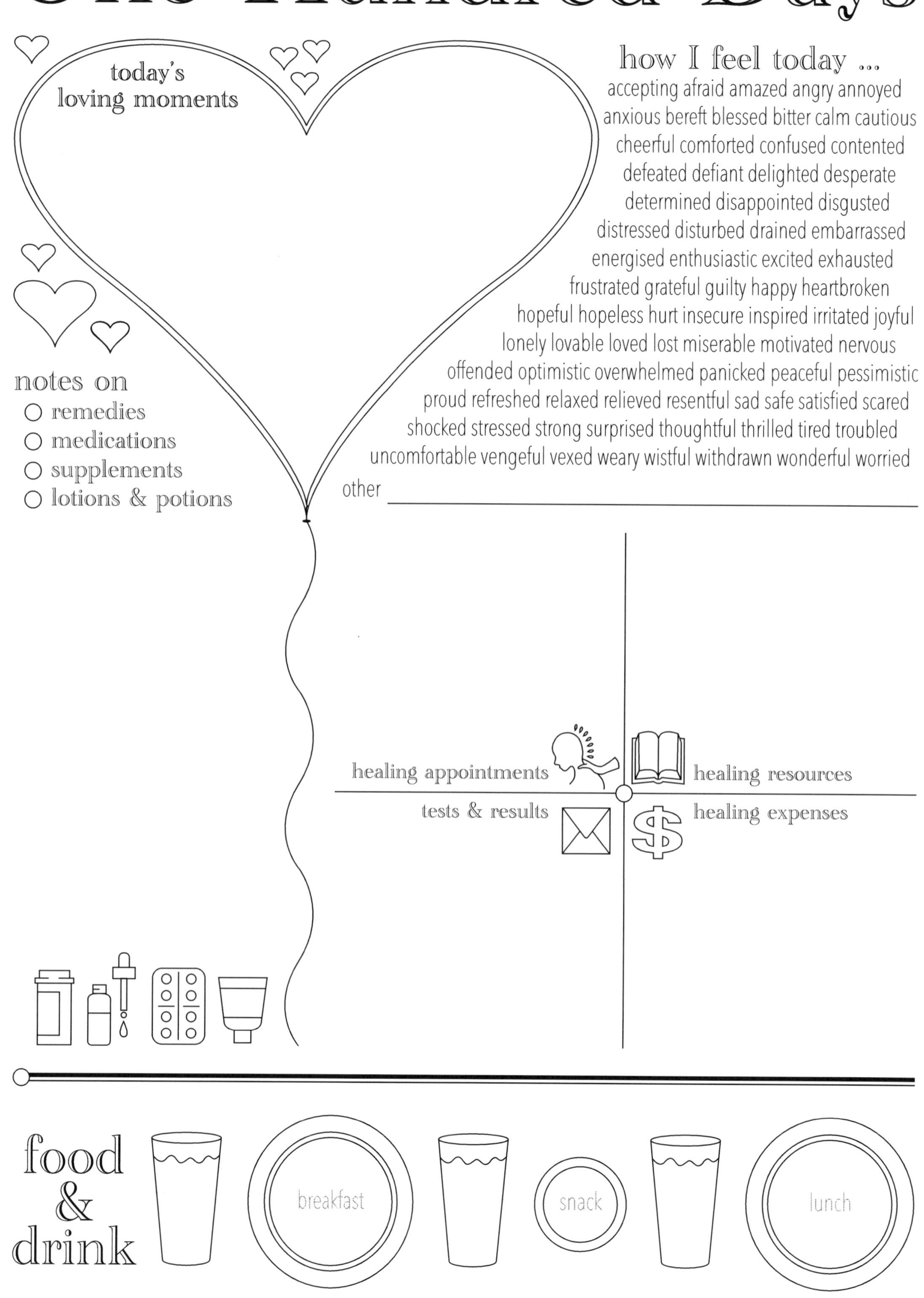

food & drink

breakfast

snack

lunch

# of Healing

physical activity

social activity

screen time

resting time

connections with nature

wondering & wandering thoughts

snack

dinner

day 15

midnight

1am

2am

3am

4am

5am

6am

7am

8am

9am

10am

11am

midday

1pm

2pm

3pm

4pm

5pm

6pm

7pm

8pm

9pm

10pm

11pm

midnight

date:

One Hundred Days

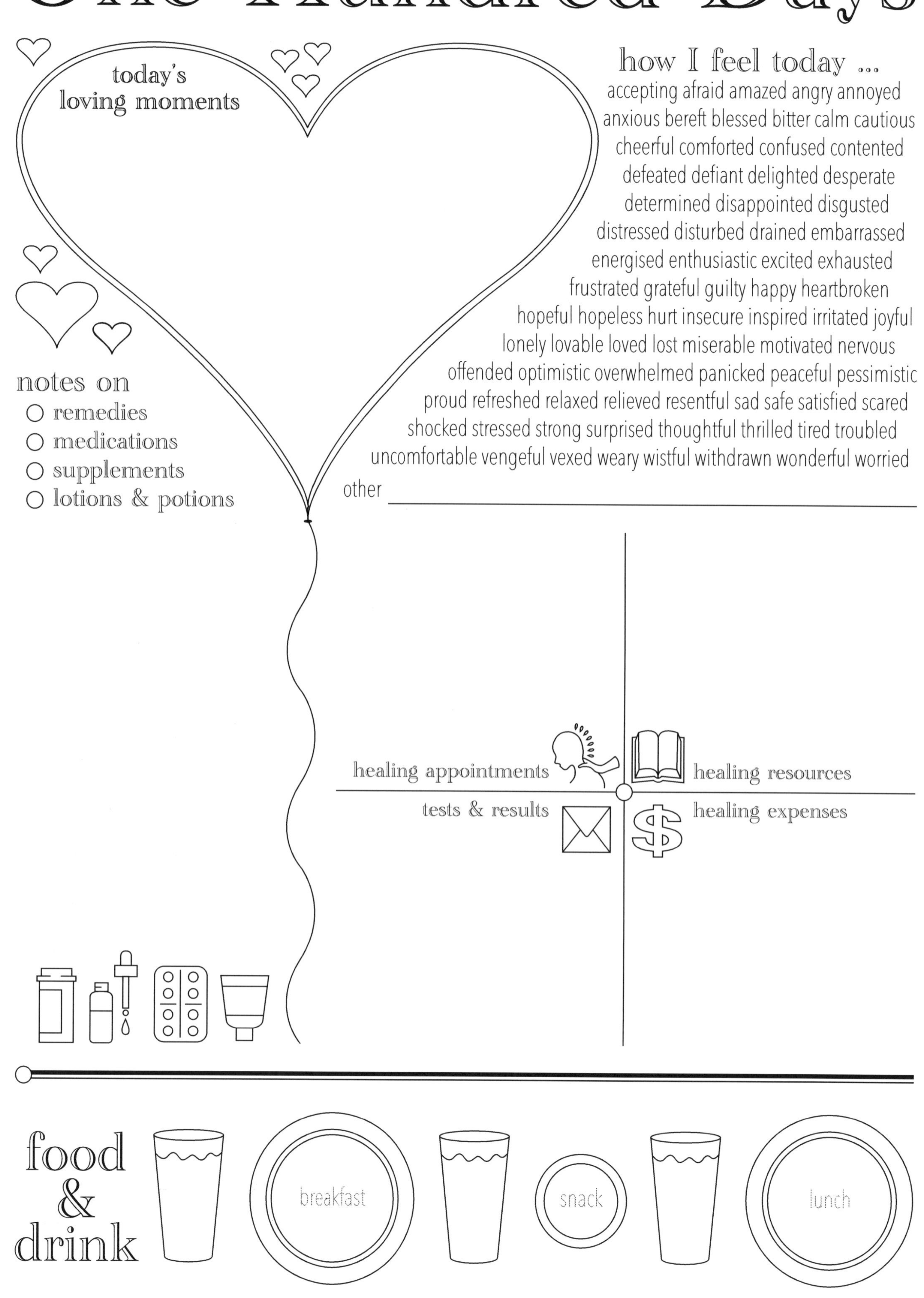

food & drink

breakfast

snack

lunch

# of Healing

physical activity

social activity

screen time

resting time

connections with nature

wondering & wandering thoughts

snack

dinner

day 16

midnight

1am

2am

3am

4am

5am

6am

7am

8am

9am

10am

11am

midday

1pm

2pm

3pm

4pm

5pm

6pm

7pm

8pm

9pm

10pm

11pm

midnight

date:

One Hundred Days

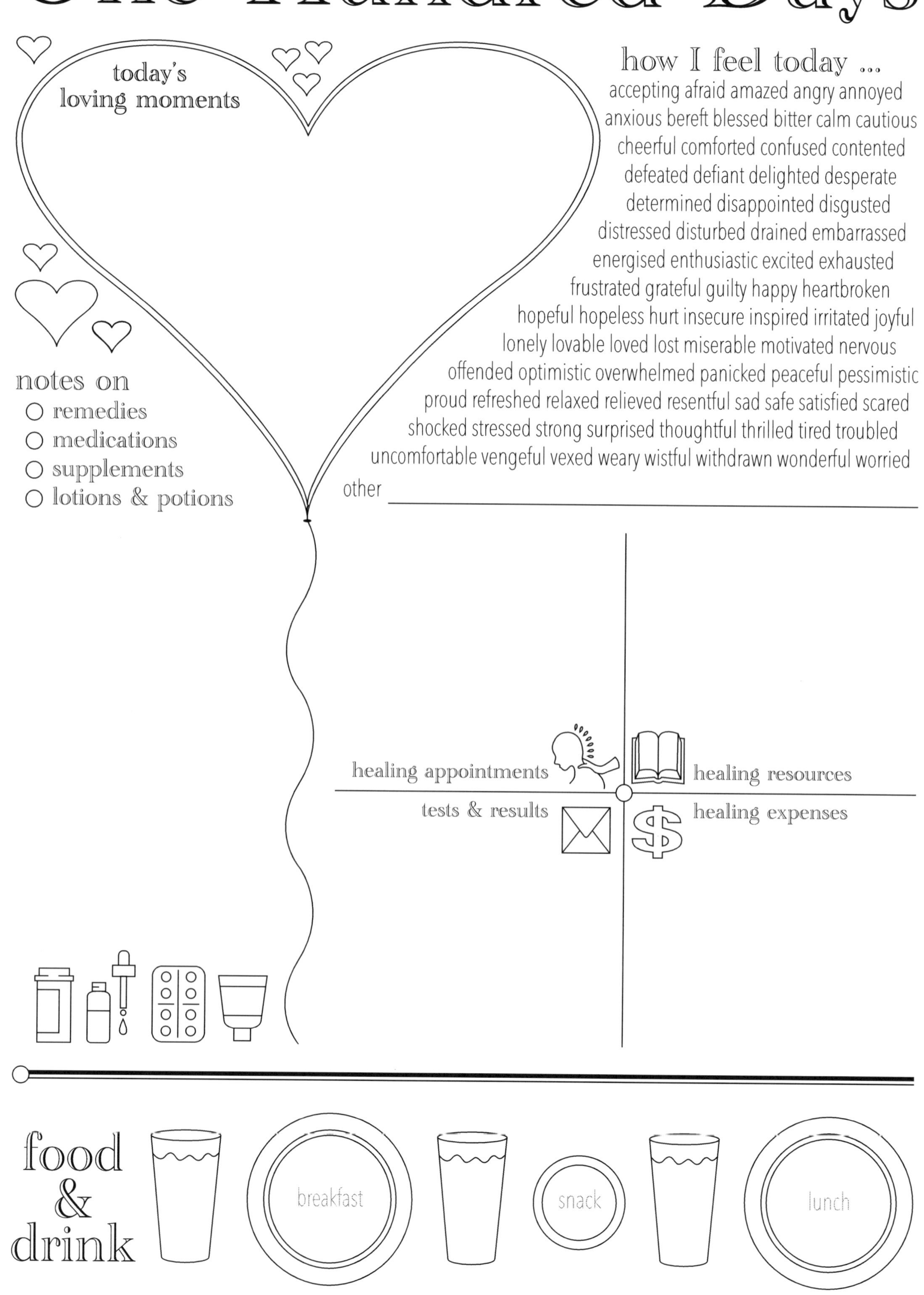

food & drink

breakfast

snack

lunch

# of Healing

physical activity

social activity

screen time

resting time

connections with nature

wondering & wandering thoughts

snack

dinner

day 17

midnight

1am

2am

3am

4am

5am

6am

7am

8am

9am

10am

11am

midday

1pm

2pm

3pm

4pm

5pm

6pm

7pm

8pm

9pm

10pm

11pm

midnight

date:

One Hundred Days

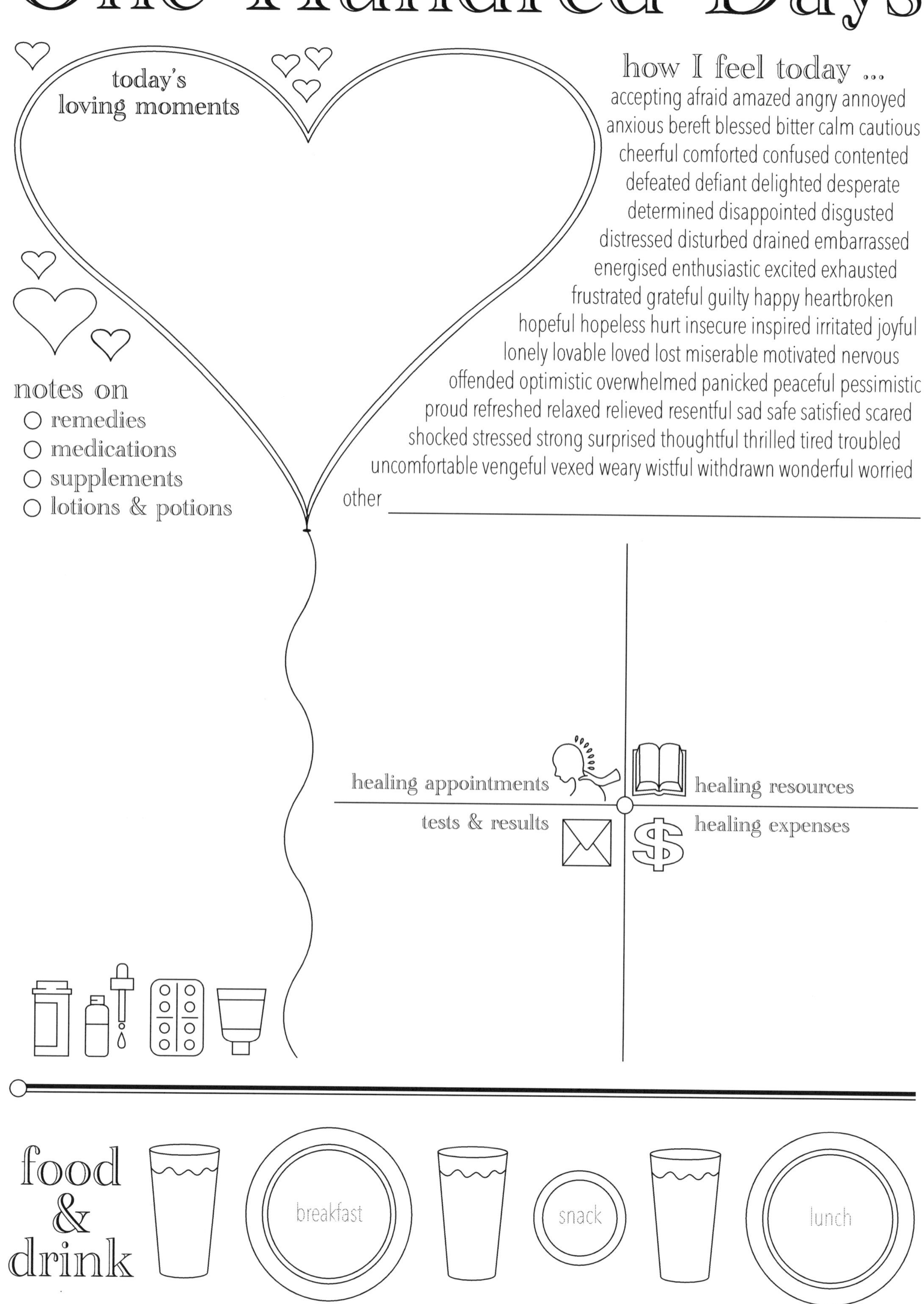

food & drink

breakfast

snack

lunch

# of Healing

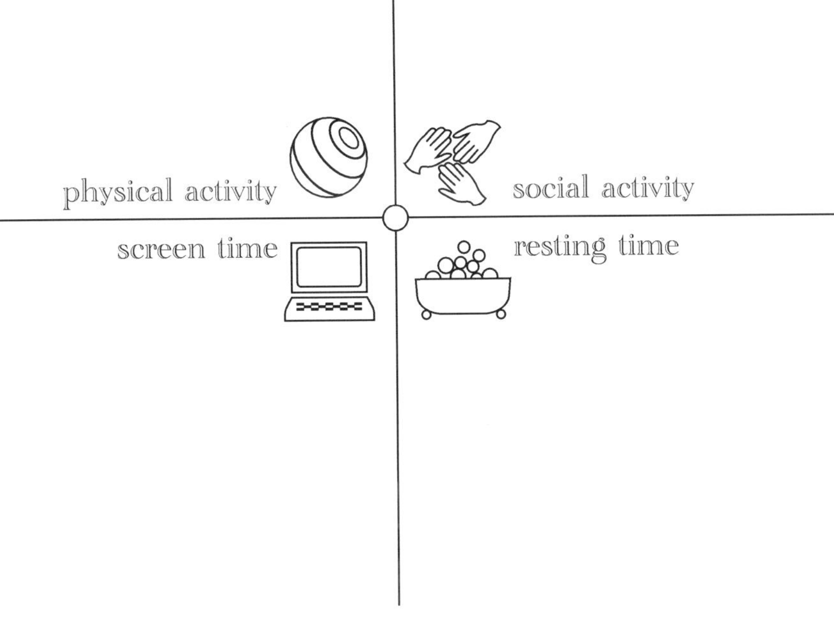

day 18

midnight
1am
2am
3am
4am
5am
6am
7am
8am
9am
10am
11am
midday
1pm
2pm
3pm
4pm
5pm
6pm
7pm
8pm
9pm
10pm
11pm
midnight

date:

One Hundred Days

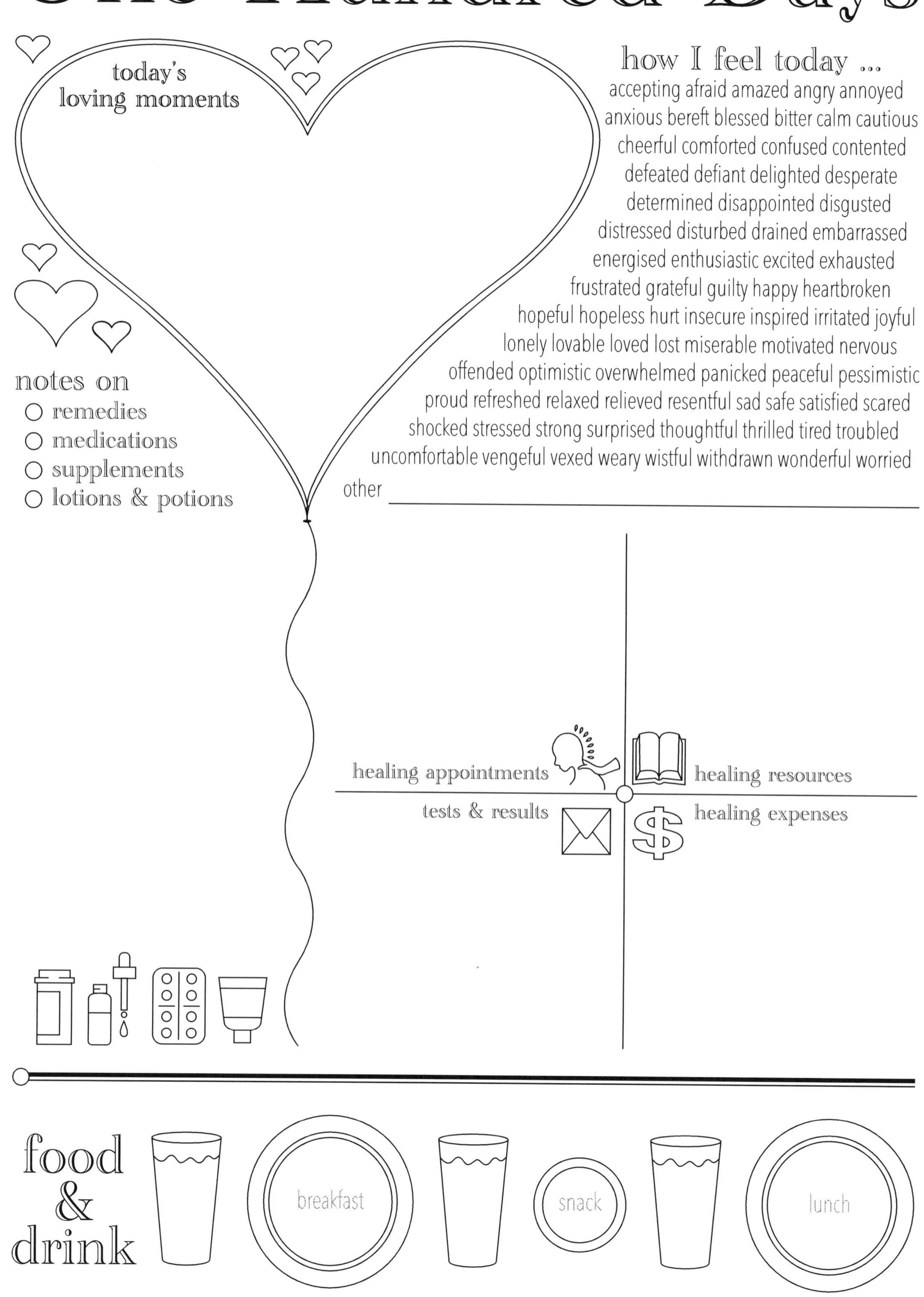

# of Healing

physical activity

social activity

screen time

resting time

connections with nature

wondering & wandering thoughts

snack

dinner

day 19

midnight

1am

2am

3am

4am

5am

6am

7am

8am

9am

10am

11am

midday

1pm

2pm

3pm

4pm

5pm

6pm

7pm

8pm

9pm

10pm

11pm

midnight

date:

One Hundred Days

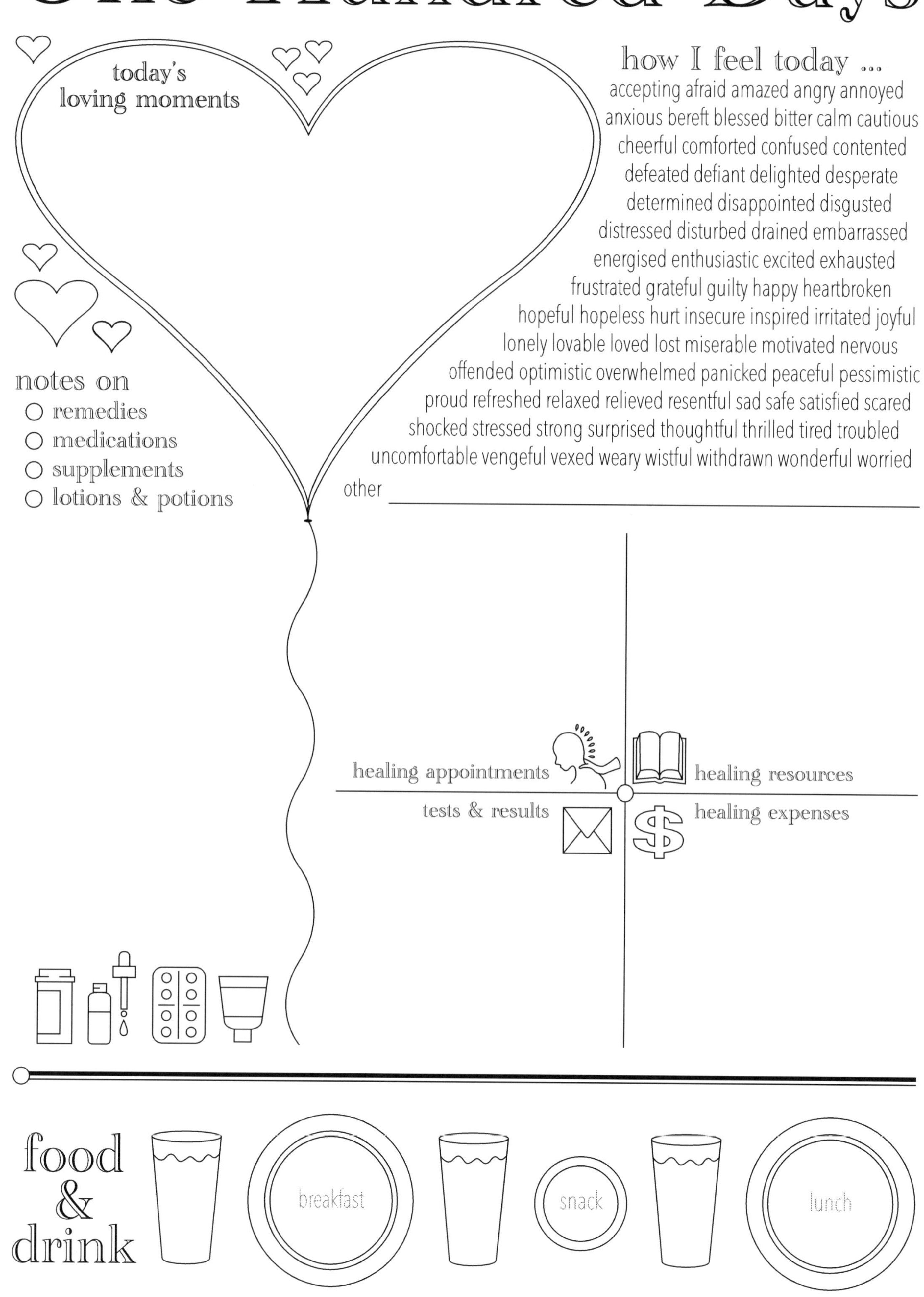

# of Healing

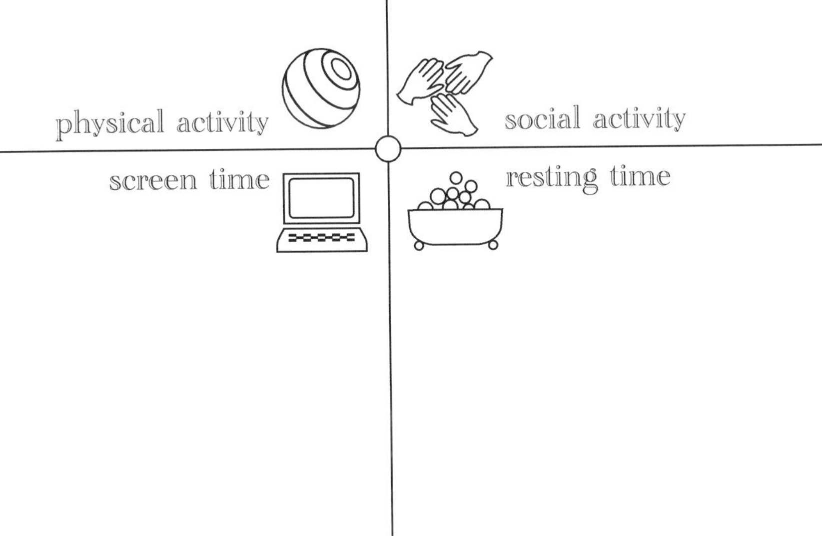

day 20

midnight

1am

2am

3am

4am

5am

6am

7am

8am

9am

10am

11am

midday

1pm

2pm

3pm

4pm

5pm

6pm

7pm

8pm

9pm

10pm

11pm

midnight

date:

One Hundred Days

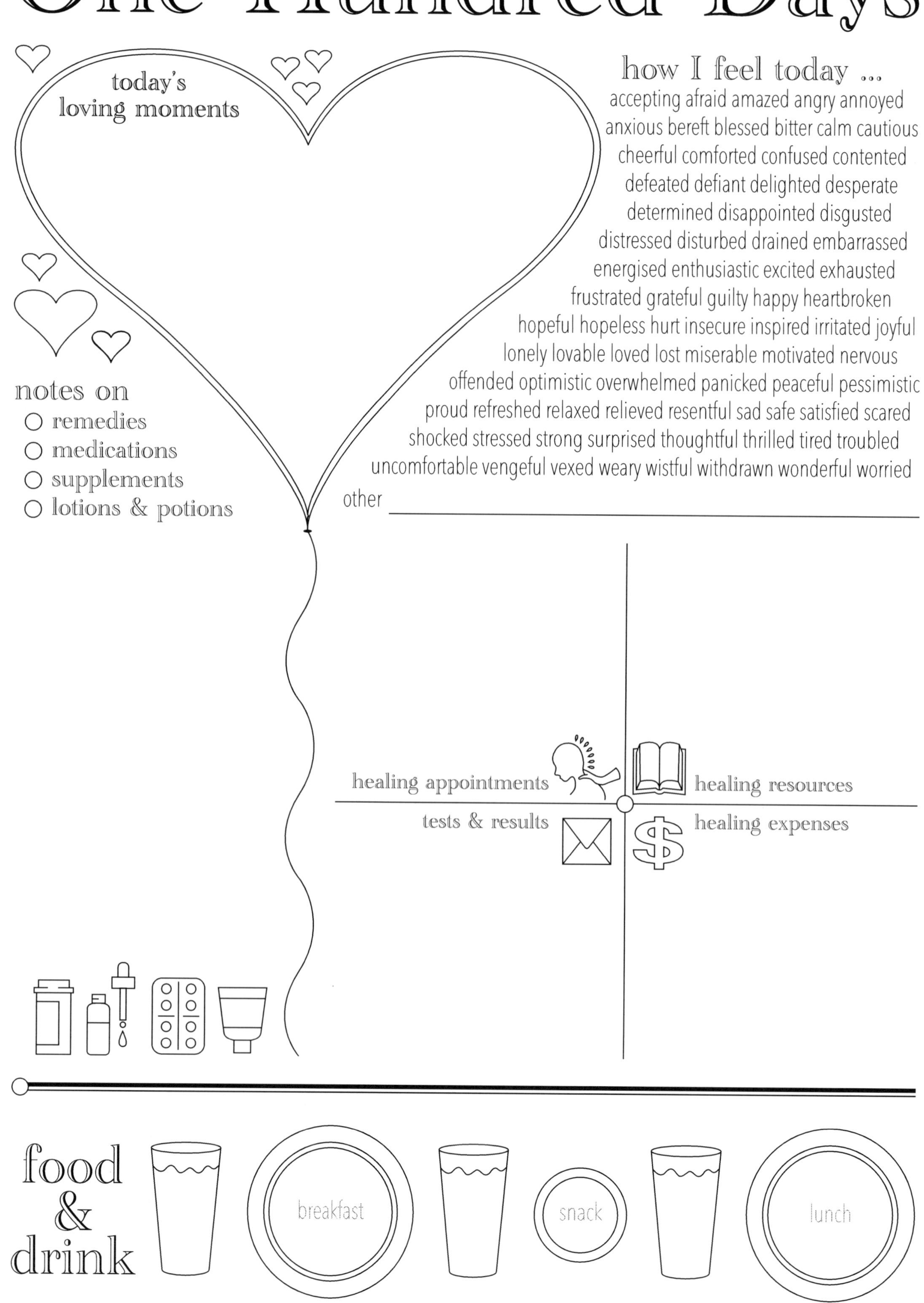

# of Healing

physical activity

social activity

screen time

resting time

connections with nature

wondering & wandering thoughts

snack

dinner

day 21

midnight

1am

2am

3am

4am

5am

6am

7am

8am

9am

10am

11am

midday

1pm

2pm

3pm

4pm

5pm

6pm

7pm

8pm

9pm

10pm

11pm

midnight

date:

One Hundred Days

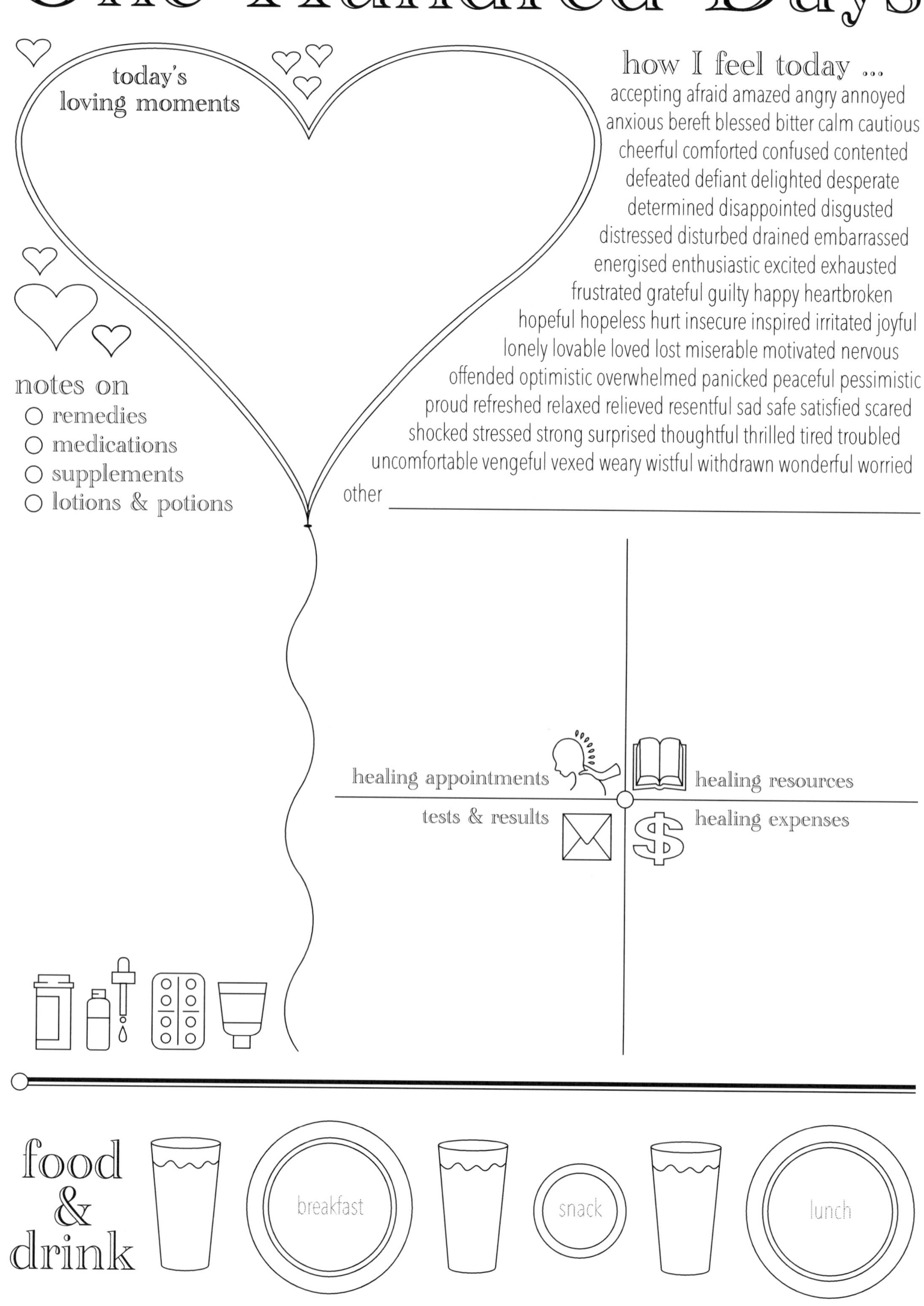

# of Healing

physical activity

social activity

screen time

resting time

connections with nature

wondering & wandering thoughts

snack

dinner

day 22

midnight

1am

2am

3am

4am

5am

6am

7am

8am

9am

10am

11am

midday

1pm

2pm

3pm

4pm

5pm

6pm

7pm

8pm

9pm

10pm

11pm

midnight

date:

One Hundred Days

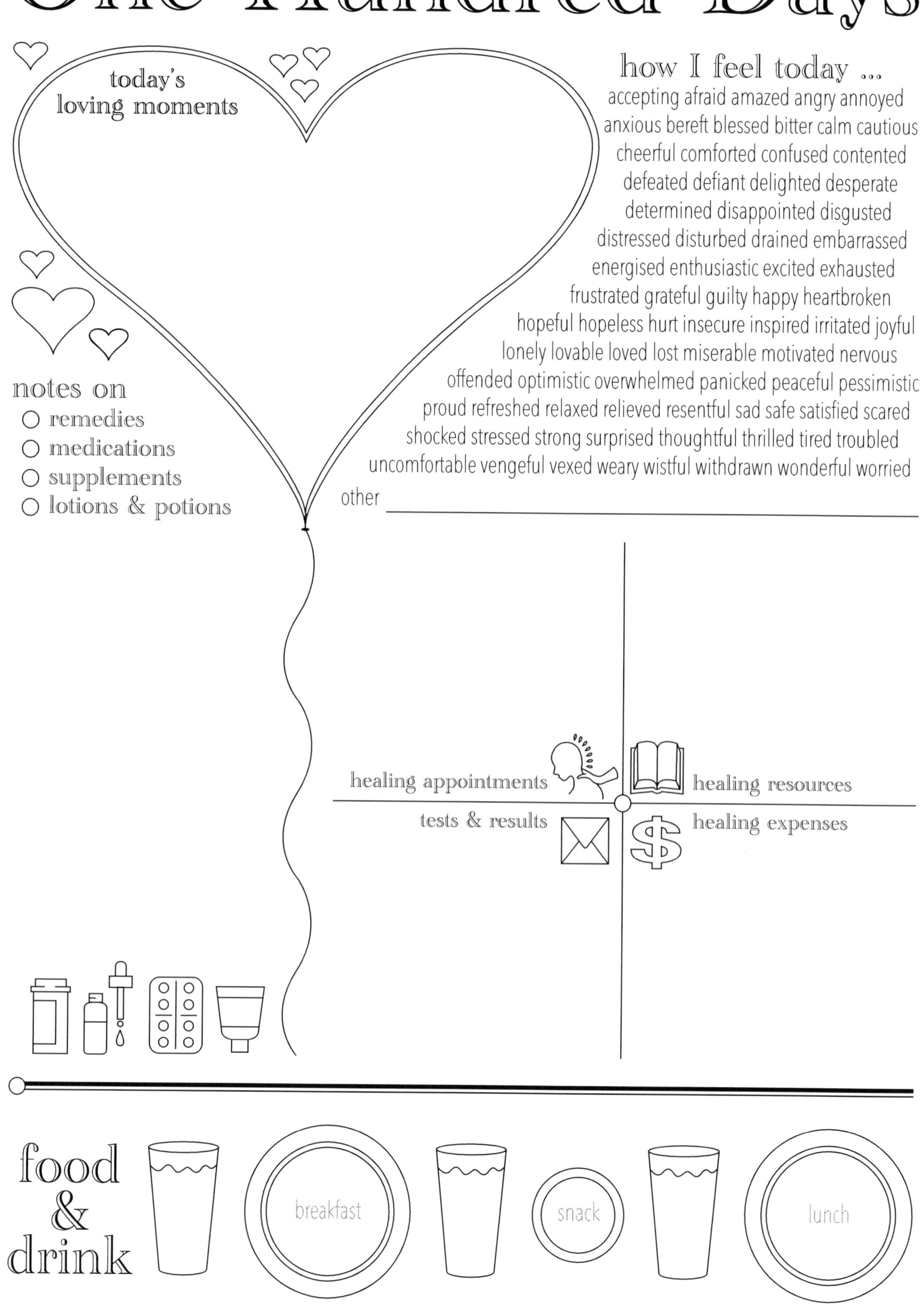

# of Healing

physical activity

social activity

screen time

resting time

connections with nature

wondering & wandering thoughts

snack

dinner

day 23

midnight

1am

2am

3am

4am

5am

6am

7am

8am

9am

10am

11am

midday

1pm

2pm

3pm

4pm

5pm

6pm

7pm

8pm

9pm

10pm

11pm

midnight

date:

One Hundred Days

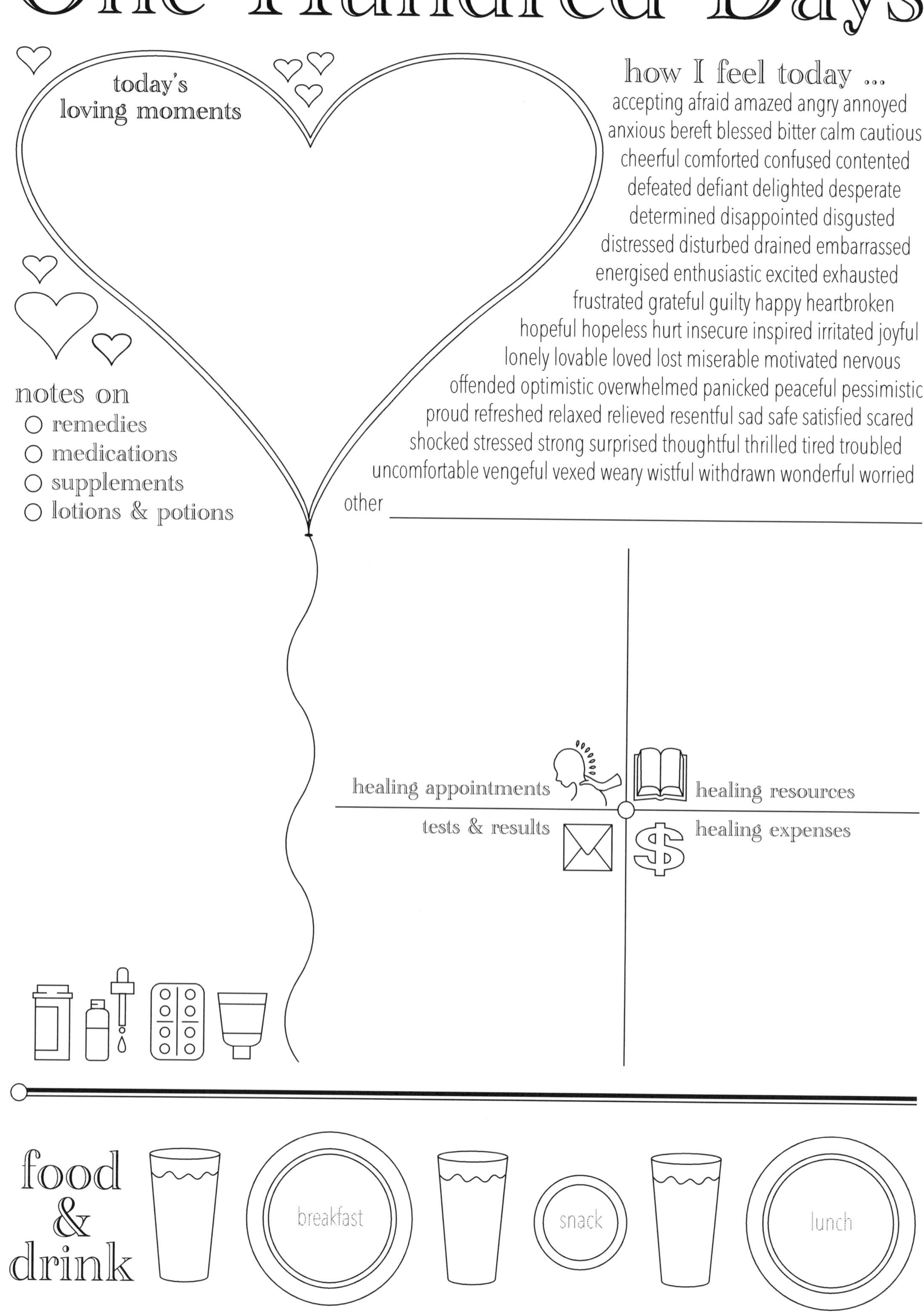

# of Healing

physical activity

social activity

screen time

resting time

connections with nature

wondering & wandering thoughts

snack

dinner

day 24

midnight

1am

2am

3am

4am

5am

6am

7am

8am

9am

10am

11am

midday

1pm

2pm

3pm

4pm

5pm

6pm

7pm

8pm

9pm

10pm

11pm

midnight

date:

One Hundred Days

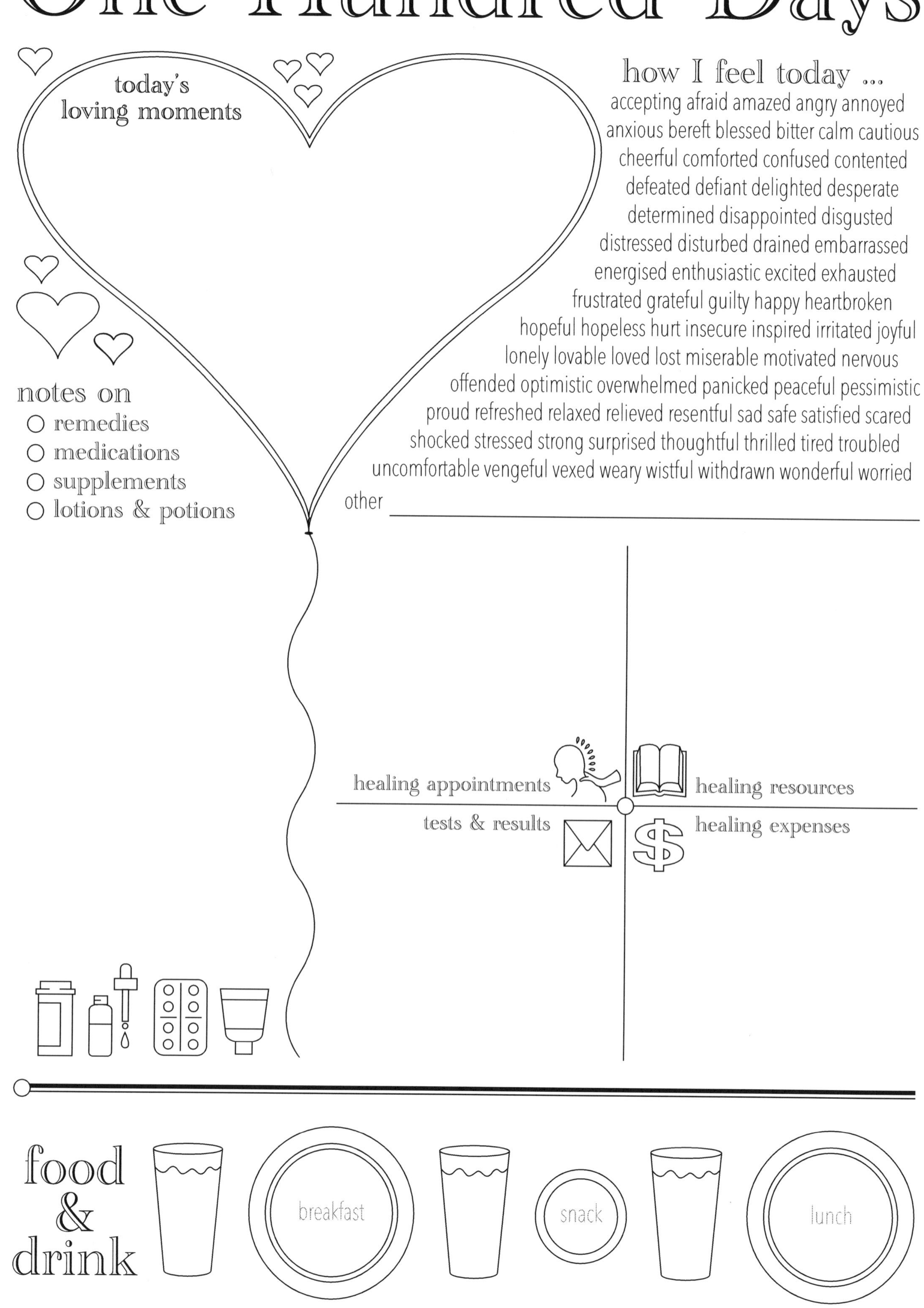

food & drink

# of Healing

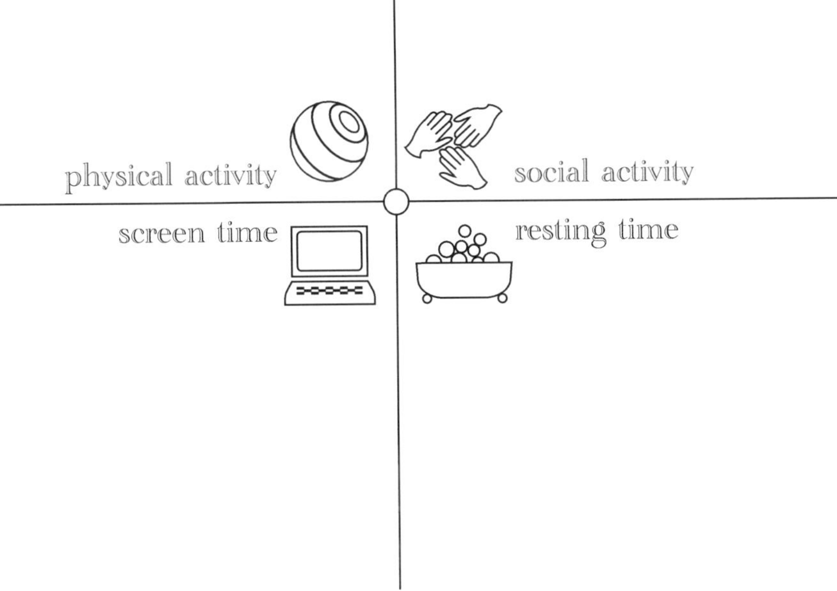

day 25

midnight
1am
2am
3am
4am
5am
6am
7am
8am
9am
10am
11am
midday
1pm
2pm
3pm
4pm
5pm
6pm
7pm
8pm
9pm
10pm
11pm
midnight

date:

One Hundred Days

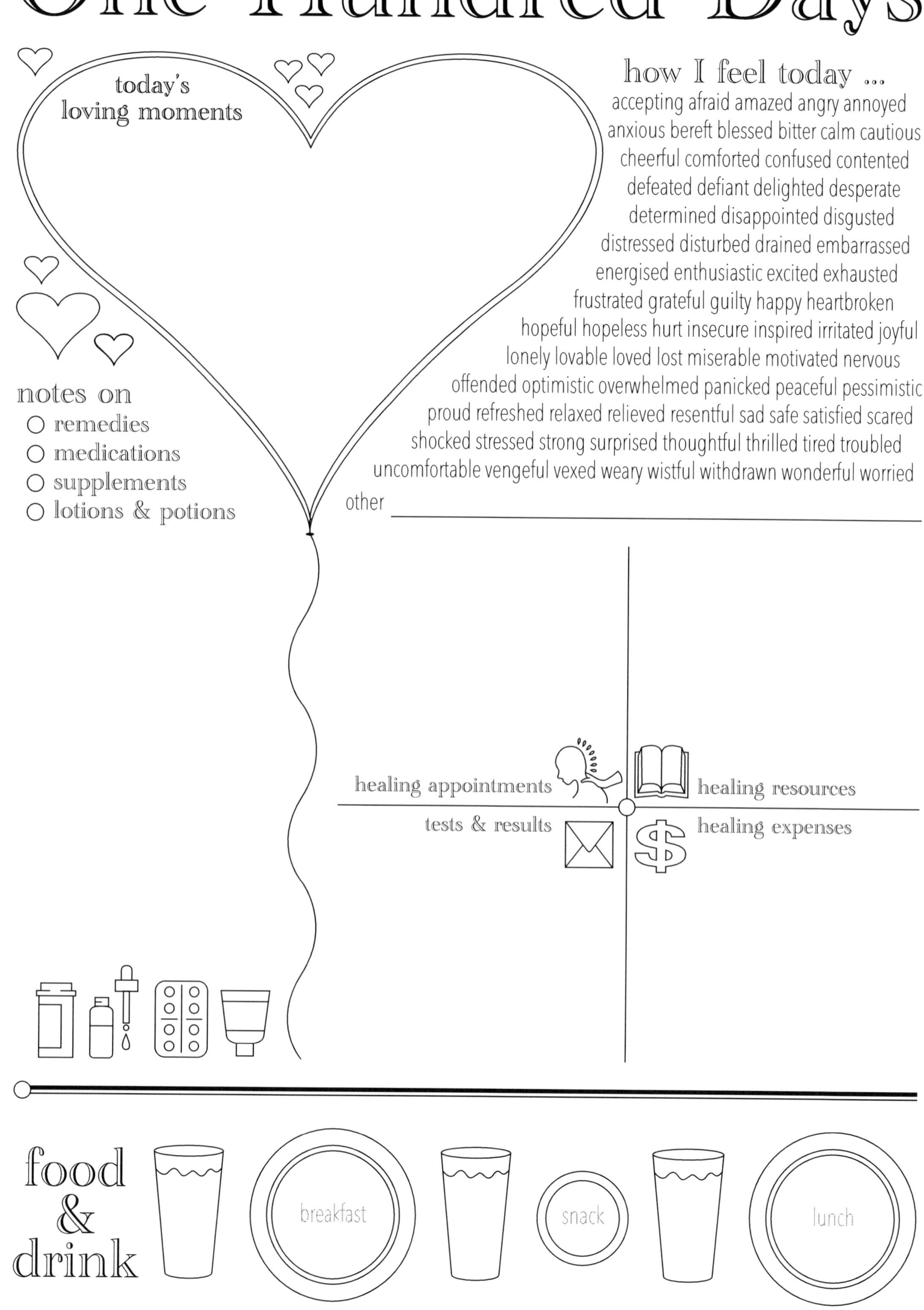

# of Healing

physical activity

social activity

screen time

resting time

connections with nature

wondering & wandering thoughts

snack

dinner

day 26

midnight

1am

2am

3am

4am

5am

6am

7am

8am

9am

10am

11am

midday

1pm

2pm

3pm

4pm

5pm

6pm

7pm

8pm

9pm

10pm

11pm

midnight

date:

One Hundred Days

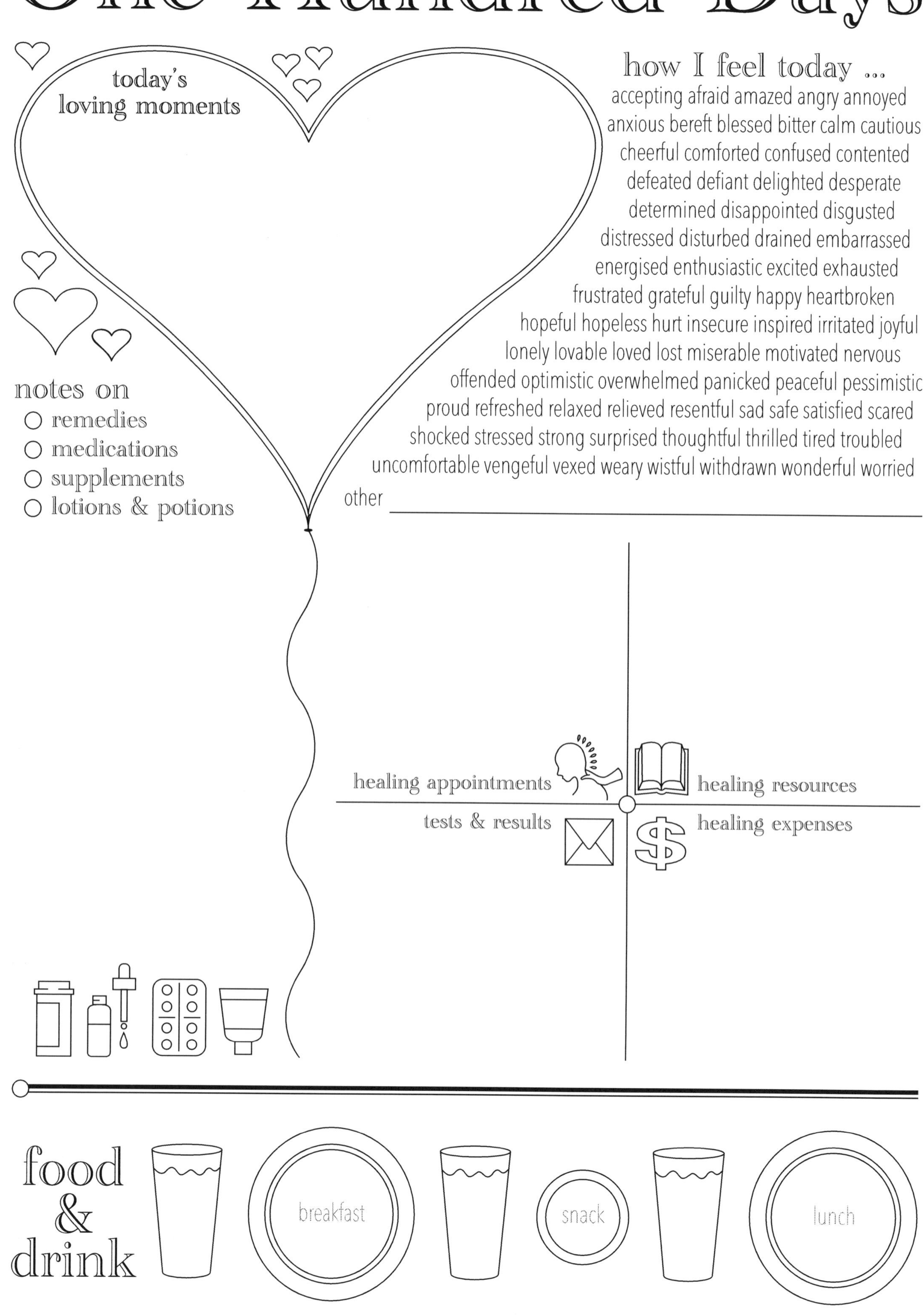

# of Healing

physical activity

social activity

screen time

resting time

connections with nature

wondering & wandering thoughts

snack

dinner

day 27

midnight

1am

2am

3am

4am

5am

6am

7am

8am

9am

10am

11am

midday

1pm

2pm

3pm

4pm

5pm

6pm

7pm

8pm

9pm

10pm

11pm

midnight

date:

One Hundred Days

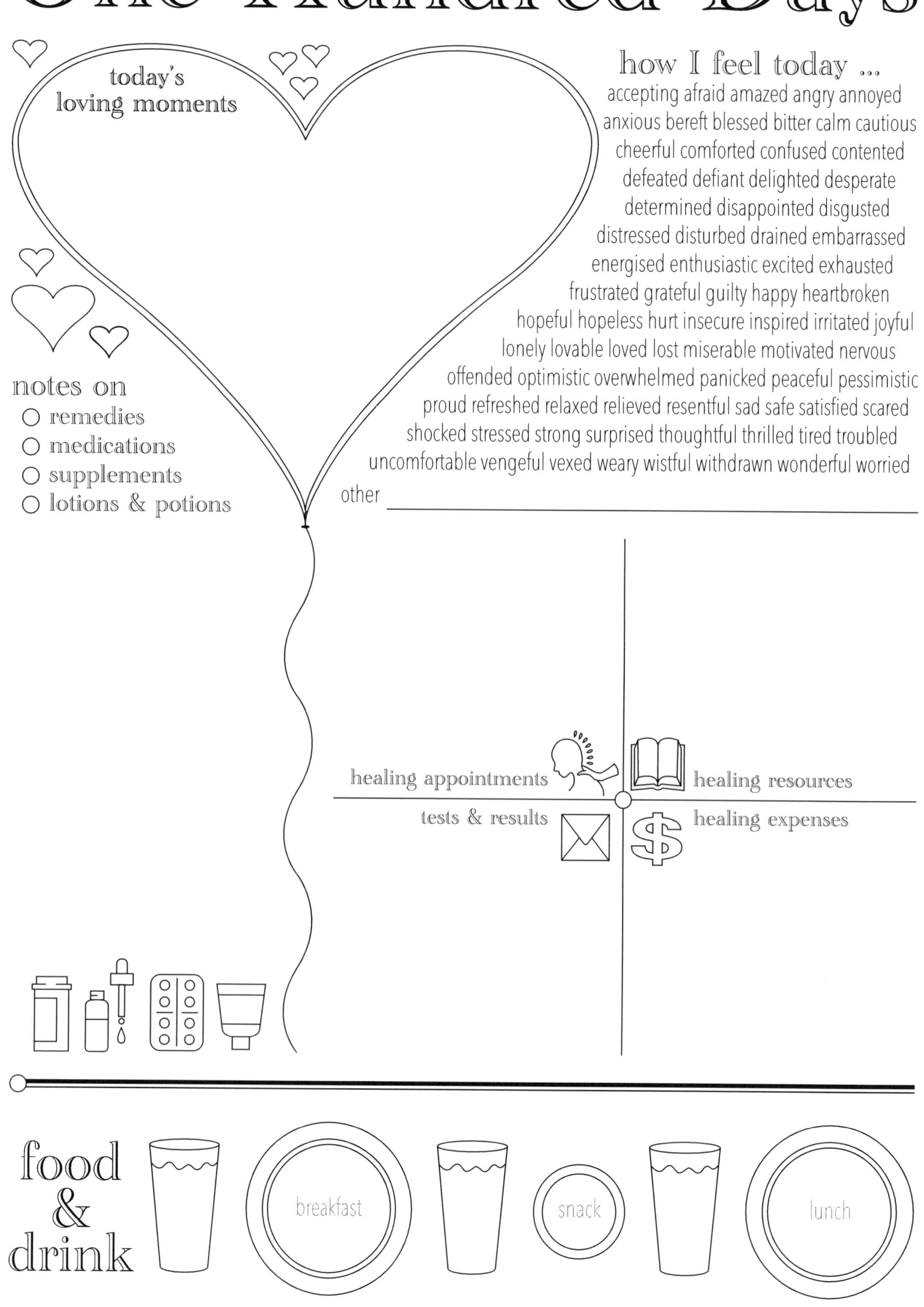

today's loving moments

how I feel today ...

accepting afraid amazed angry annoyed
anxious bereft blessed bitter calm cautious
cheerful comforted confused contented
defeated defiant delighted desperate
determined disappointed disgusted
distressed disturbed drained embarrassed
energised enthusiastic excited exhausted
frustrated grateful guilty happy heartbroken
hopeful hopeless hurt insecure inspired irritated joyful
lonely lovable loved lost miserable motivated nervous
offended optimistic overwhelmed panicked peaceful pessimistic
proud refreshed relaxed relieved resentful sad safe satisfied scared
shocked stressed strong surprised thoughtful thrilled tired troubled
uncomfortable vengeful vexed weary wistful withdrawn wonderful worried

other ____________________

notes on

- ○ remedies
- ○ medications
- ○ supplements
- ○ lotions & potions

healing appointments

healing resources

tests & results

healing expenses

food & drink

breakfast

snack

lunch

# of Healing

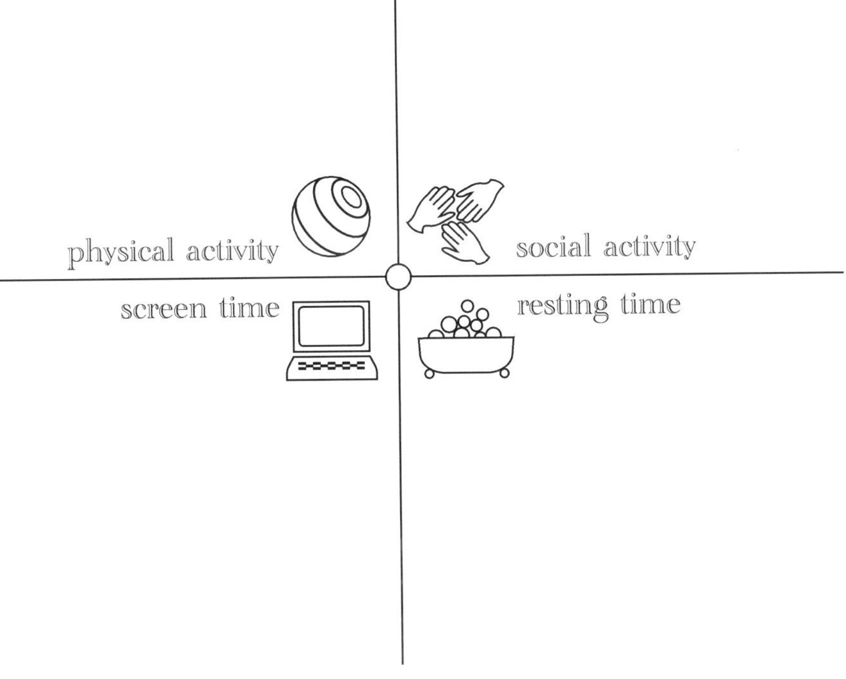

day 28

midnight

1am

2am

3am

4am

5am

6am

7am

8am

9am

10am

11am

midday

1pm

2pm

3pm

4pm

5pm

6pm

7pm

8pm

9pm

10pm

11pm

midnight

date:

One Hundred Days

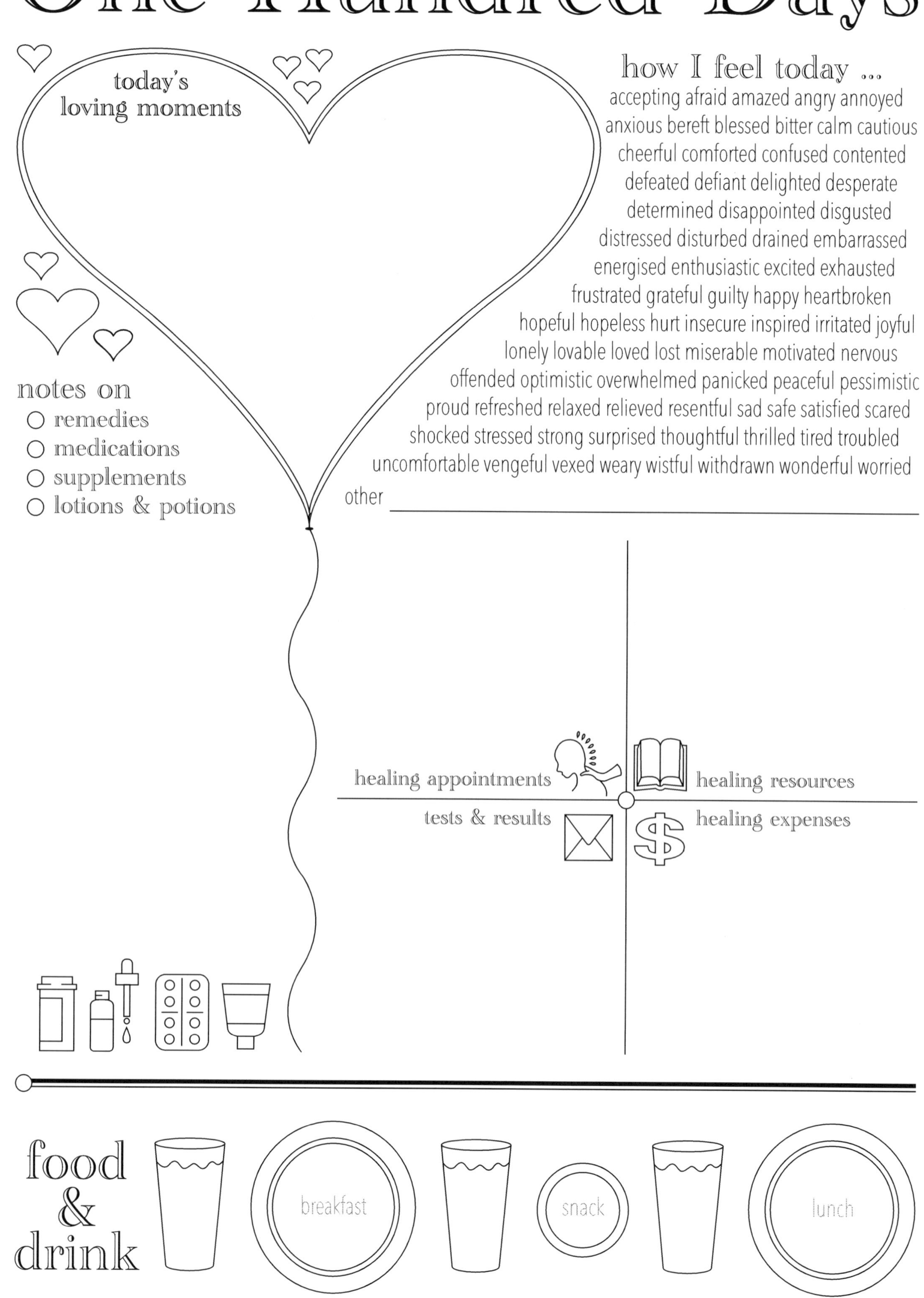

# of Healing

physical activity

social activity

screen time

resting time

connections with nature

wondering & wandering thoughts

snack

dinner

day 29

midnight

1am

2am

3am

4am

5am

6am

7am

8am

9am

10am

11am

midday

1pm

2pm

3pm

4pm

5pm

6pm

7pm

8pm

9pm

10pm

11pm

midnight

date:

One Hundred Days

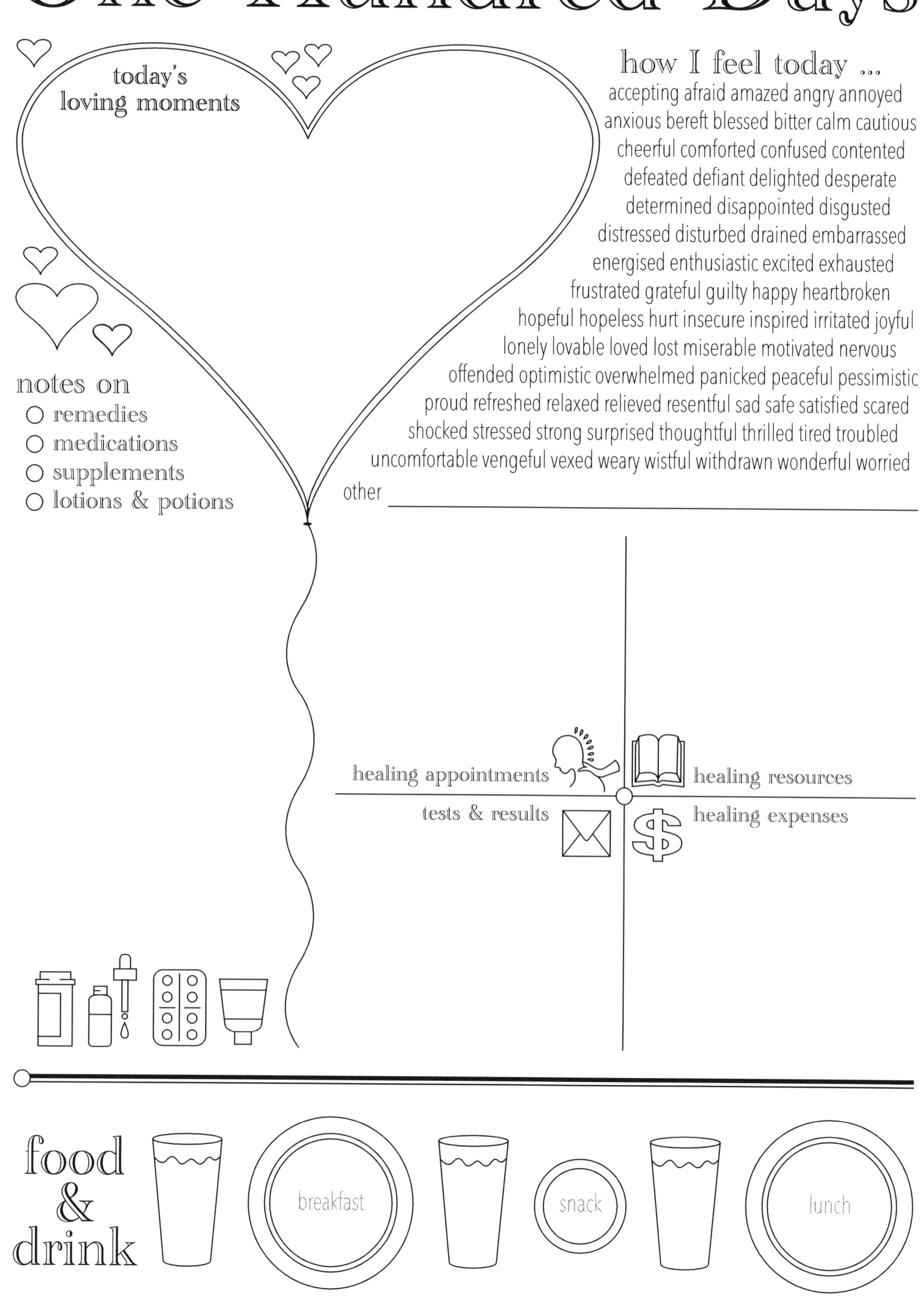

food & drink

breakfast

snack

lunch

# of Healing

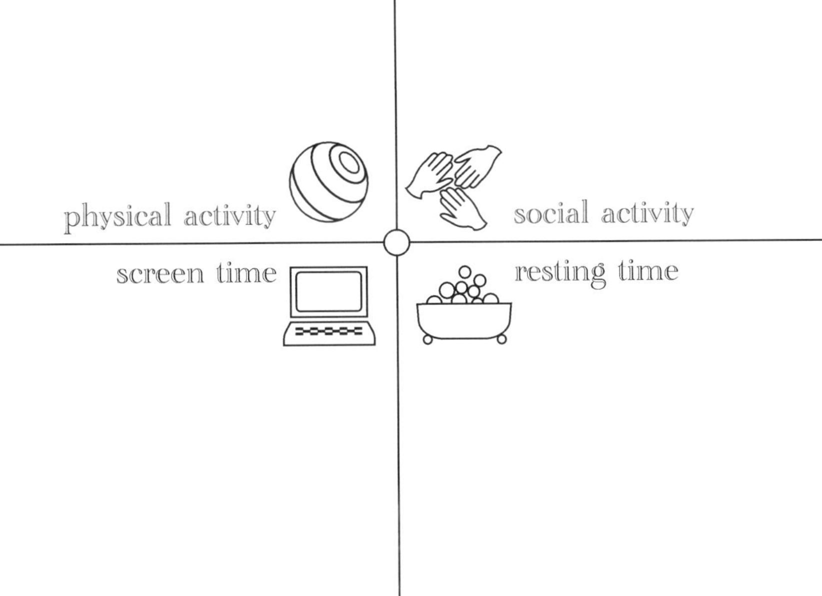

day 30

midnight

1am

2am

3am

4am

5am

6am

7am

8am

9am

10am

11am

midday

1pm

2pm

3pm

4pm

5pm

6pm

7pm

8pm

9pm

10pm

11pm

midnight

date:

One Hundred Days

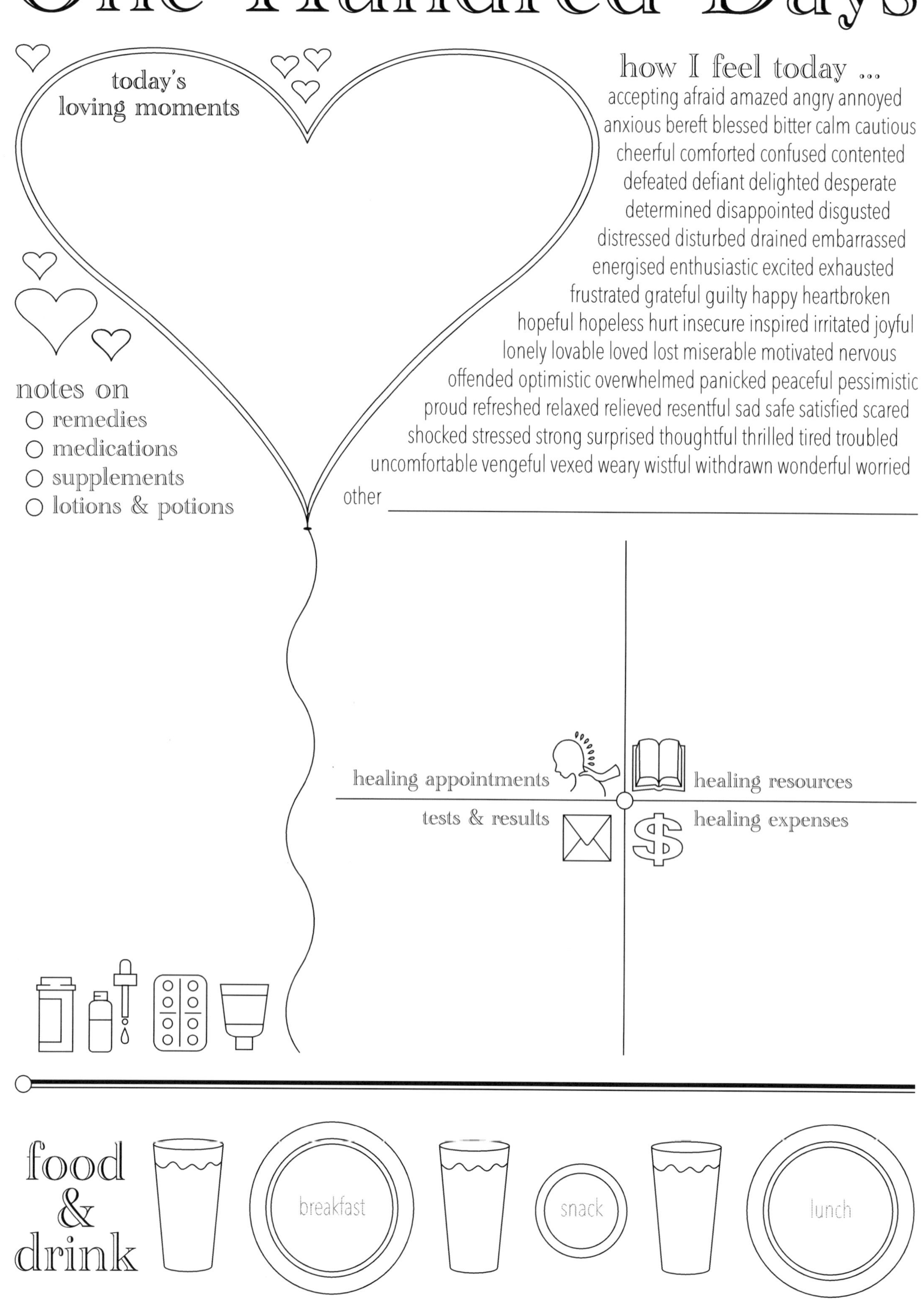

food & drink

breakfast

snack

lunch

# of Healing

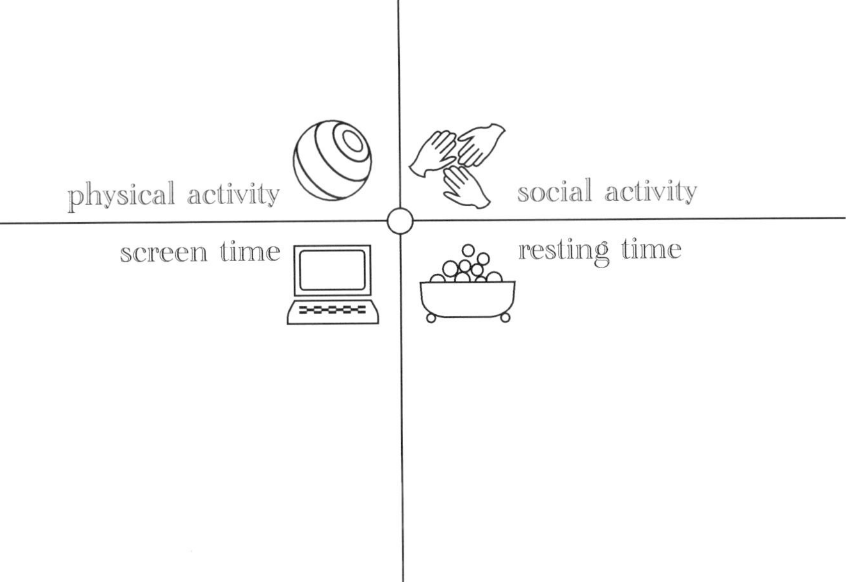

day 31

midnight

1am

2am

3am

4am

5am

6am

7am

8am

9am

10am

11am

midday

1pm

2pm

3pm

4pm

5pm

6pm

7pm

8pm

9pm

10pm

11pm

midnight

date:

One Hundred Days

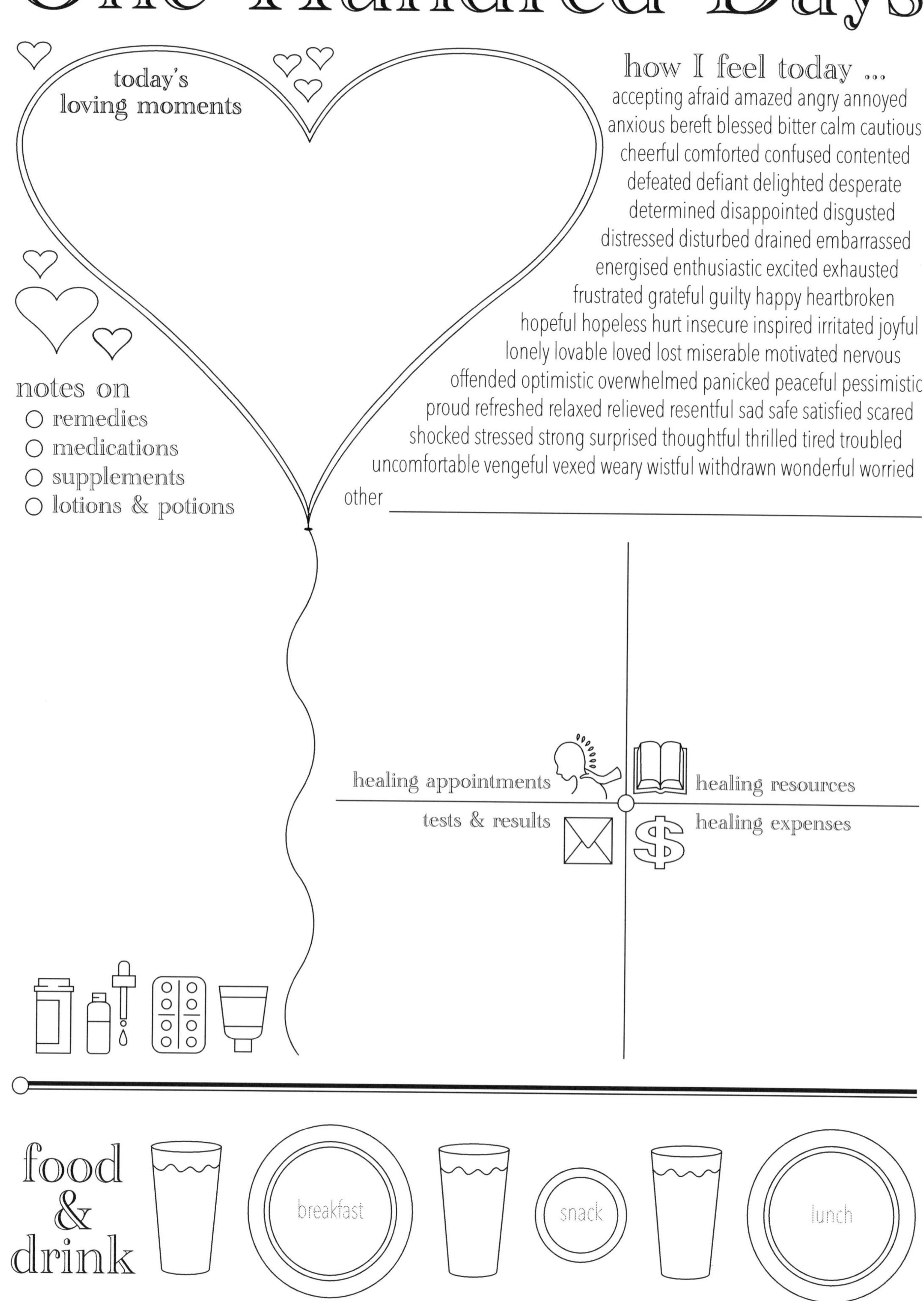

# of Healing

physical activity

social activity

screen time

resting time

connections with nature

day 32

midnight

1am

2am

3am

4am

5am

6am

7am

8am

9am

10am

11am

midday

1pm

2pm

3pm

4pm

5pm

6pm

7pm

8pm

9pm

10pm

11pm

midnight

date:

One Hundred Days

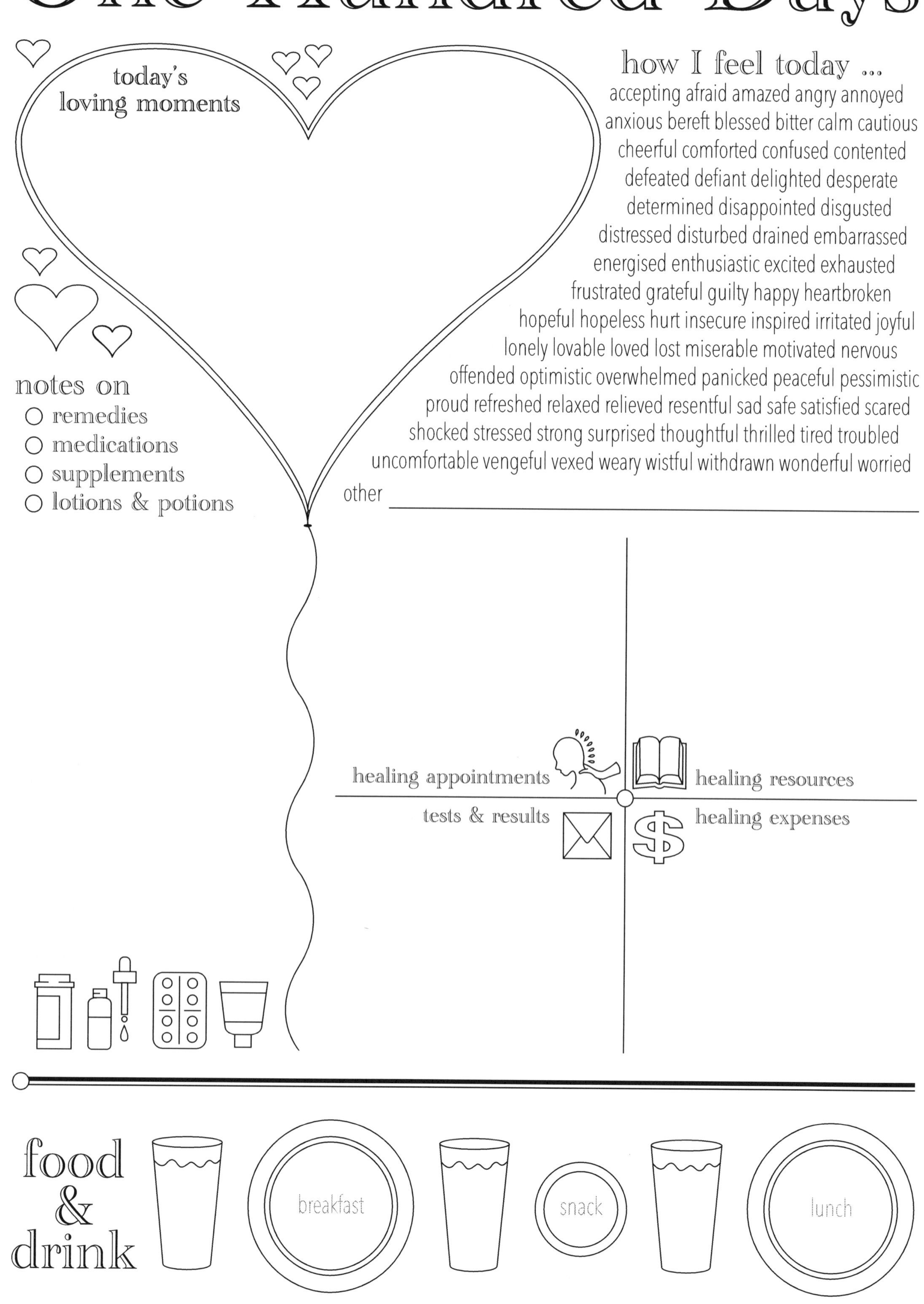

# of Healing

physical activity

social activity

screen time

resting time

connections with nature

wondering & wandering thoughts

snack

dinner

day 33

midnight

1am

2am

3am

4am

5am

6am

7am

8am

9am

10am

11am

midday

1pm

2pm

3pm

4pm

5pm

6pm

7pm

8pm

9pm

10pm

11pm

midnight

date:

One Hundred Days

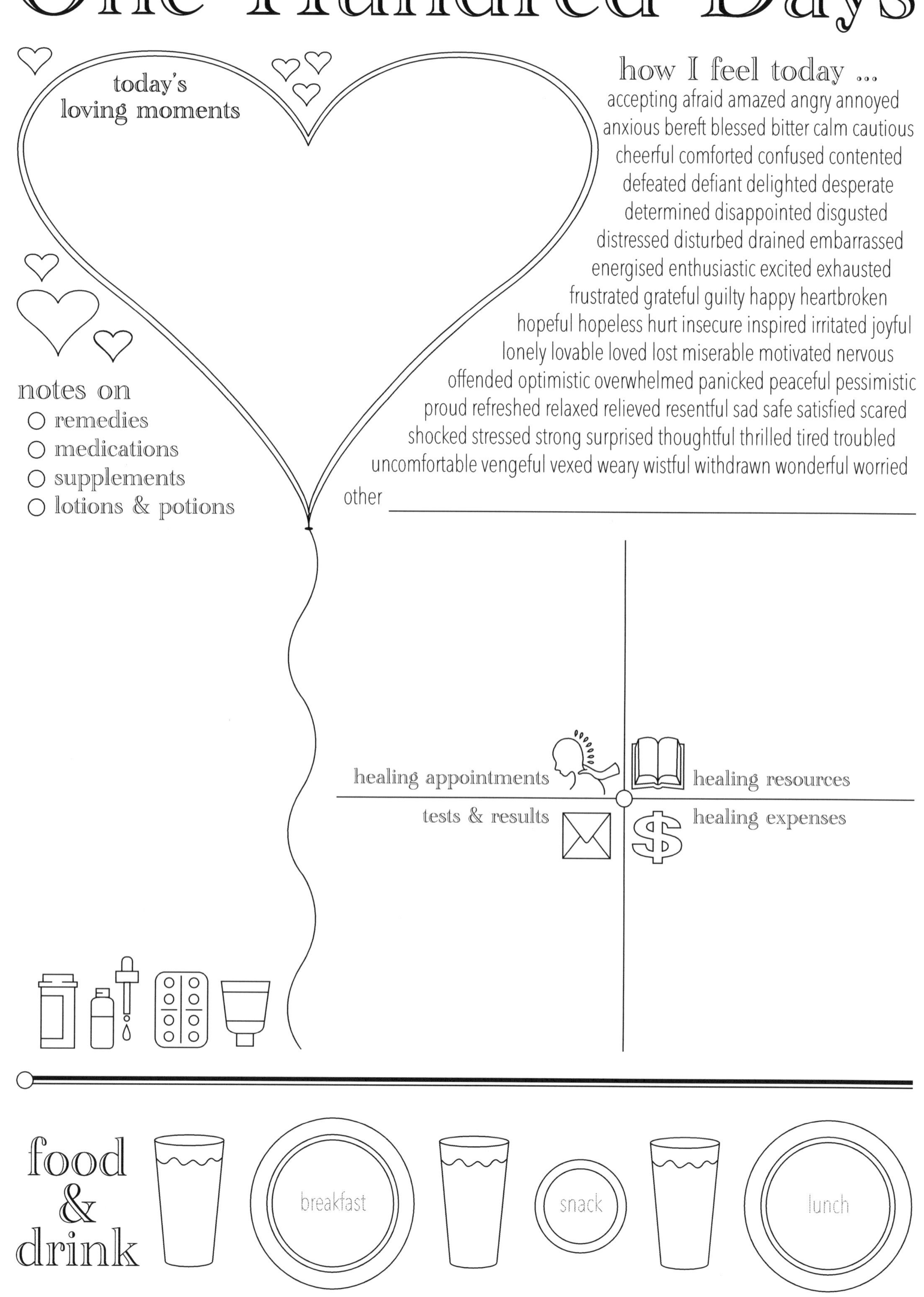

food & drink

breakfast

snack

lunch

# of Healing

physical activity

social activity

screen time

resting time

connections with nature

wondering & wandering thoughts

snack

dinner

day 34

midnight

1am

2am

3am

4am

5am

6am

7am

8am

9am

10am

11am

midday

1pm

2pm

3pm

4pm

5pm

6pm

7pm

8pm

9pm

10pm

11pm

midnight

date:

One Hundred Days

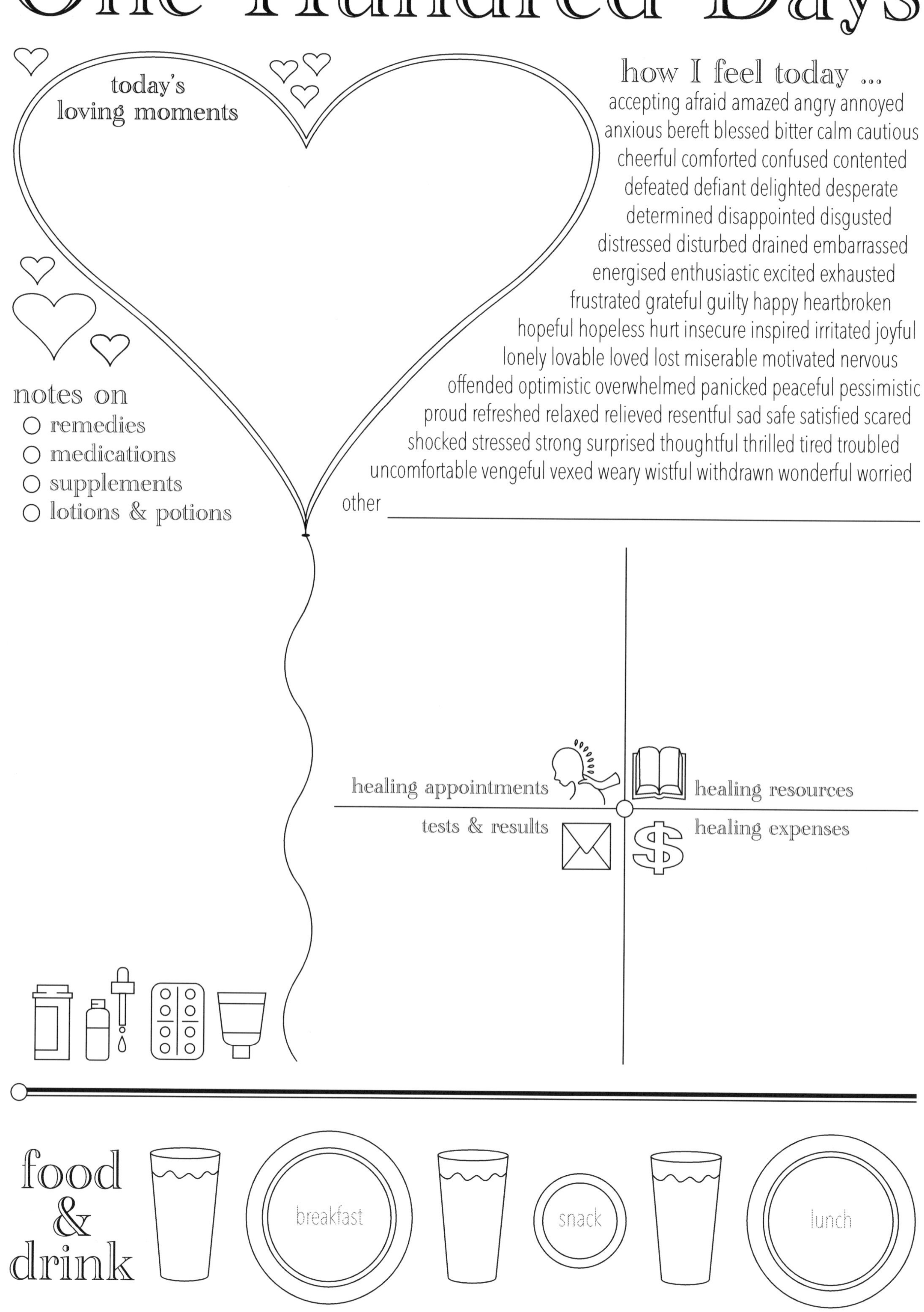

# of Healing

physical activity

social activity

screen time

resting time

connections with nature

wondering & wandering thoughts

snack

dinner

day 35

midnight

1am

2am

3am

4am

5am

6am

7am

8am

9am

10am

11am

midday

1pm

2pm

3pm

4pm

5pm

6pm

7pm

8pm

9pm

10pm

11pm

midnight

date:

One Hundred Days

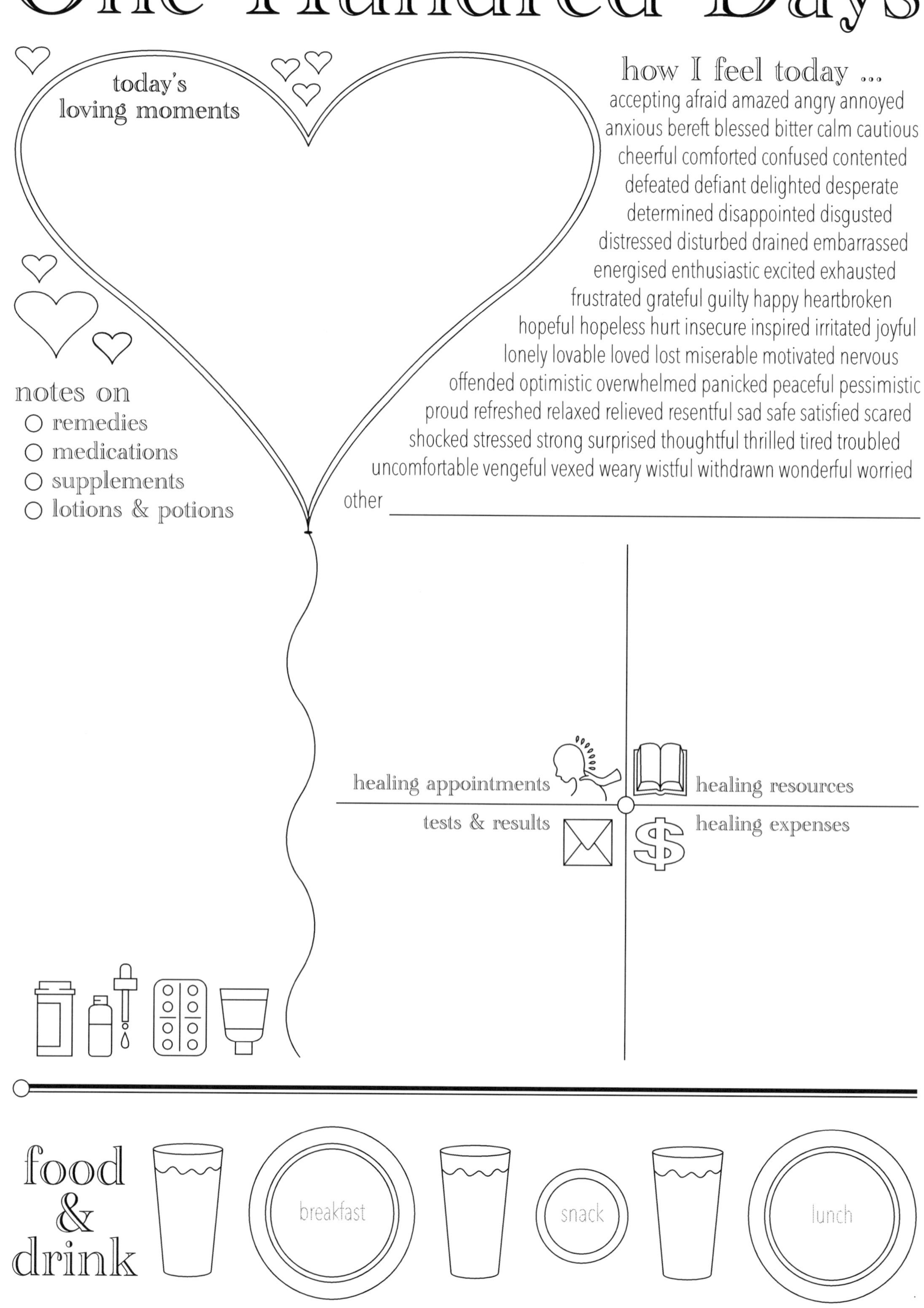

# of Healing

day 36

midnight
1am
2am
3am
4am
5am
6am
7am
8am
9am
10am
11am
midday
1pm
2pm
3pm
4pm
5pm
6pm
7pm
8pm
9pm
10pm
11pm
midnight

date:

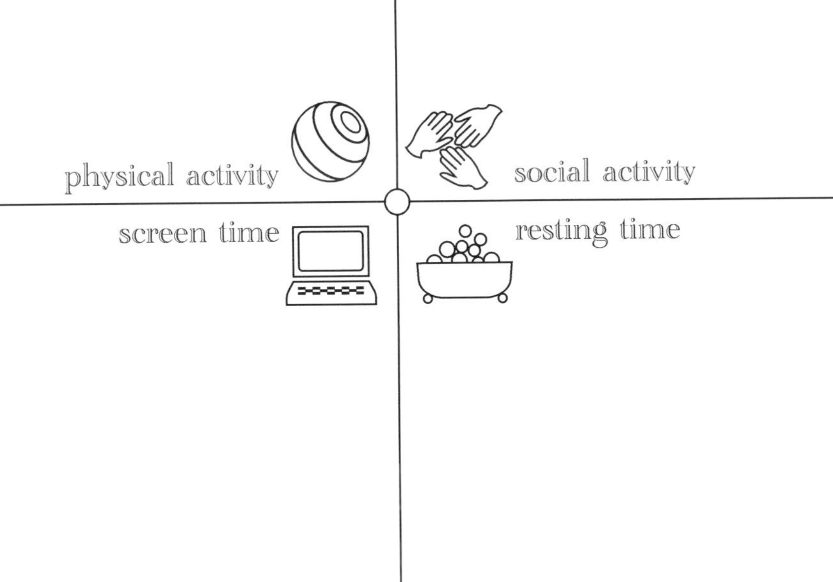

One Hundred Days

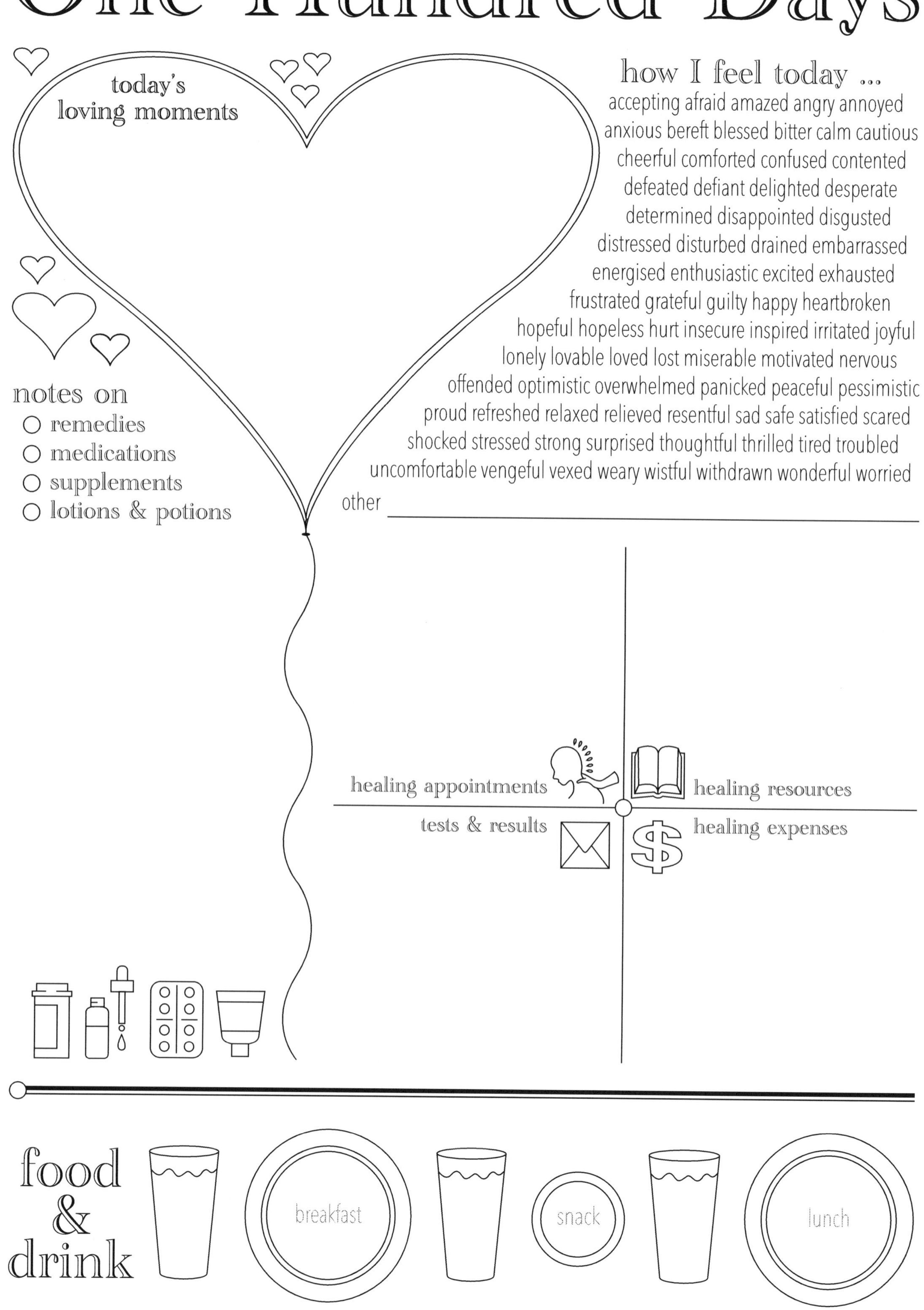

# of Healing

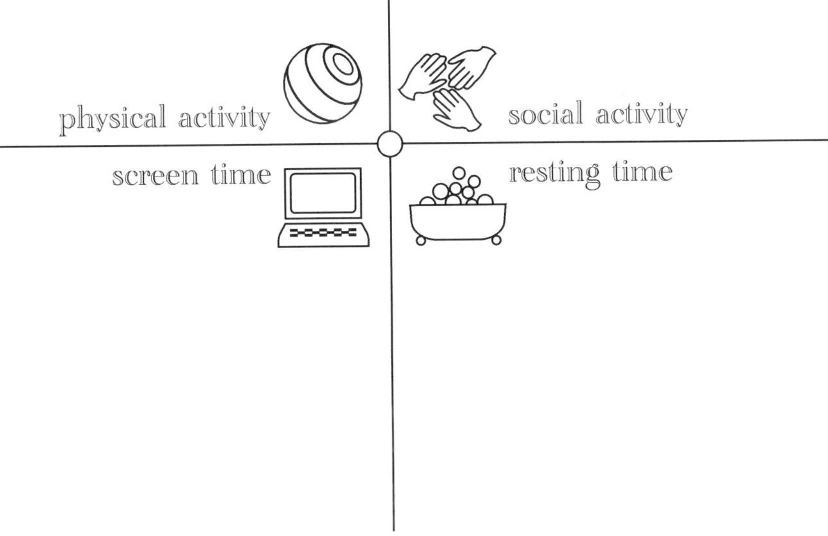

day 37

midnight

1am

2am

3am

4am

5am

6am

7am

8am

9am

10am

11am

midday

1pm

2pm

3pm

4pm

5pm

6pm

7pm

8pm

9pm

10pm

11pm

midnight

date:

One Hundred Days

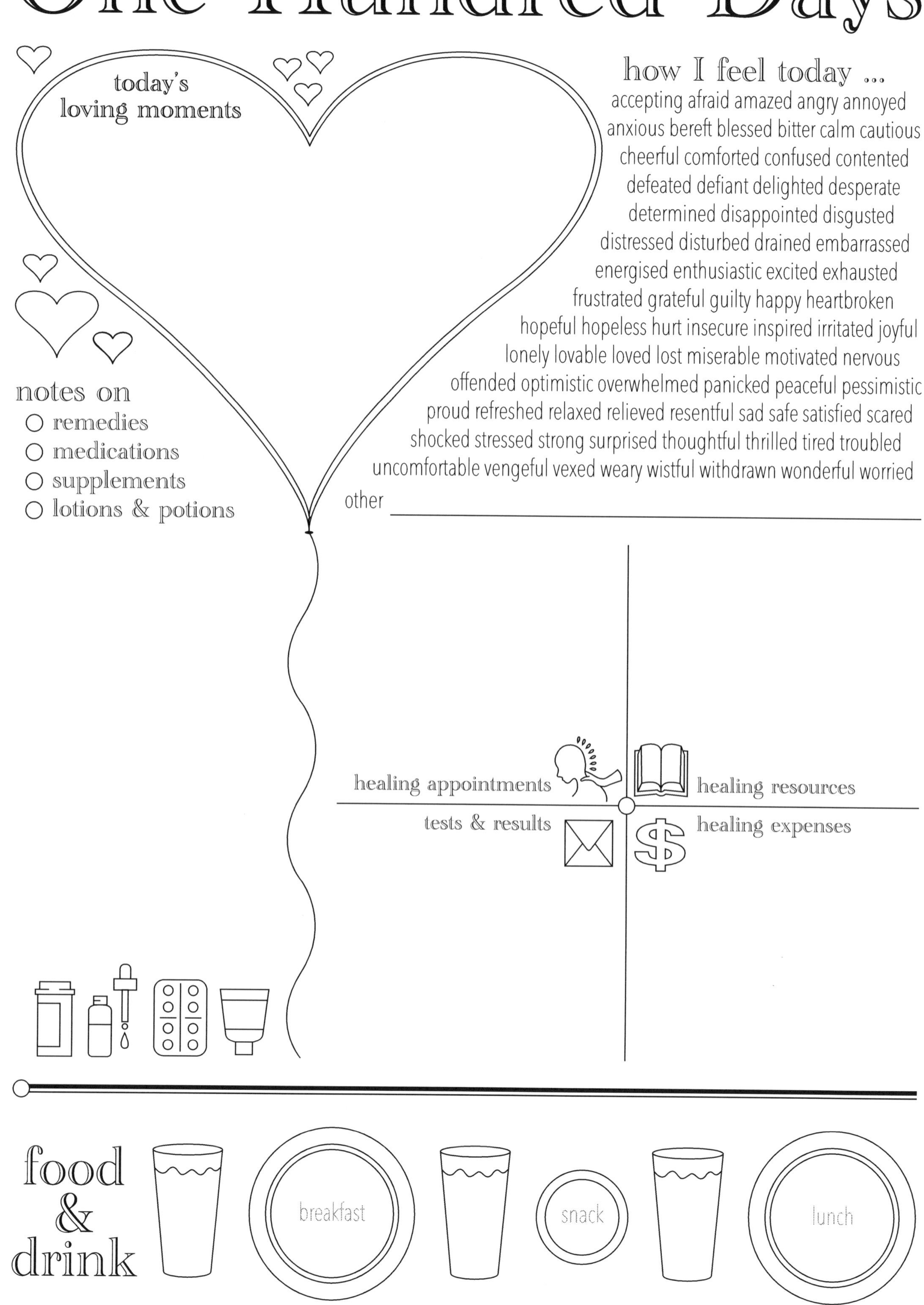

# of Healing

day 38

midnight
1am
2am
3am
4am
5am
6am
7am
8am
9am
10am
11am
midday
1pm
2pm
3pm
4pm
5pm
6pm
7pm
8pm
9pm
10pm
11pm
midnight

date:

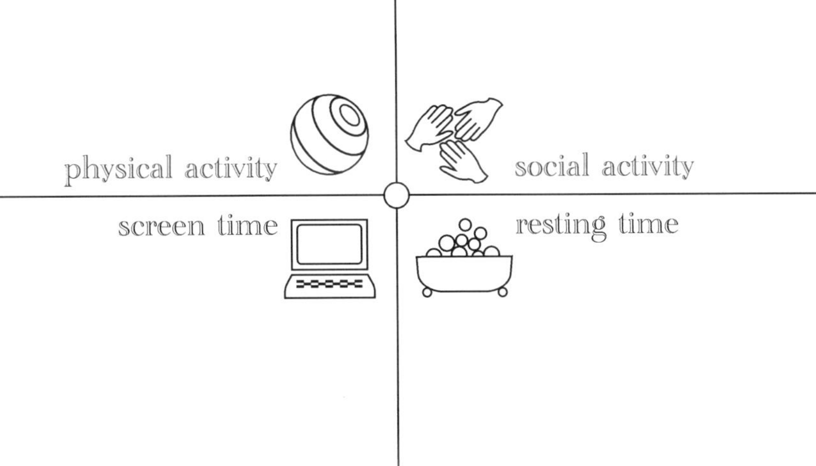

One Hundred Days

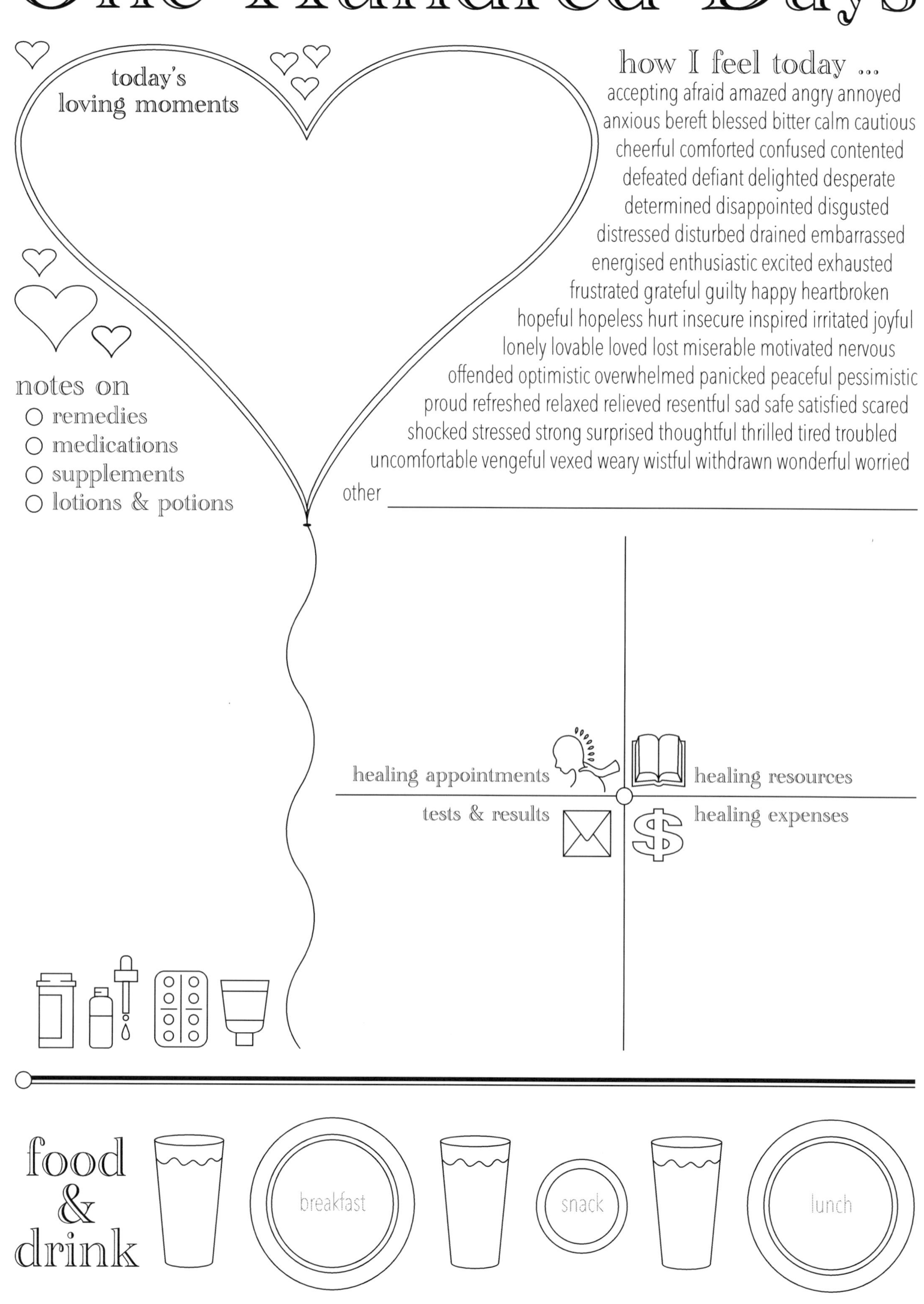

# of Healing

physical activity

social activity

screen time

resting time

connections with nature

day 39

midnight
1am
2am
3am
4am
5am
6am
7am
8am
9am
10am
11am
midday
1pm
2pm
3pm
4pm
5pm
6pm
7pm
8pm
9pm
10pm
11pm
midnight

date:

One Hundred Days

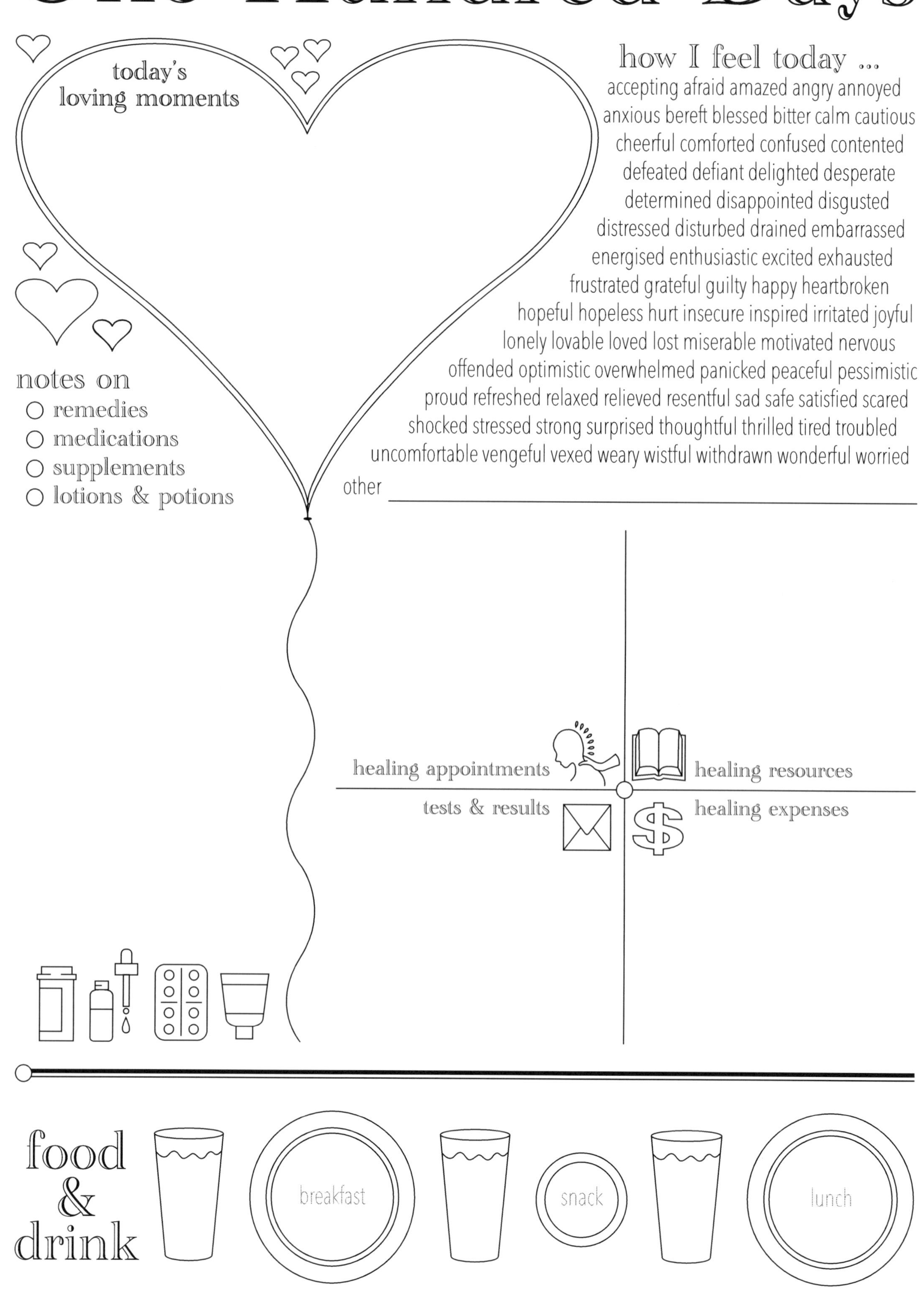

food & drink

breakfast

snack

lunch

# of Healing

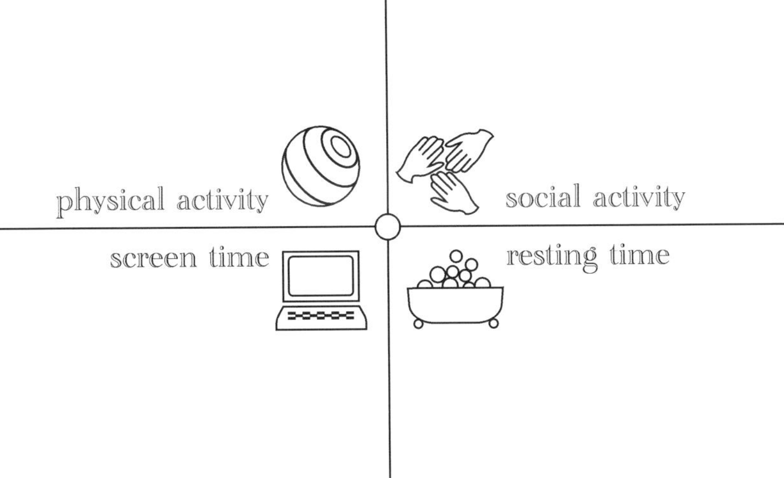

connections with nature

day 40

midnight
1am
2am
3am
4am
5am
6am
7am
8am
9am
10am
11am
midday
1pm
2pm
3pm
4pm
5pm
6pm
7pm
8pm
9pm
10pm
11pm
midnight

date:

One Hundred Days

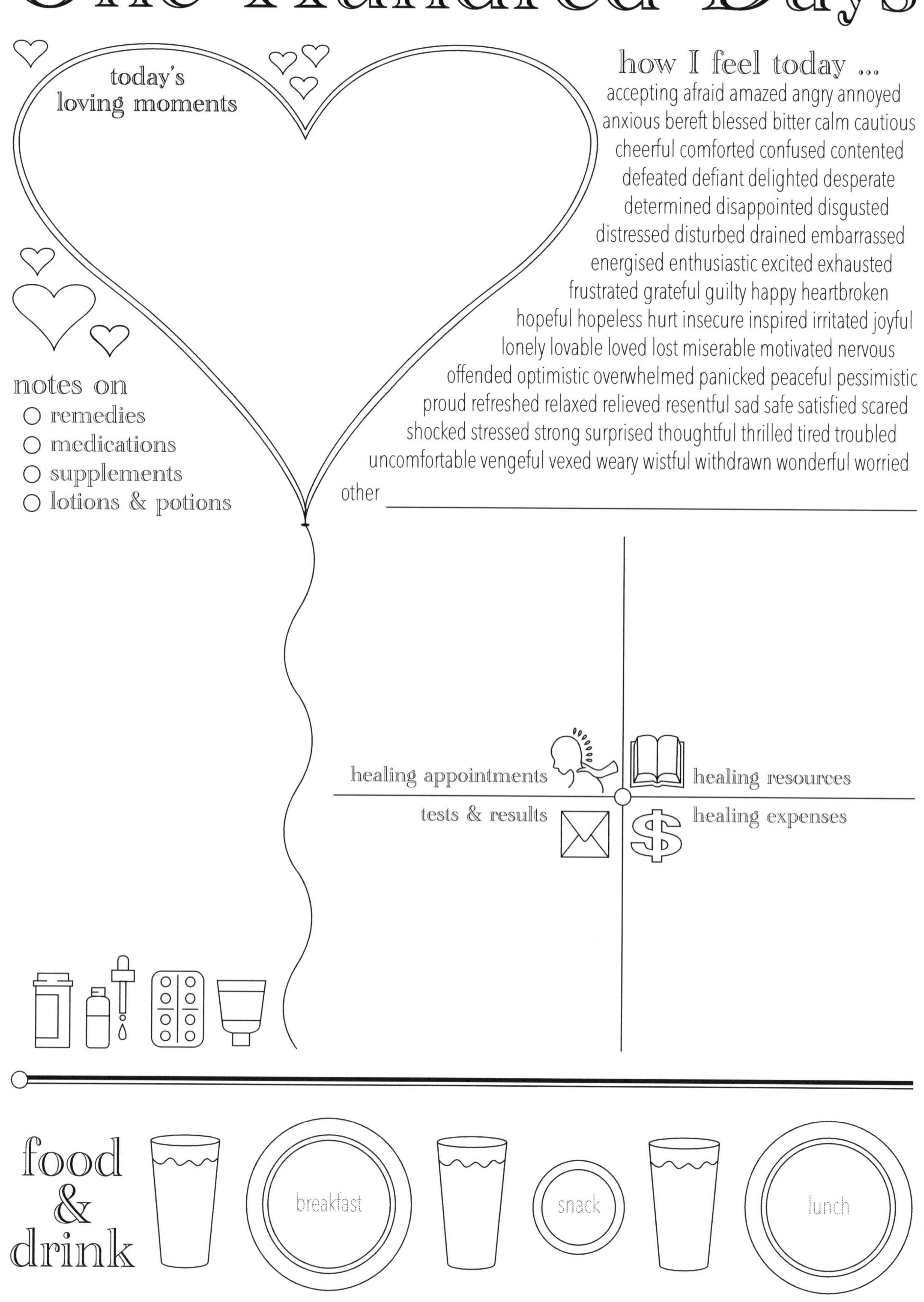

food & drink

breakfast

snack

lunch

# of Healing

physical activity

social activity

screen time

resting time

connections with nature

day 41

midnight

1am

2am

3am

4am

5am

6am

7am

8am

9am

10am

11am

midday

1pm

2pm

3pm

4pm

5pm

6pm

7pm

8pm

9pm

10pm

11pm

midnight

date:

One Hundred Days

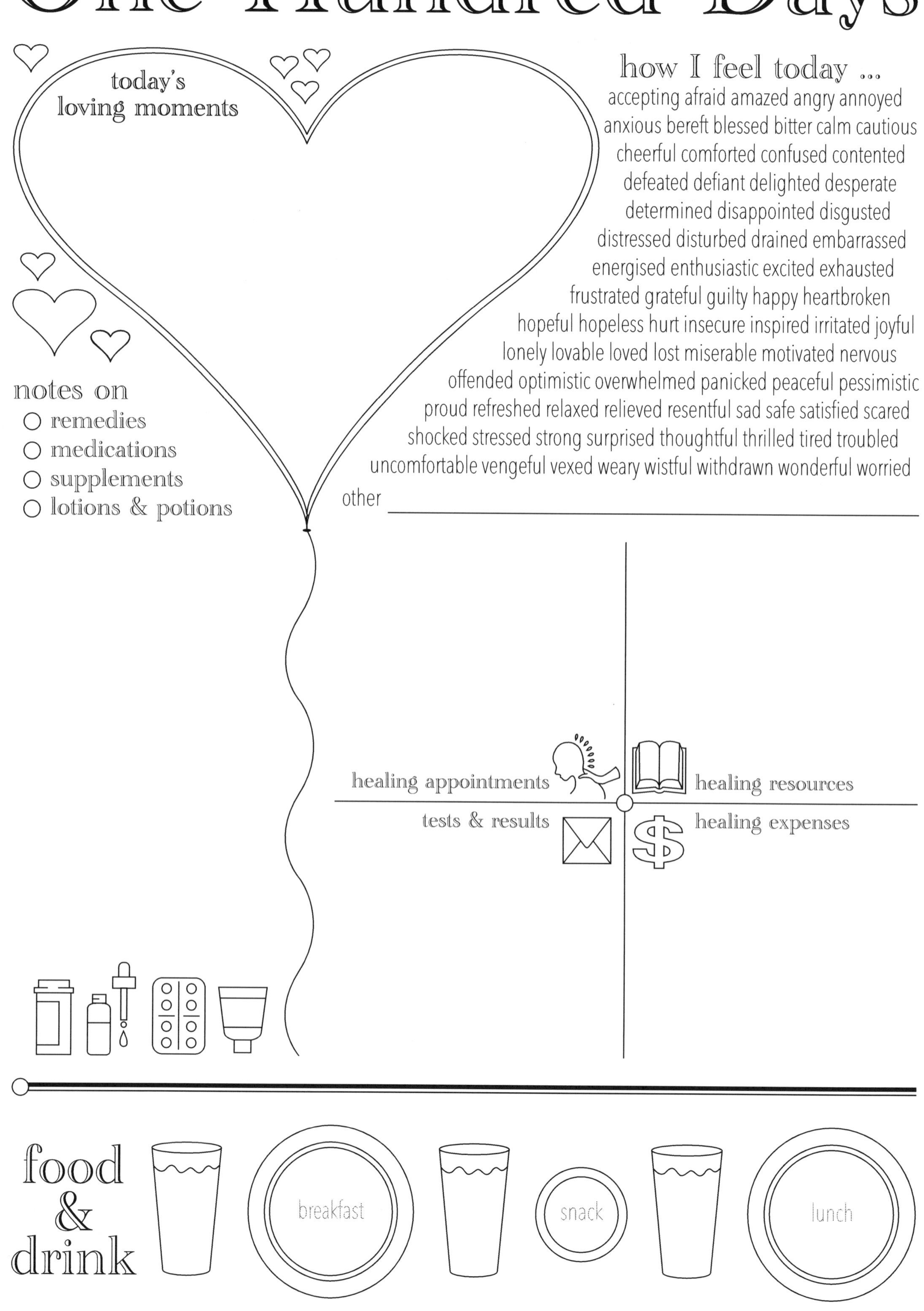

# of Healing

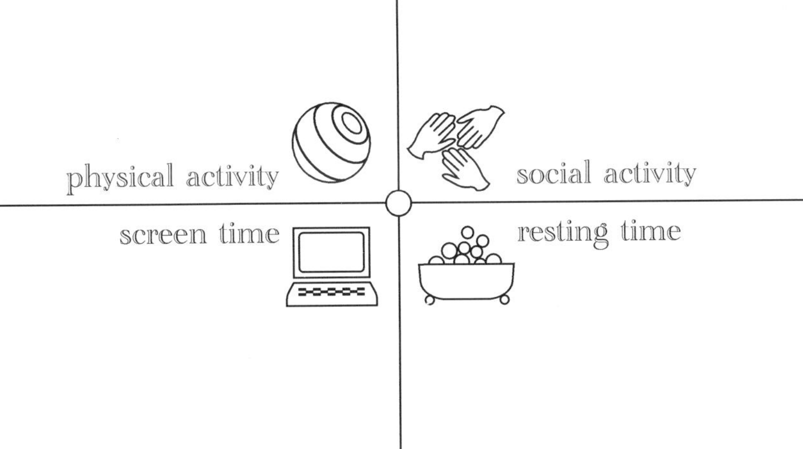

day 42

midnight

1am

2am

3am

4am

5am

6am

7am

8am

9am

10am

11am

midday

1pm

2pm

3pm

4pm

5pm

6pm

7pm

8pm

9pm

10pm

11pm

midnight

date:

One Hundred Days

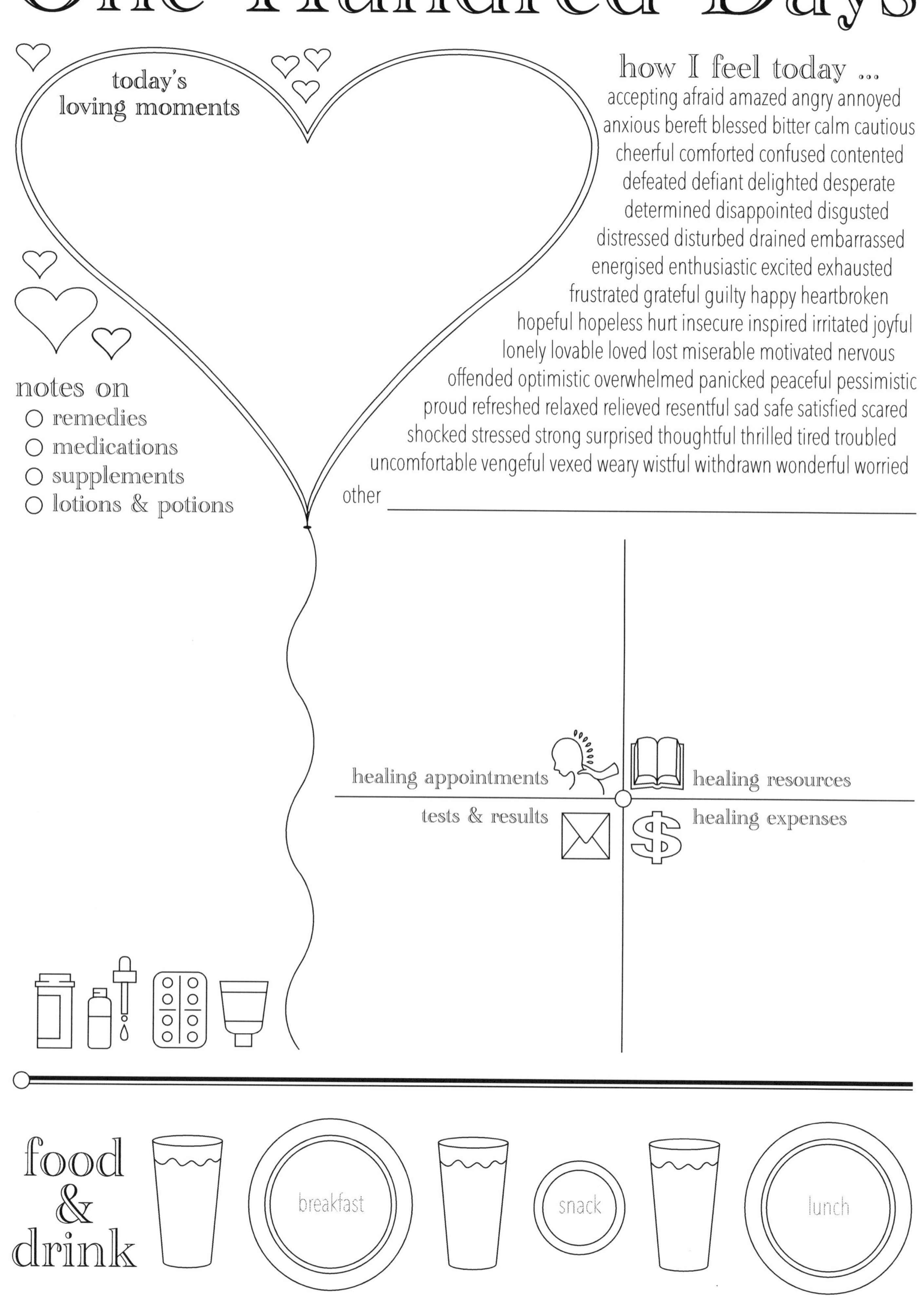

# of Healing

physical activity

social activity

screen time

resting time

connections with nature

wondering & wandering thoughts

snack

dinner

day 43

midnight

1am

2am

3am

4am

5am

6am

7am

8am

9am

10am

11am

midday

1pm

2pm

3pm

4pm

5pm

6pm

7pm

8pm

9pm

10pm

11pm

midnight

date:

One Hundred Days

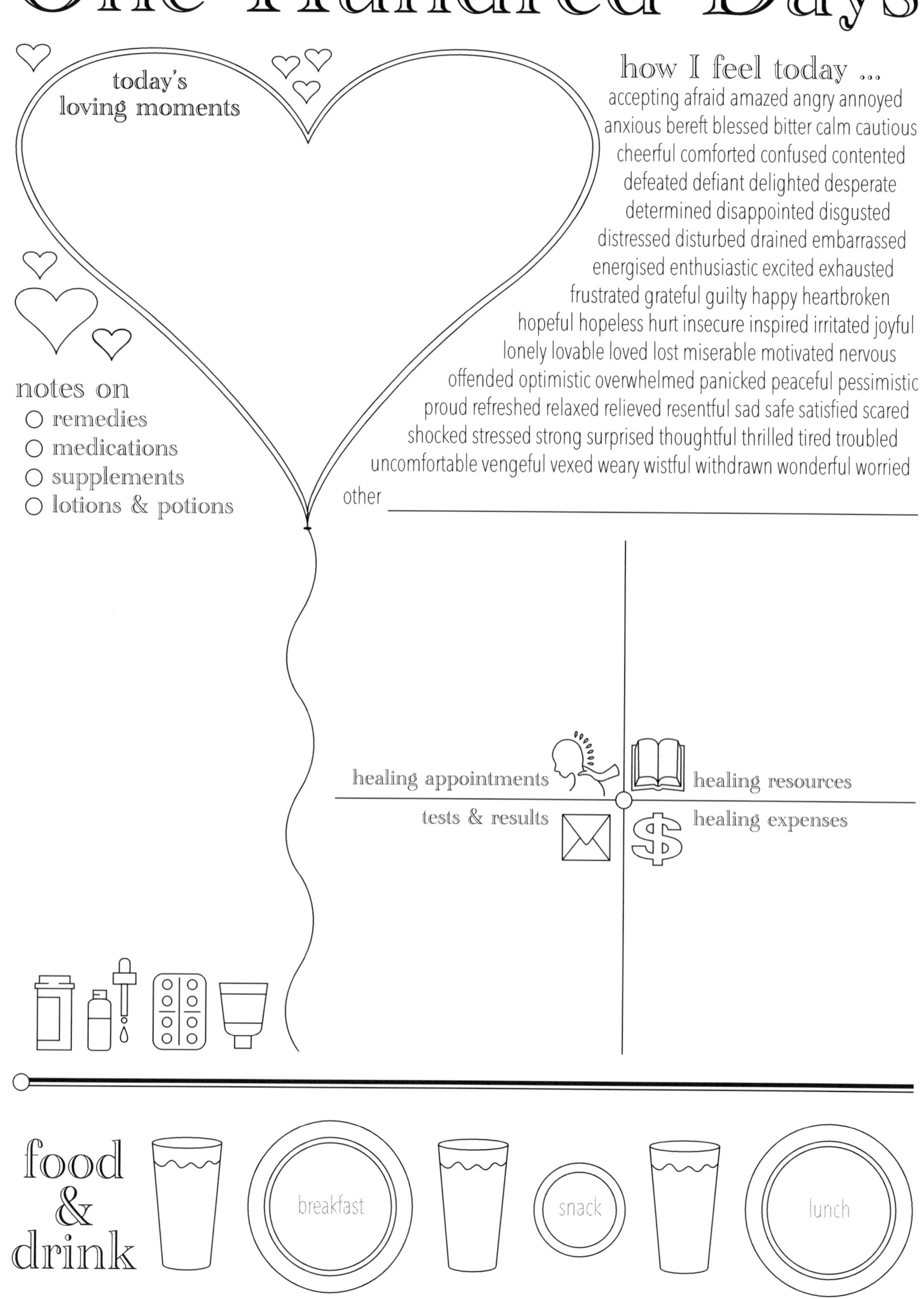

food & drink

breakfast

snack

lunch

# of Healing

physical activity

social activity

screen time

resting time

connections with nature

wondering & wandering thoughts

snack

dinner

day 44

midnight

1am

2am

3am

4am

5am

6am

7am

8am

9am

10am

11am

midday

1pm

2pm

3pm

4pm

5pm

6pm

7pm

8pm

9pm

10pm

11pm

midnight

date:

One Hundred Days

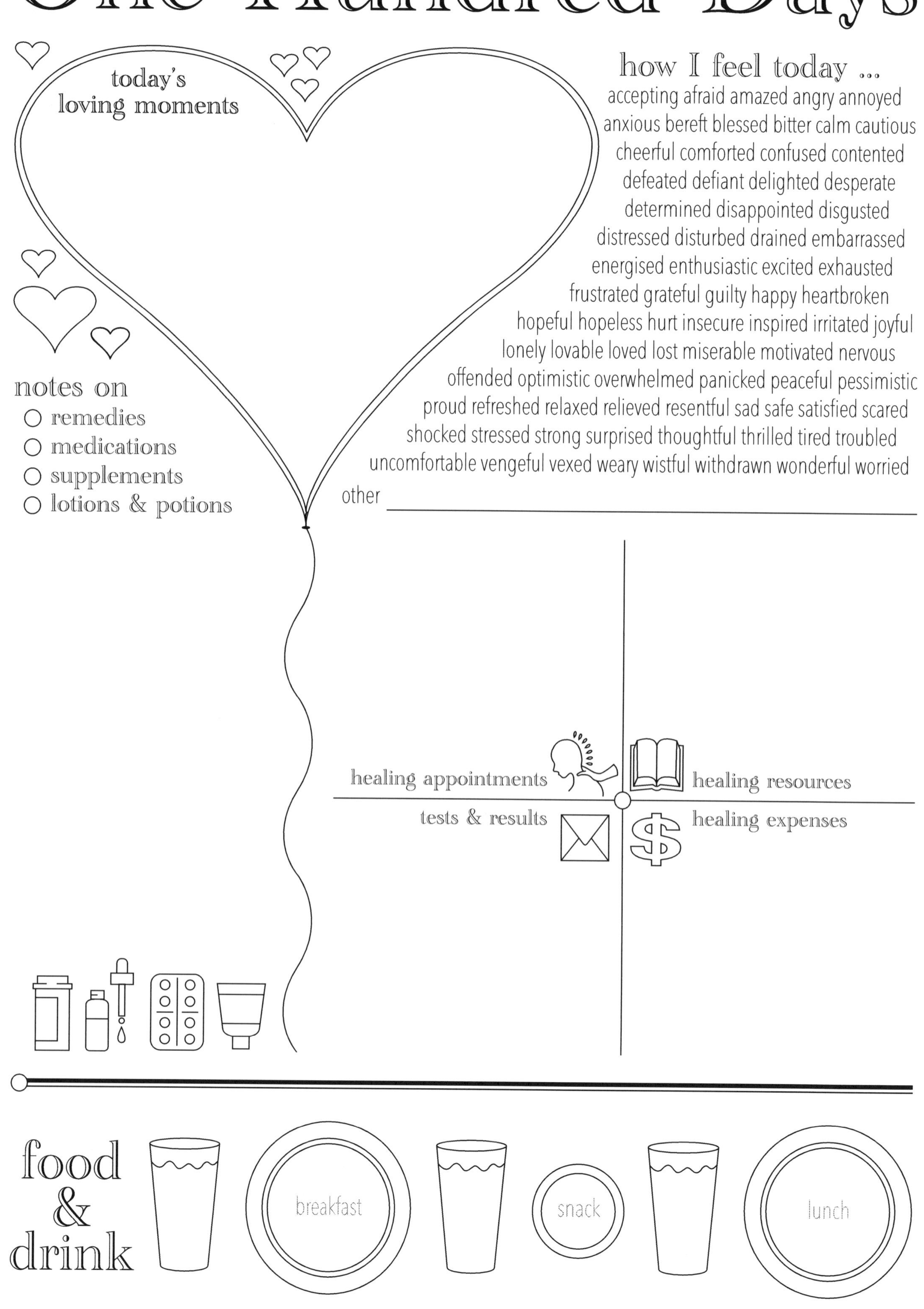

# of Healing

physical activity

social activity

screen time

resting time

connections with nature

wondering & wandering thoughts

snack

dinner

day 45

midnight

1am

2am

3am

4am

5am

6am

7am

8am

9am

10am

11am

midday

1pm

2pm

3pm

4pm

5pm

6pm

7pm

8pm

9pm

10pm

11pm

midnight

date:

One Hundred Days

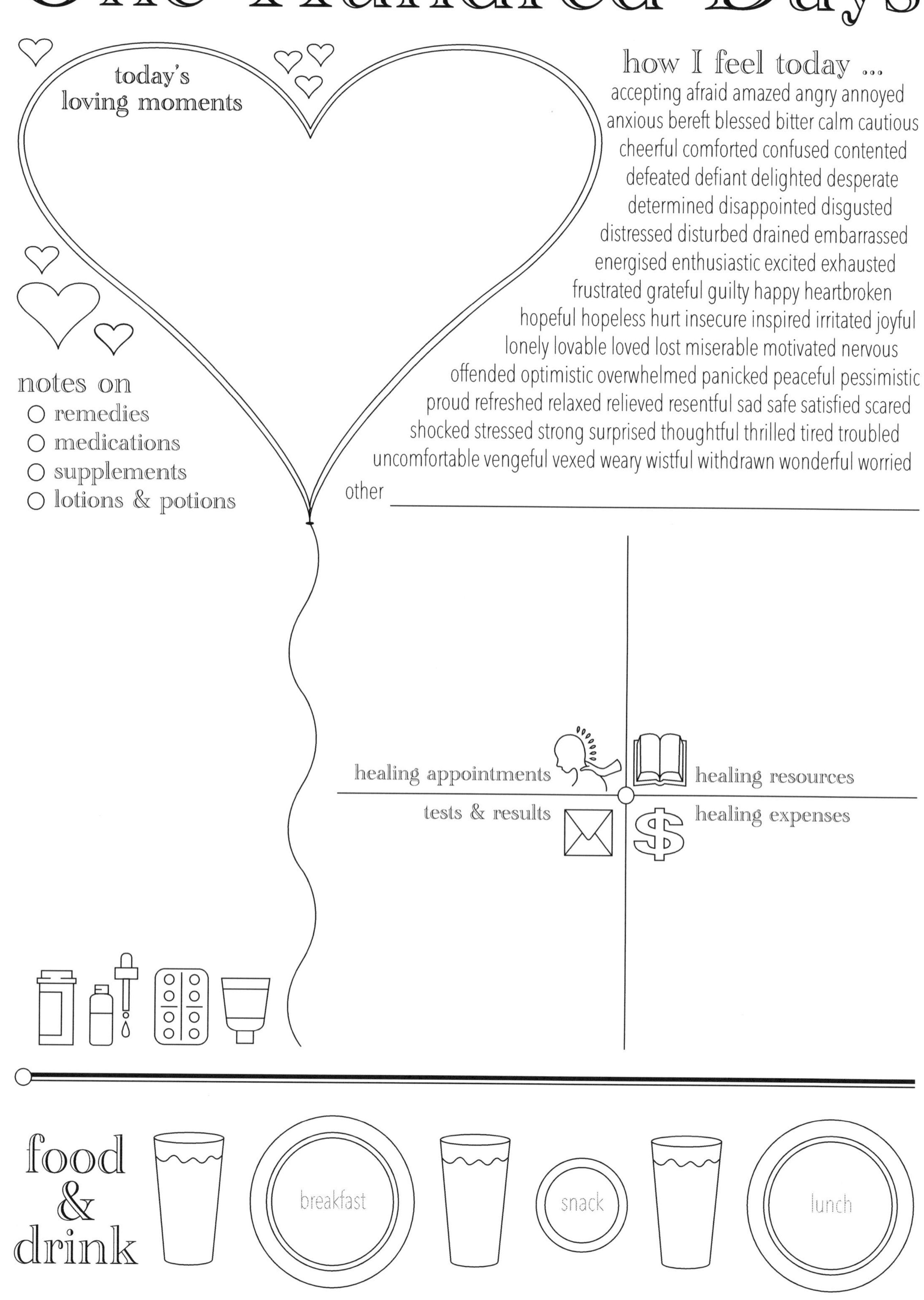

# of Healing

physical activity

social activity

screen time

resting time

connections with nature

wondering & wandering thoughts

snack

dinner

day 46

midnight
1am
2am
3am
4am
5am
6am
7am
8am
9am
10am
11am
midday
1pm
2pm
3pm
4pm
5pm
6pm
7pm
8pm
9pm
10pm
11pm
midnight

date:

One Hundred Days

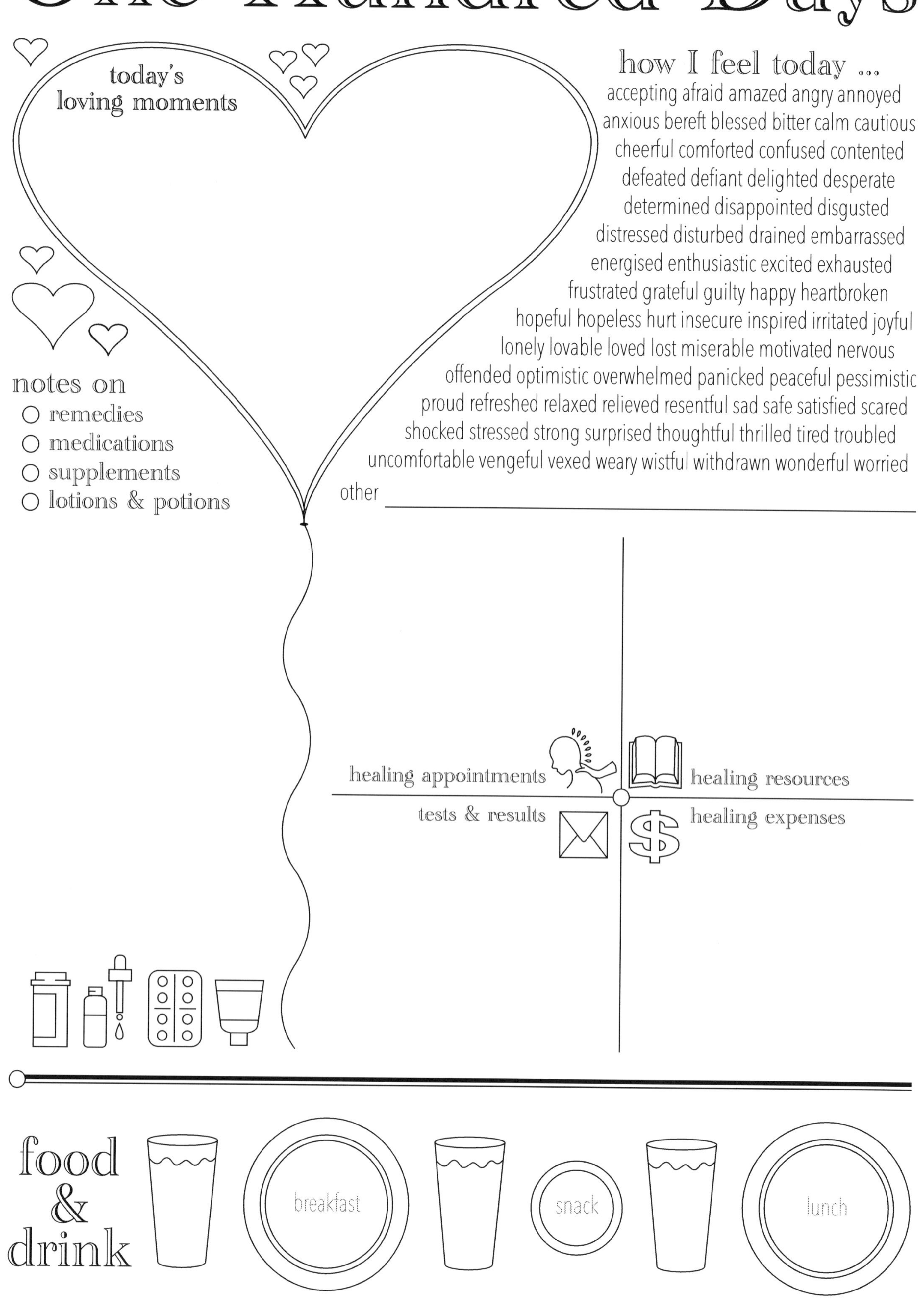

food & drink

breakfast

snack

lunch

# of Healing

day 47

midnight
1am
2am
3am
4am
5am
6am
7am
8am
9am
10am
11am
midday
1pm
2pm
3pm
4pm
5pm
6pm
7pm
8pm
9pm
10pm
11pm
midnight

date:

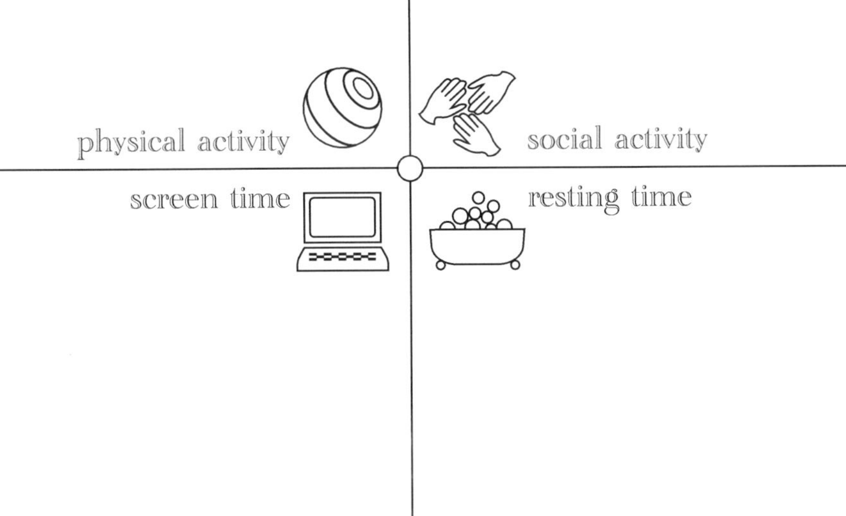

One Hundred Days

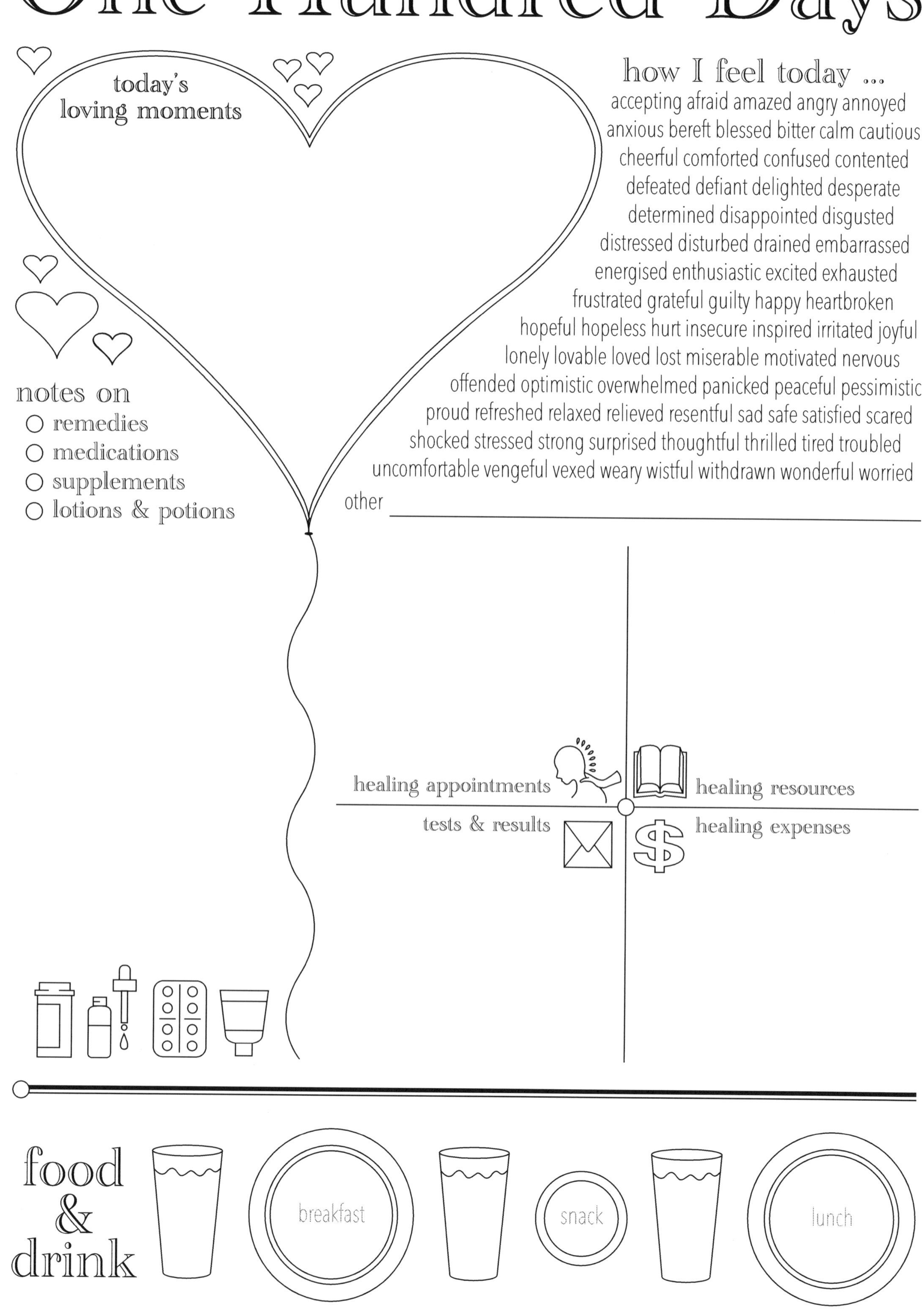

# of Healing

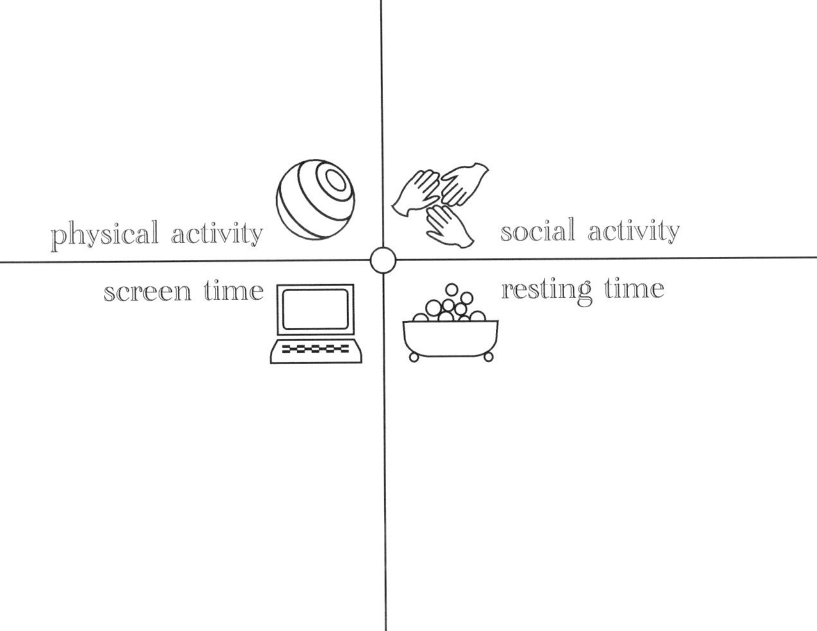

day 48

midnight

1am

2am

3am

4am

5am

6am

7am

8am

9am

10am

11am

midday

1pm

2pm

3pm

4pm

5pm

6pm

7pm

8pm

9pm

10pm

11pm

midnight

date:

One Hundred Days

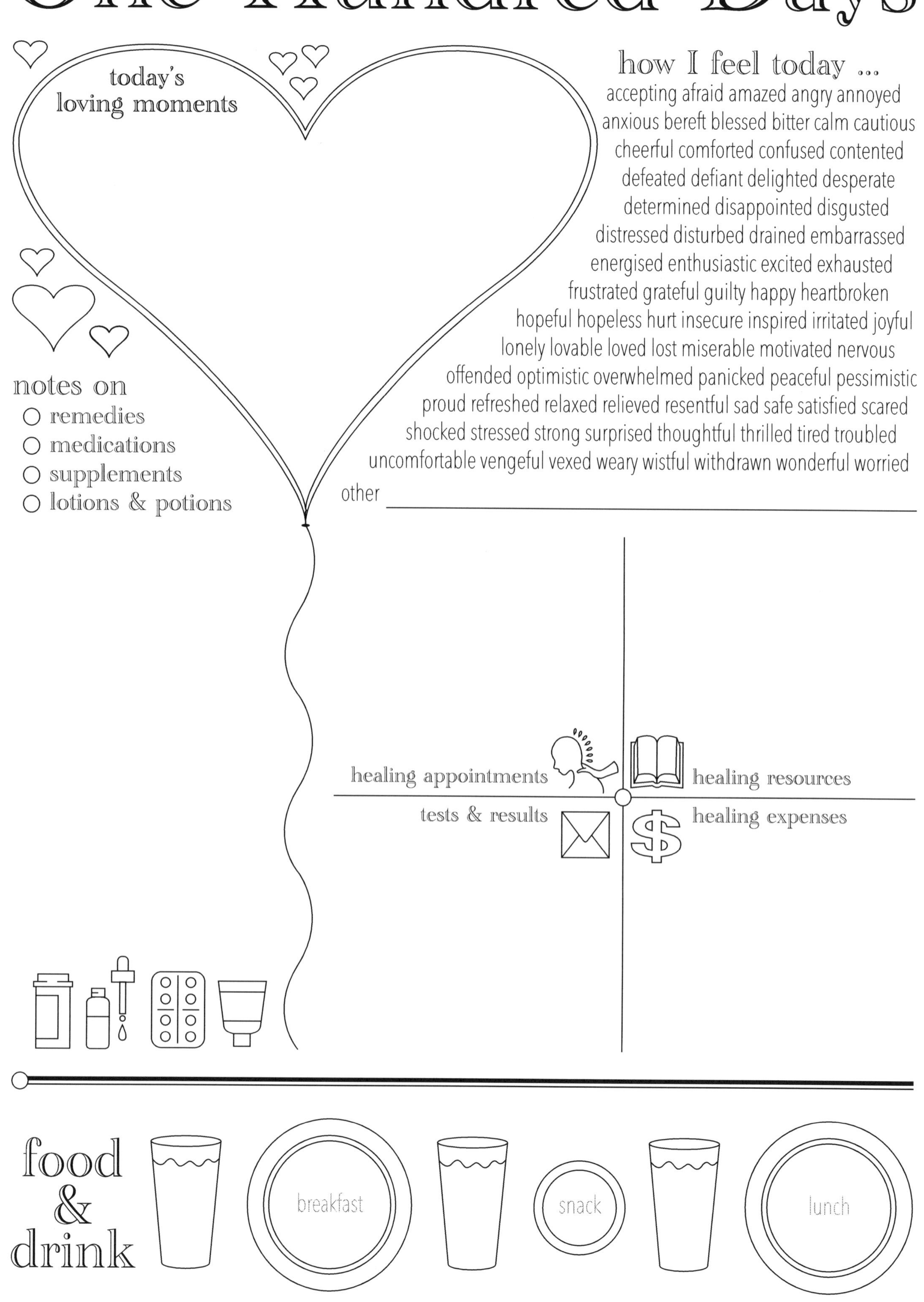

# of Healing

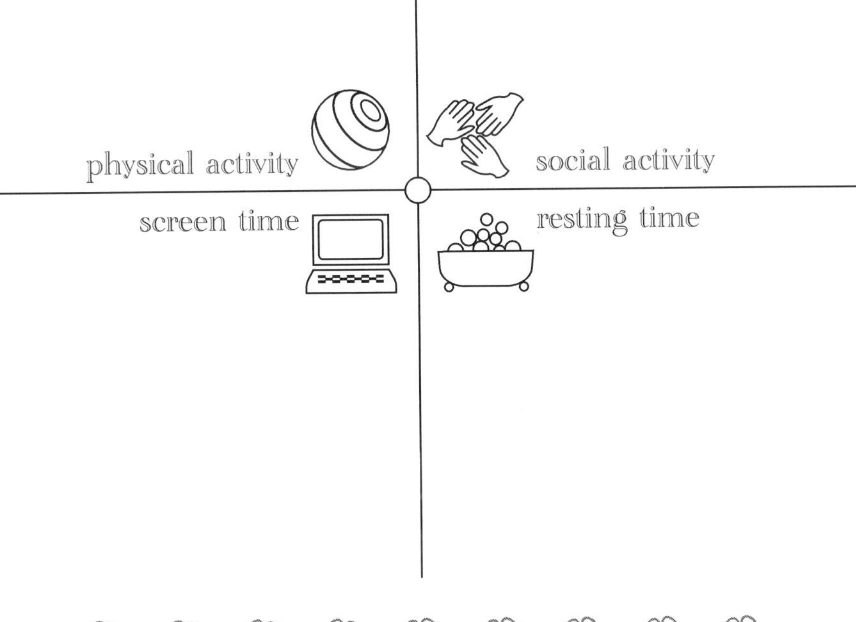

day 49

midnight

1am

2am

3am

4am

5am

6am

7am

8am

9am

10am

11am

midday

1pm

2pm

3pm

4pm

5pm

6pm

7pm

8pm

9pm

10pm

11pm

midnight

date:

One Hundred Days

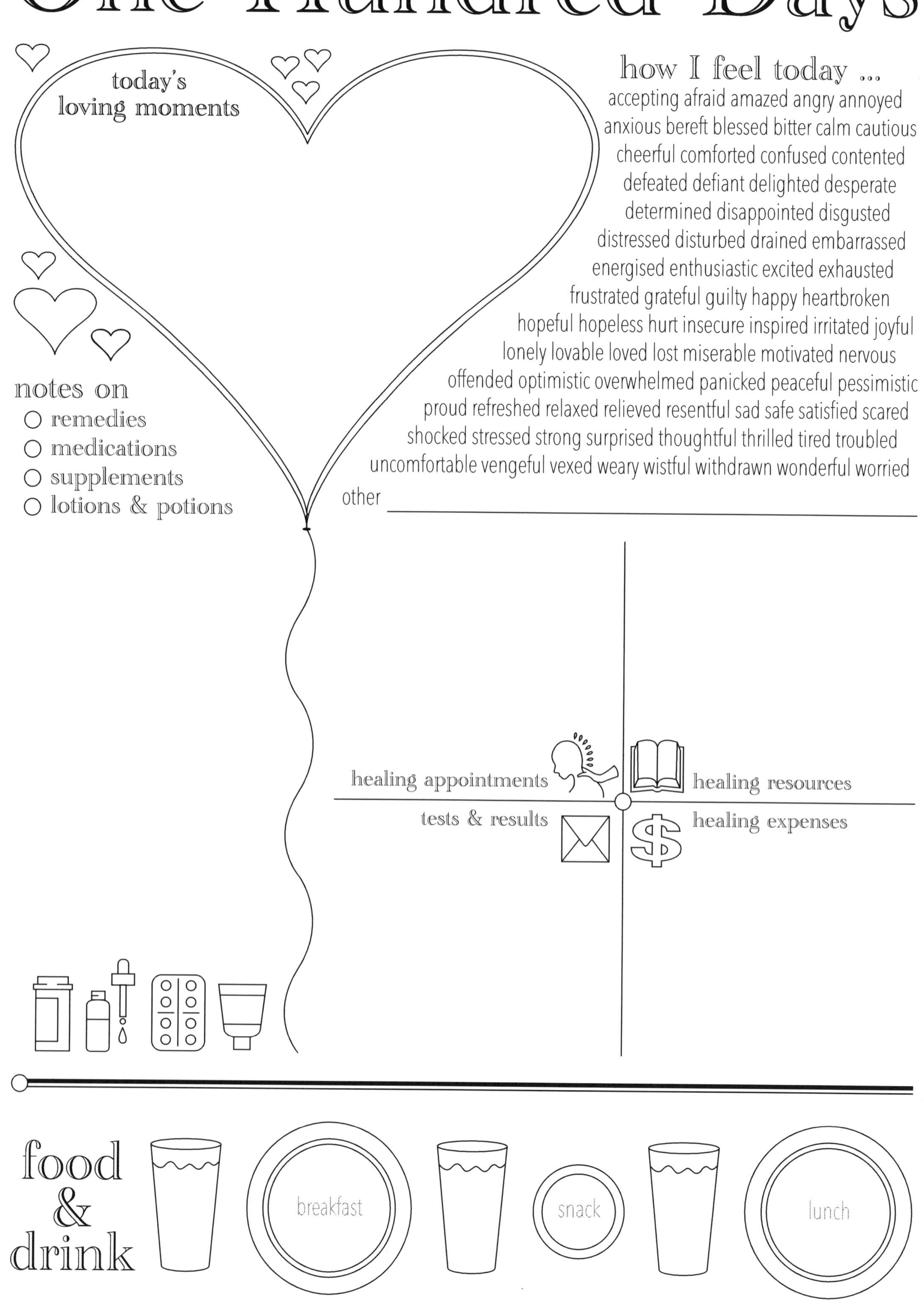

food & drink

breakfast

snack

lunch

# of Healing

physical activity

social activity

screen time

resting time

connections with nature

wondering & wandering thoughts

snack

dinner

day 50

midnight

1am

2am

3am

4am

5am

6am

7am

8am

9am

10am

11am

midday

1pm

2pm

3pm

4pm

5pm

6pm

7pm

8pm

9pm

10pm

11pm

midnight

date:

One Hundred Days

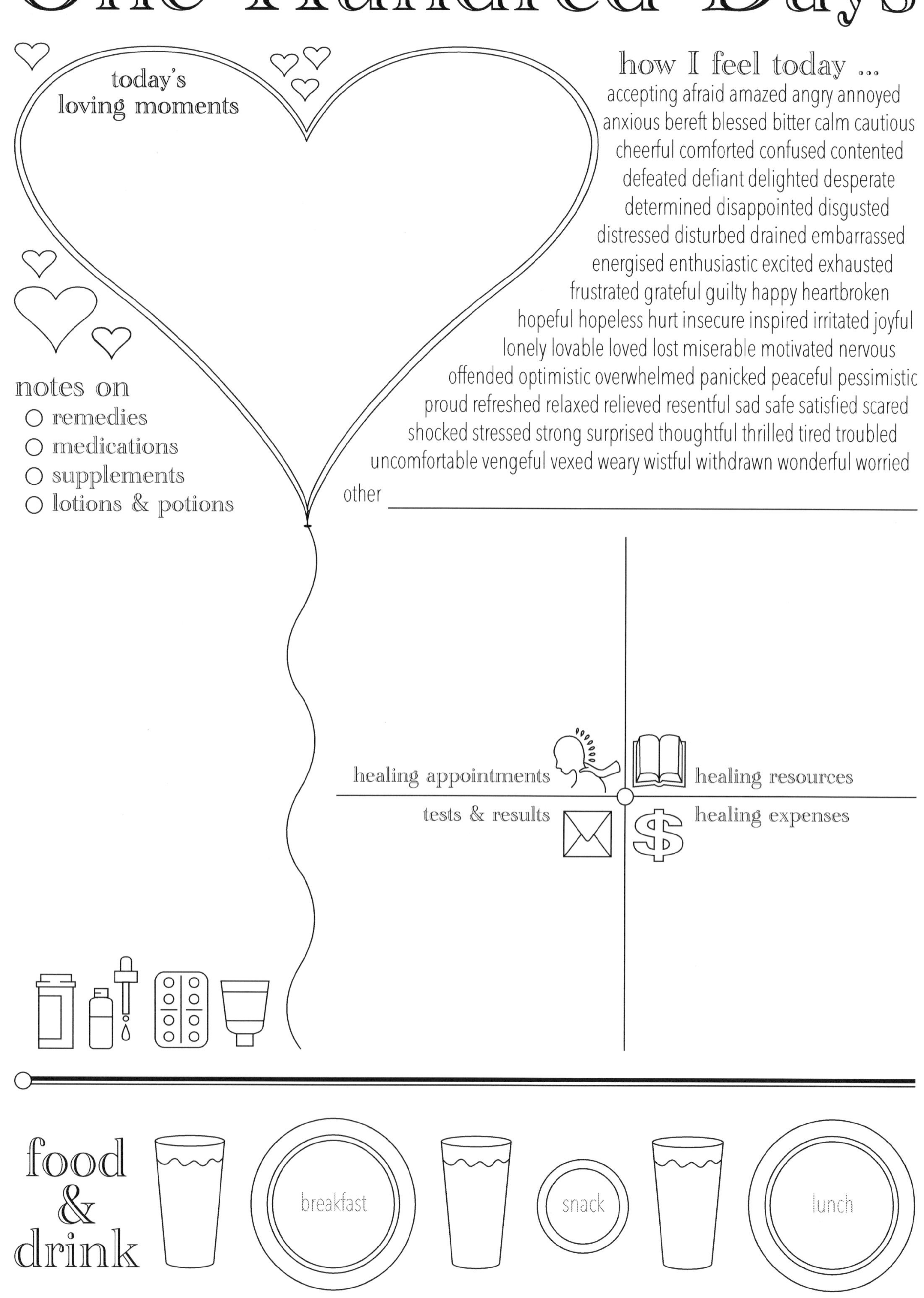

# of Healing

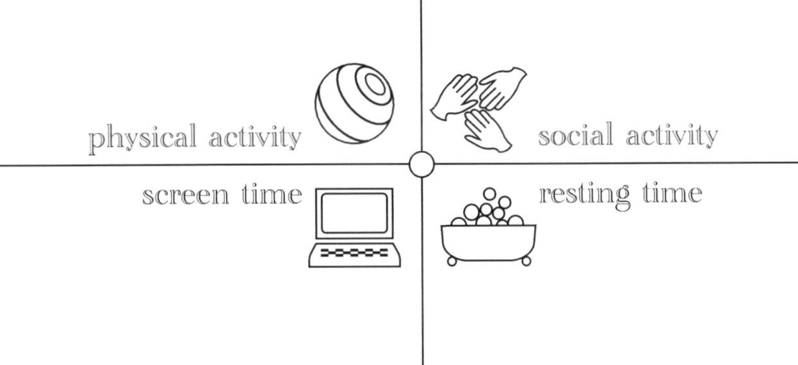

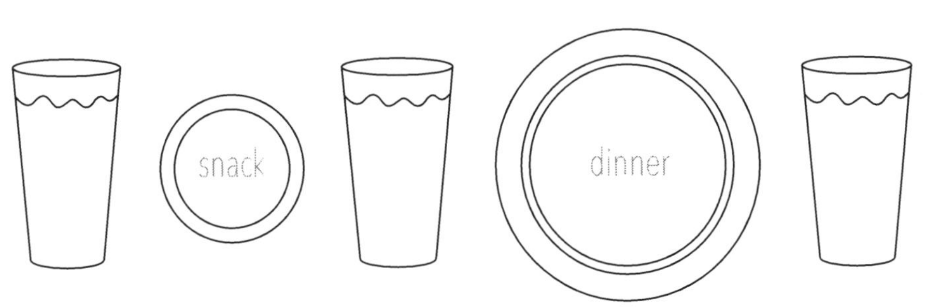

day 51

midnight

1am

2am

3am

4am

5am

6am

7am

8am

9am

10am

11am

midday

1pm

2pm

3pm

4pm

5pm

6pm

7pm

8pm

9pm

10pm

11pm

midnight

date:

One Hundred Days

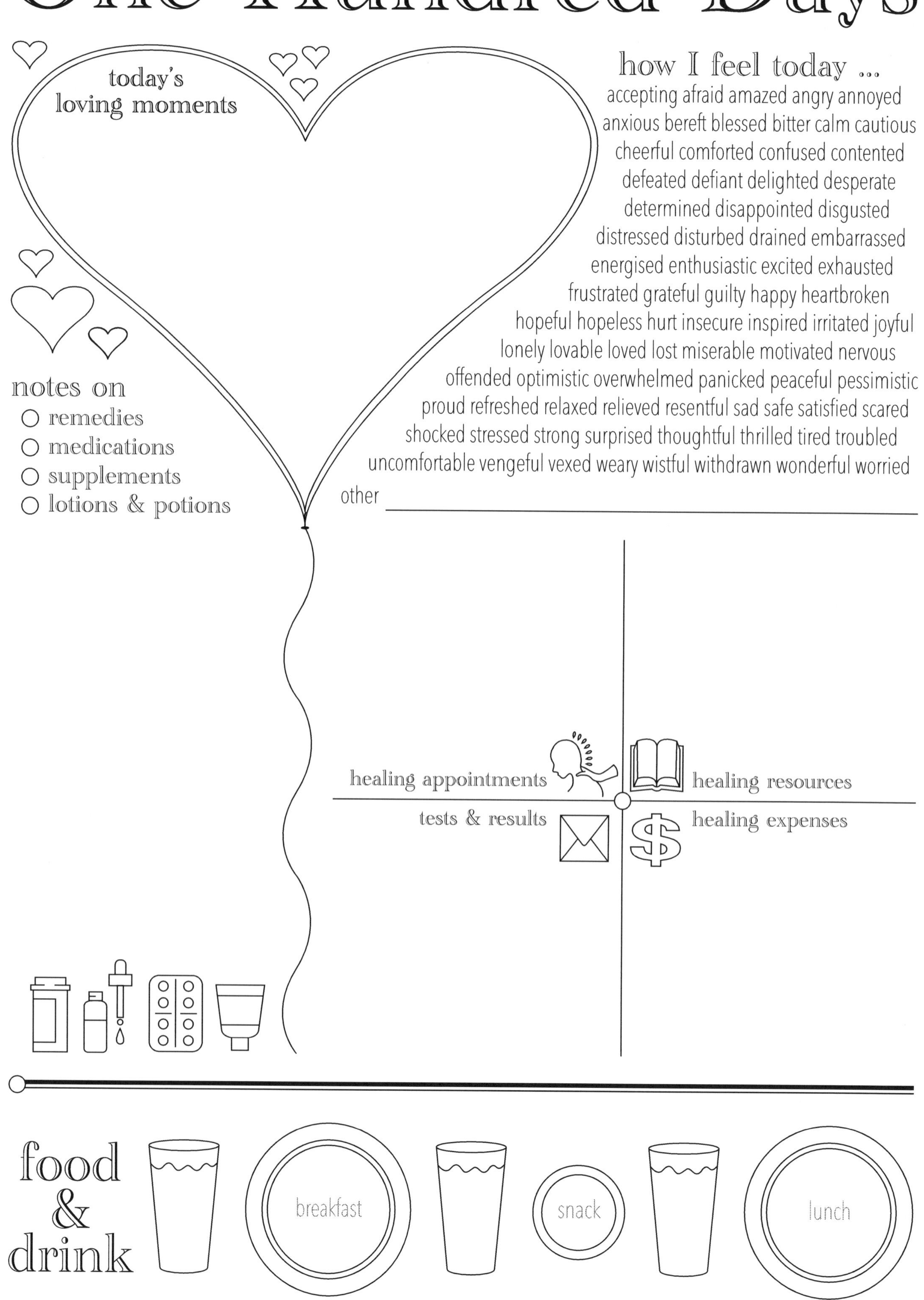

food & drink

breakfast

snack

lunch

# of Healing

day 52

midnight
1am
2am
3am
4am
5am
6am
7am
8am
9am
10am
11am
midday
1pm
2pm
3pm
4pm
5pm
6pm
7pm
8pm
9pm
10pm
11pm
midnight

date:

physical activity

social activity

screen time

resting time

connections with nature

wondering & wandering thoughts

snack

dinner

One Hundred Days

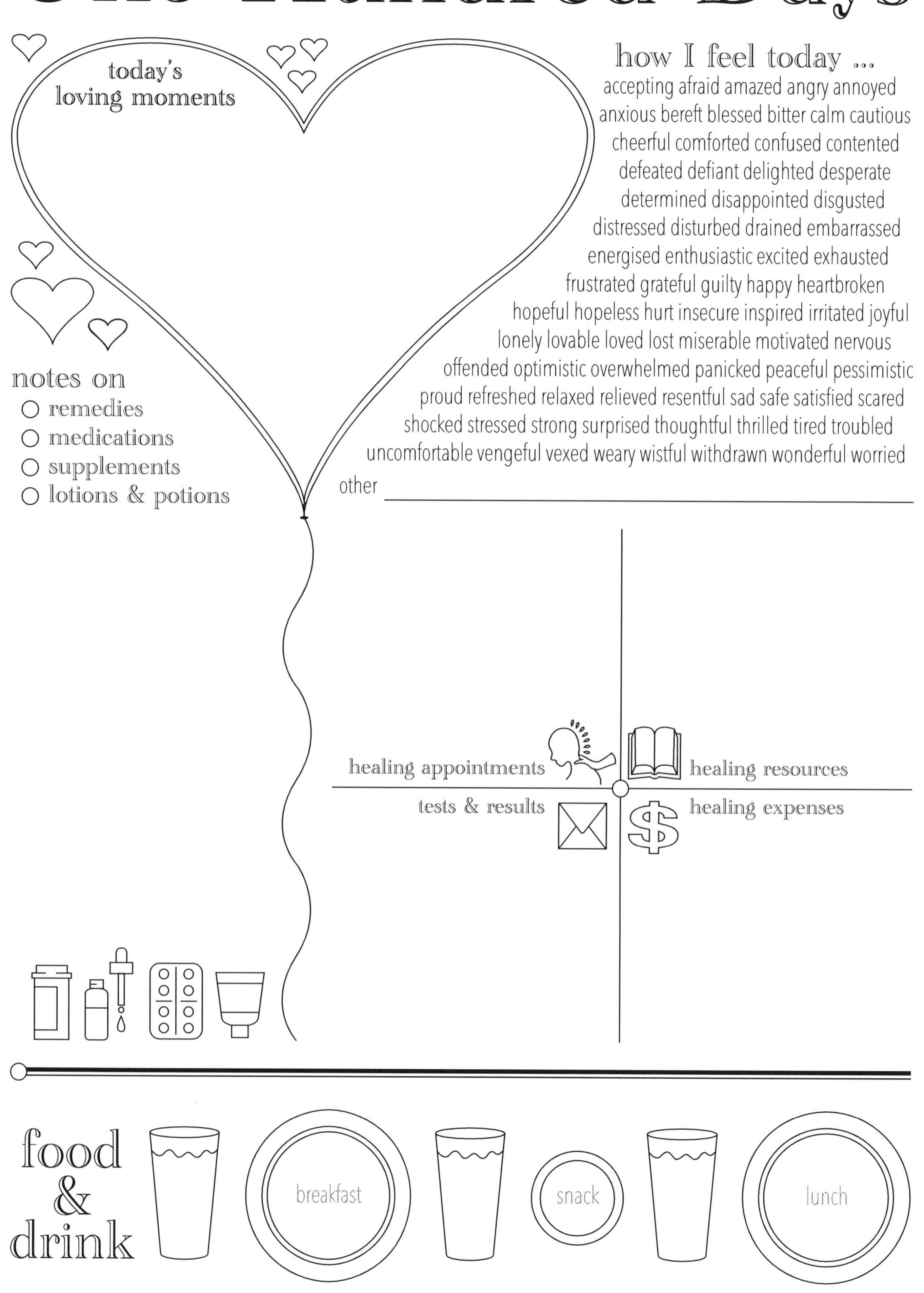

# of Healing

physical activity

social activity

screen time

resting time

connections with nature

wondering & wandering thoughts

snack

dinner

day 53

midnight

1am

2am

3am

4am

5am

6am

7am

8am

9am

10am

11am

midday

1pm

2pm

3pm

4pm

5pm

6pm

7pm

8pm

9pm

10pm

11pm

midnight

date:

One Hundred Days

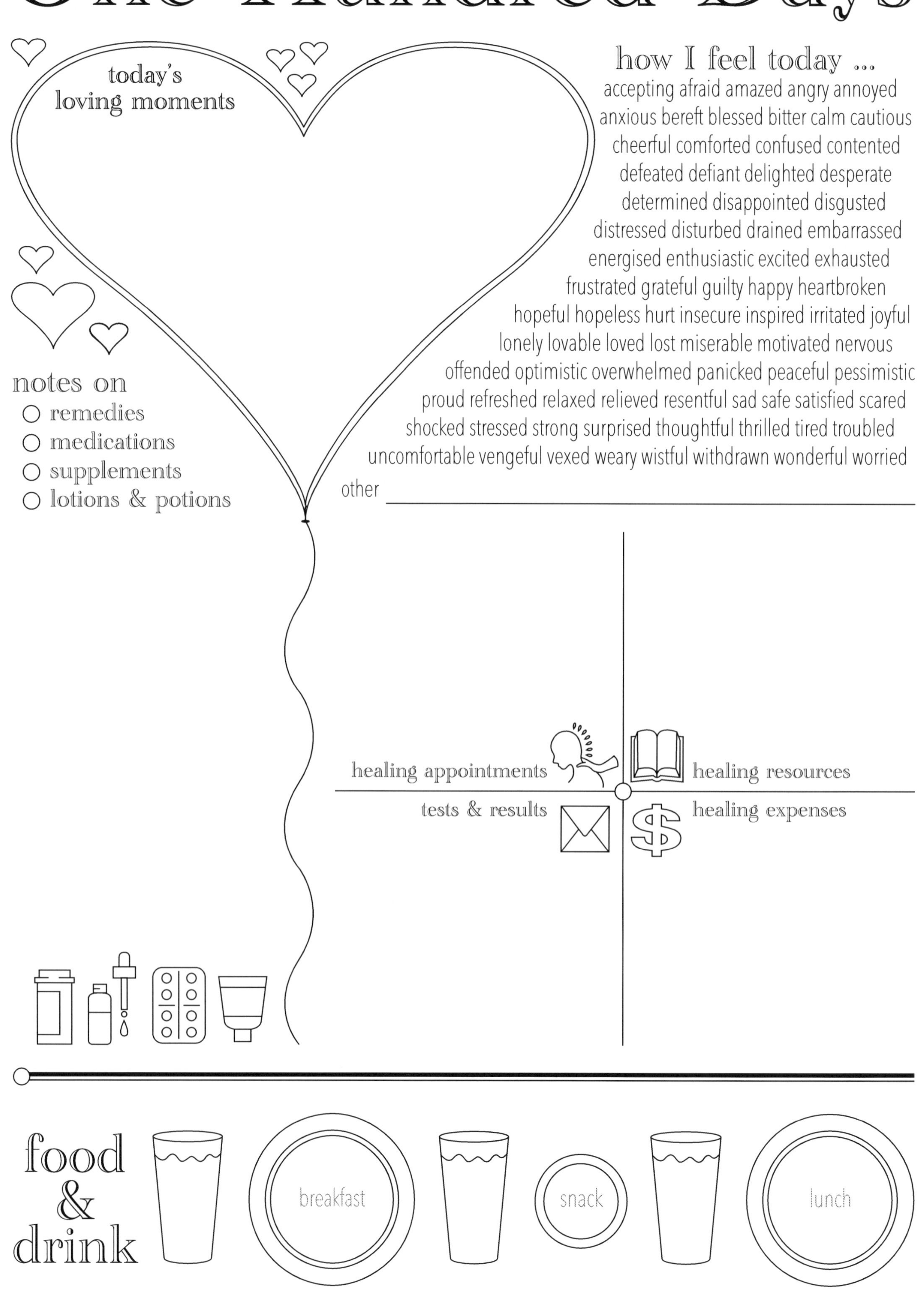

# of Healing

physical activity

social activity

screen time

resting time

connections with nature

wondering & wandering thoughts

snack

dinner

day 54

midnight

1am

2am

3am

4am

5am

6am

7am

8am

9am

10am

11am

midday

1pm

2pm

3pm

4pm

5pm

6pm

7pm

8pm

9pm

10pm

11pm

midnight

date:

One Hundred Days

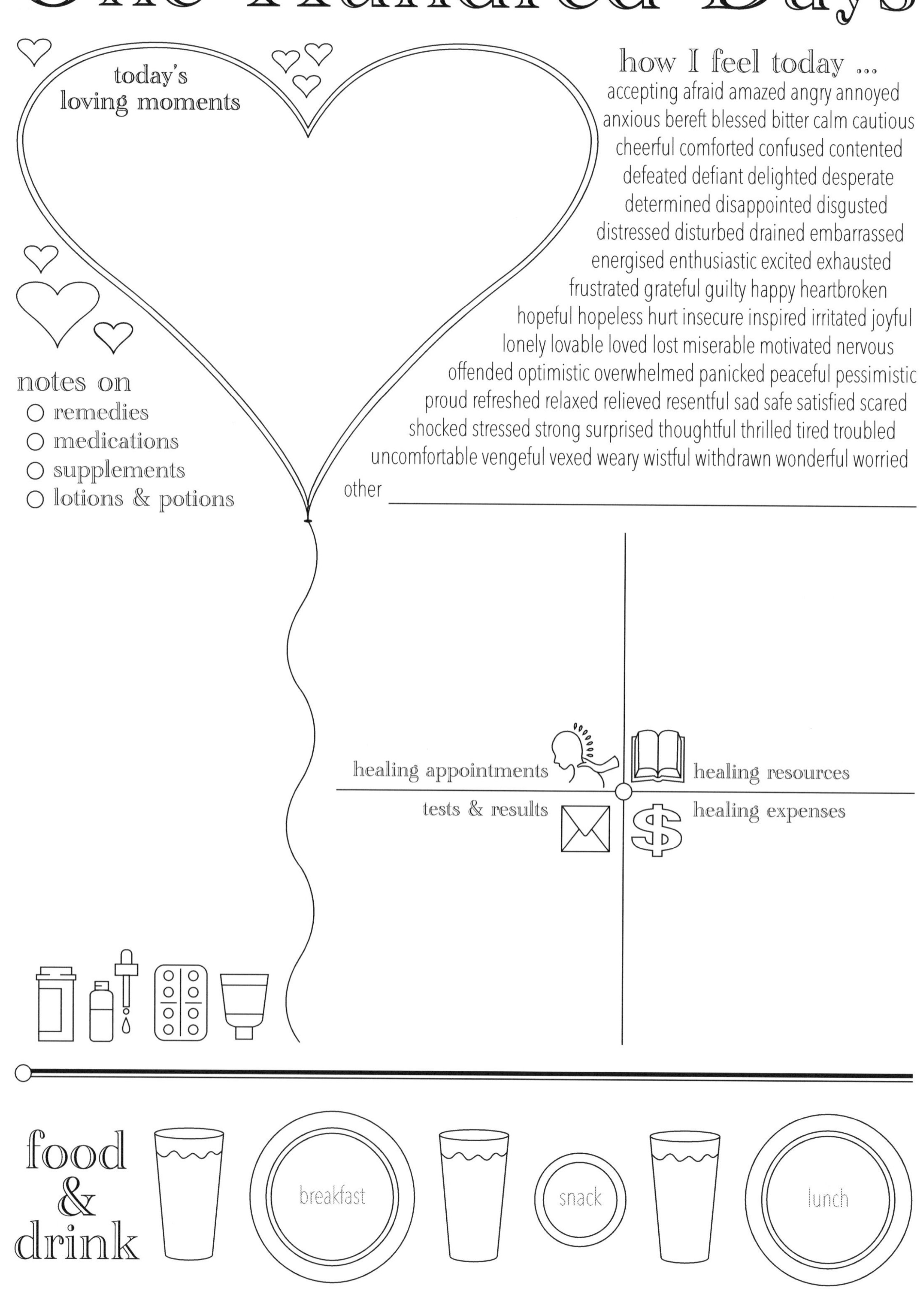

# of Healing

physical activity

social activity

screen time

resting time

connections with nature

wondering & wandering thoughts

snack

dinner

day 55

midnight

1am

2am

3am

4am

5am

6am

7am

8am

9am

10am

11am

midday

1pm

2pm

3pm

4pm

5pm

6pm

7pm

8pm

9pm

10pm

11pm

midnight

date:

One Hundred Days

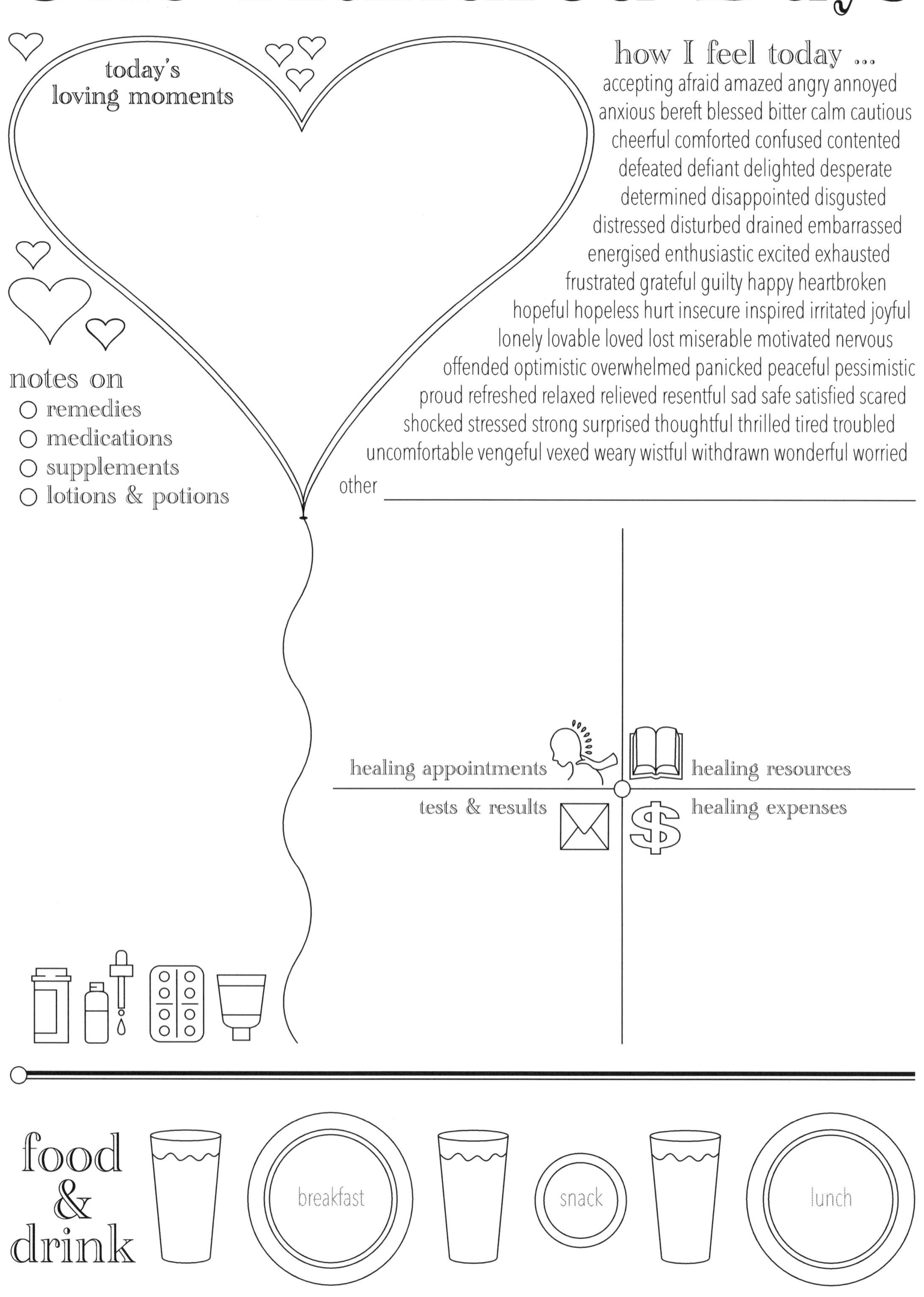

food & drink

breakfast

snack

lunch

# of Healing

physical activity

social activity

screen time

resting time

connections with nature

wondering & wandering thoughts

snack

dinner

day 56

midnight

1am

2am

3am

4am

5am

6am

7am

8am

9am

10am

11am

midday

1pm

2pm

3pm

4pm

5pm

6pm

7pm

8pm

9pm

10pm

11pm

midnight

date:

One Hundred Days

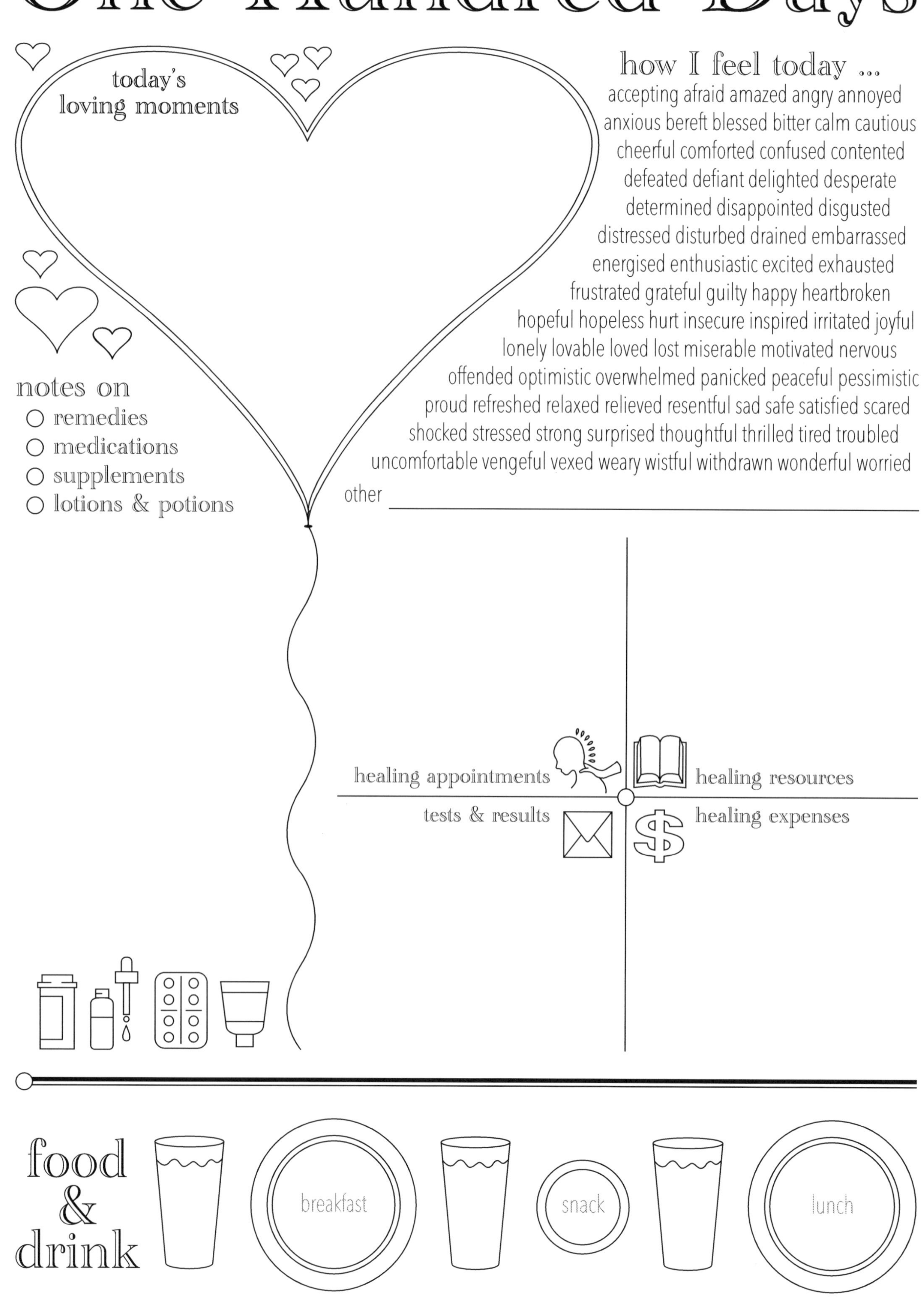

# of Healing

physical activity

social activity

screen time

resting time

connections with nature

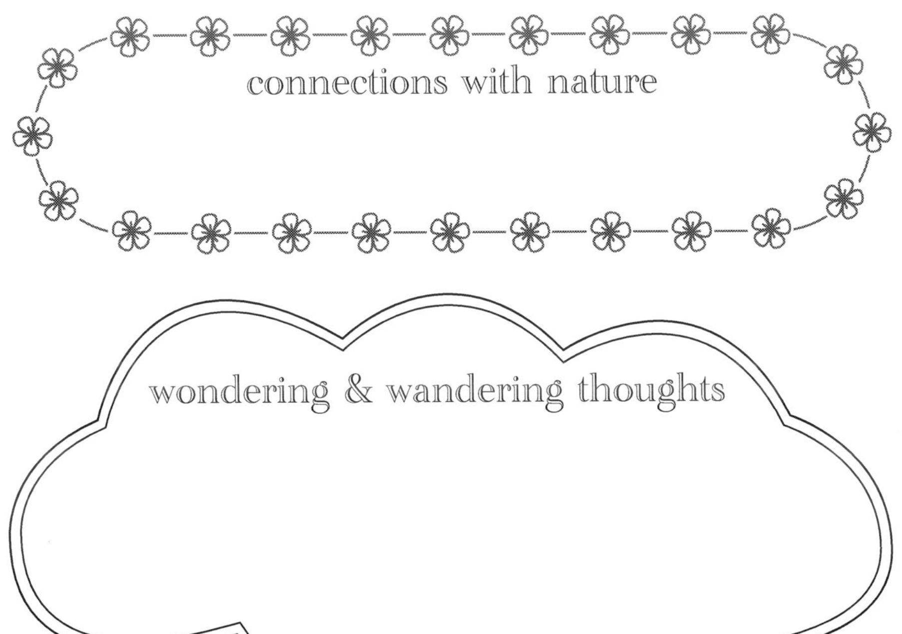

day 57

midnight

1am

2am

3am

4am

5am

6am

7am

8am

9am

10am

11am

midday

1pm

2pm

3pm

4pm

5pm

6pm

7pm

8pm

9pm

10pm

11pm

midnight

date:

One Hundred Days

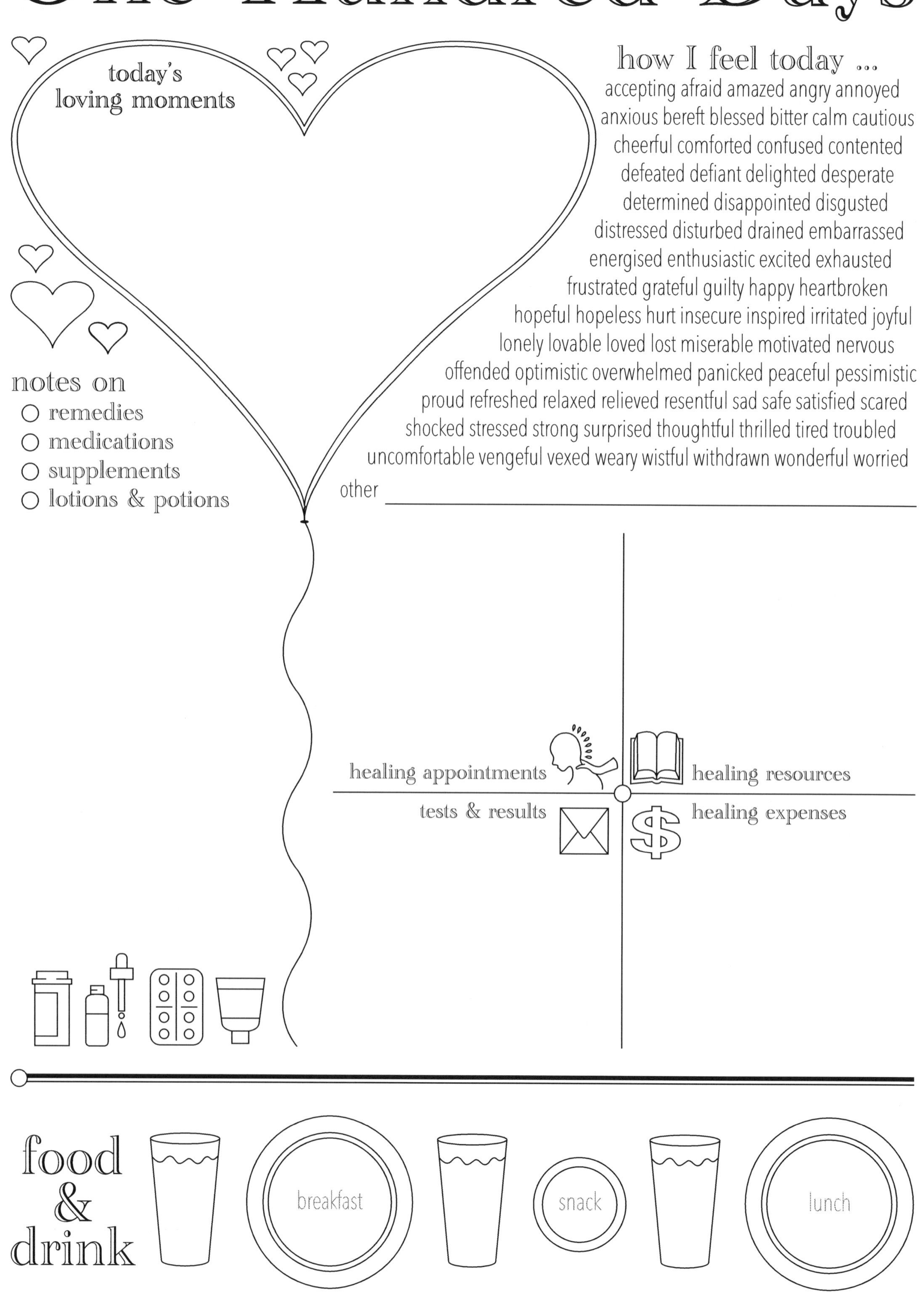

# of Healing

physical activity

social activity

screen time

resting time

connections with nature

wondering & wandering thoughts

snack

dinner

day 58

midnight

1am

2am

3am

4am

5am

6am

7am

8am

9am

10am

11am

midday

1pm

2pm

3pm

4pm

5pm

6pm

7pm

8pm

9pm

10pm

11pm

midnight

date:

One Hundred Days

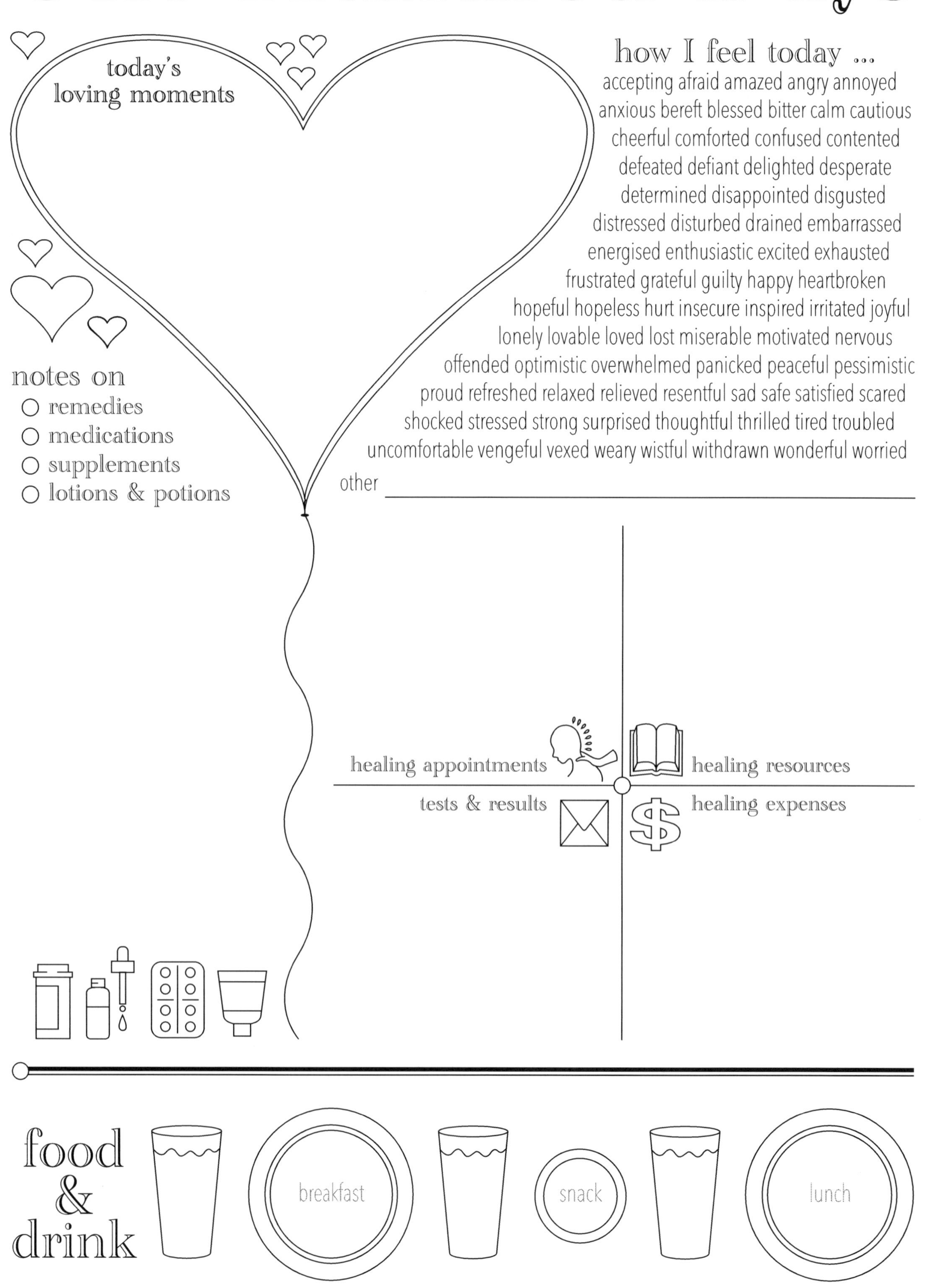

# of Healing

physical activity

social activity

screen time

resting time

connections with nature

wondering & wandering thoughts

snack

dinner

day 59

midnight

1am

2am

3am

4am

5am

6am

7am

8am

9am

10am

11am

midday

1pm

2pm

3pm

4pm

5pm

6pm

7pm

8pm

9pm

10pm

11pm

midnight

date:

One Hundred Days

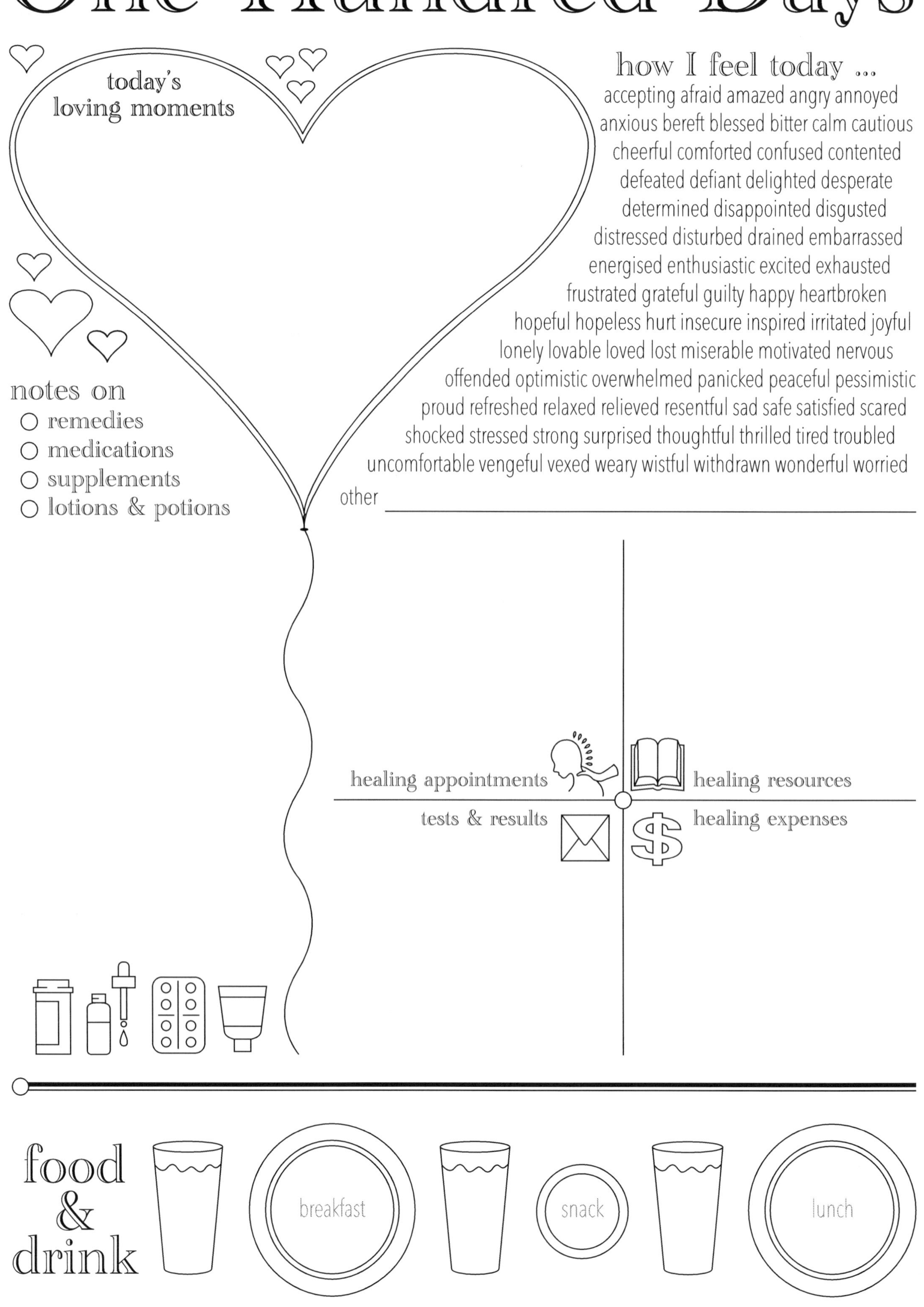

# of Healing

physical activity

social activity

screen time

resting time

connections with nature

wondering & wandering thoughts

snack

dinner

day 60

midnight

1am

2am

3am

4am

5am

6am

7am

8am

9am

10am

11am

midday

1pm

2pm

3pm

4pm

5pm

6pm

7pm

8pm

9pm

10pm

11pm

midnight

date:

One Hundred Days

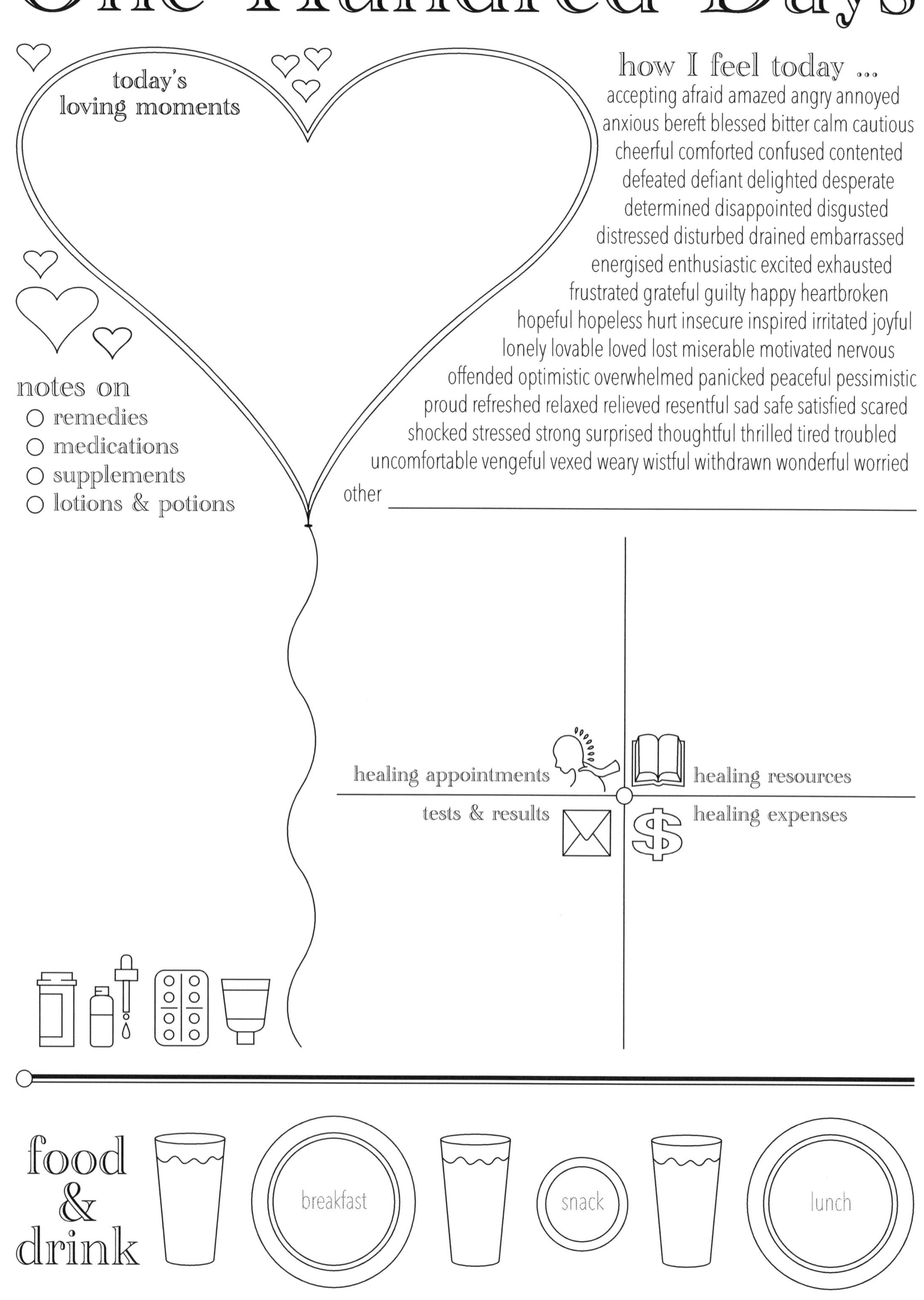

# of Healing

physical activity

social activity

screen time

resting time

connections with nature

wondering & wandering thoughts

snack

dinner

day 61

midnight

1am

2am

3am

4am

5am

6am

7am

8am

9am

10am

11am

midday

1pm

2pm

3pm

4pm

5pm

6pm

7pm

8pm

9pm

10pm

11pm

midnight

date:

One Hundred Days

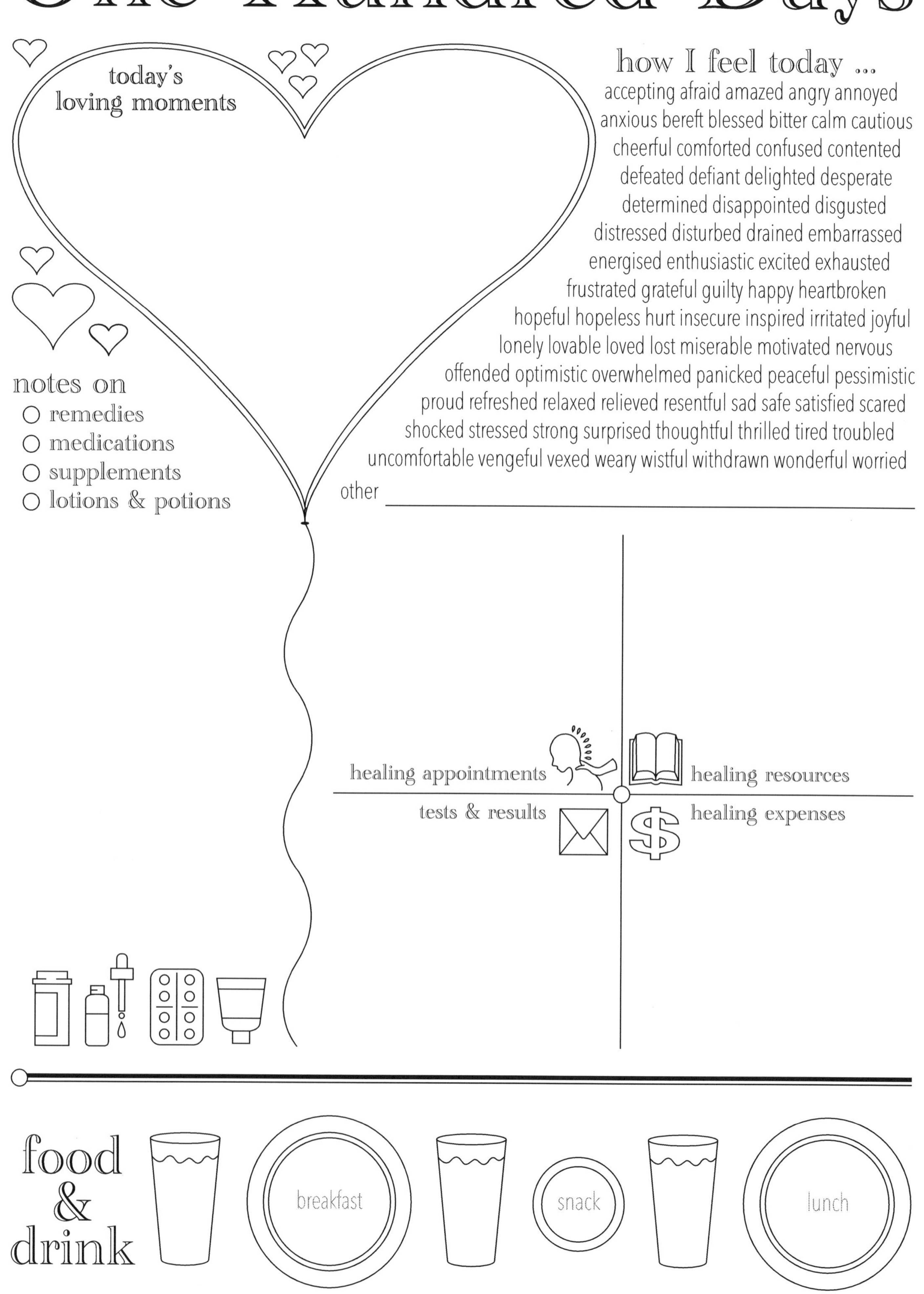

# of Healing

physical activity

social activity

screen time

resting time

connections with nature

wondering & wandering thoughts

snack

dinner

day 62

midnight

1am

2am

3am

4am

5am

6am

7am

8am

9am

10am

11am

midday

1pm

2pm

3pm

4pm

5pm

6pm

7pm

8pm

9pm

10pm

11pm

midnight

date:

One Hundred Days

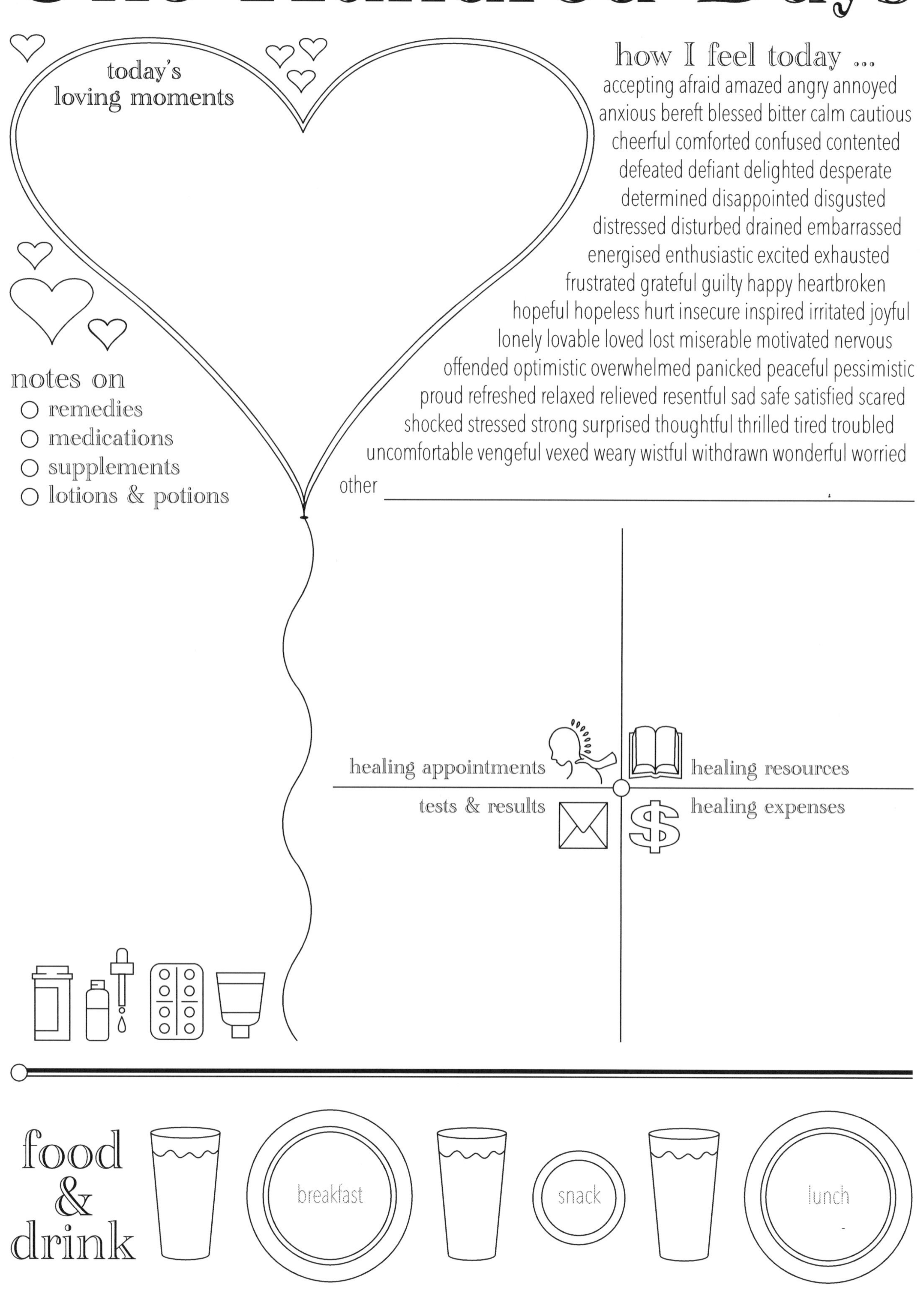

# of Healing

day 63

midnight
1am
2am
3am
4am
5am
6am
7am
8am
9am
10am
11am
midday
1pm
2pm
3pm
4pm
5pm
6pm
7pm
8pm
9pm
10pm
11pm
midnight

date:

physical activity

social activity

screen time

resting time

connections with nature

wondering & wandering thoughts

snack

dinner

One Hundred Days

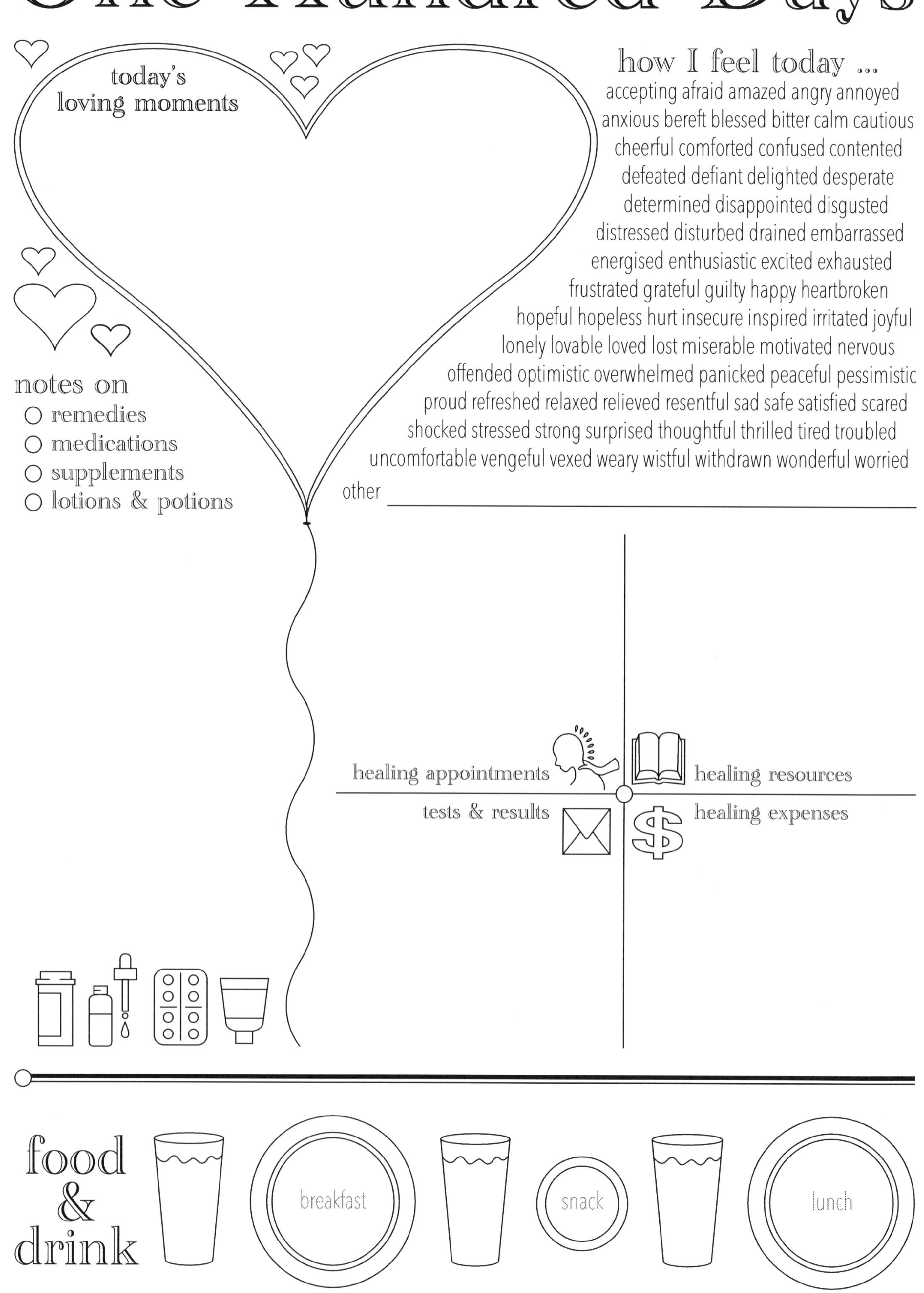

# of Healing

physical activity

social activity

screen time

resting time

connections with nature

wondering & wandering thoughts

snack

dinner

day 64

midnight

1am

2am

3am

4am

5am

6am

7am

8am

9am

10am

11am

midday

1pm

2pm

3pm

4pm

5pm

6pm

7pm

8pm

9pm

10pm

11pm

midnight

date:

One Hundred Days

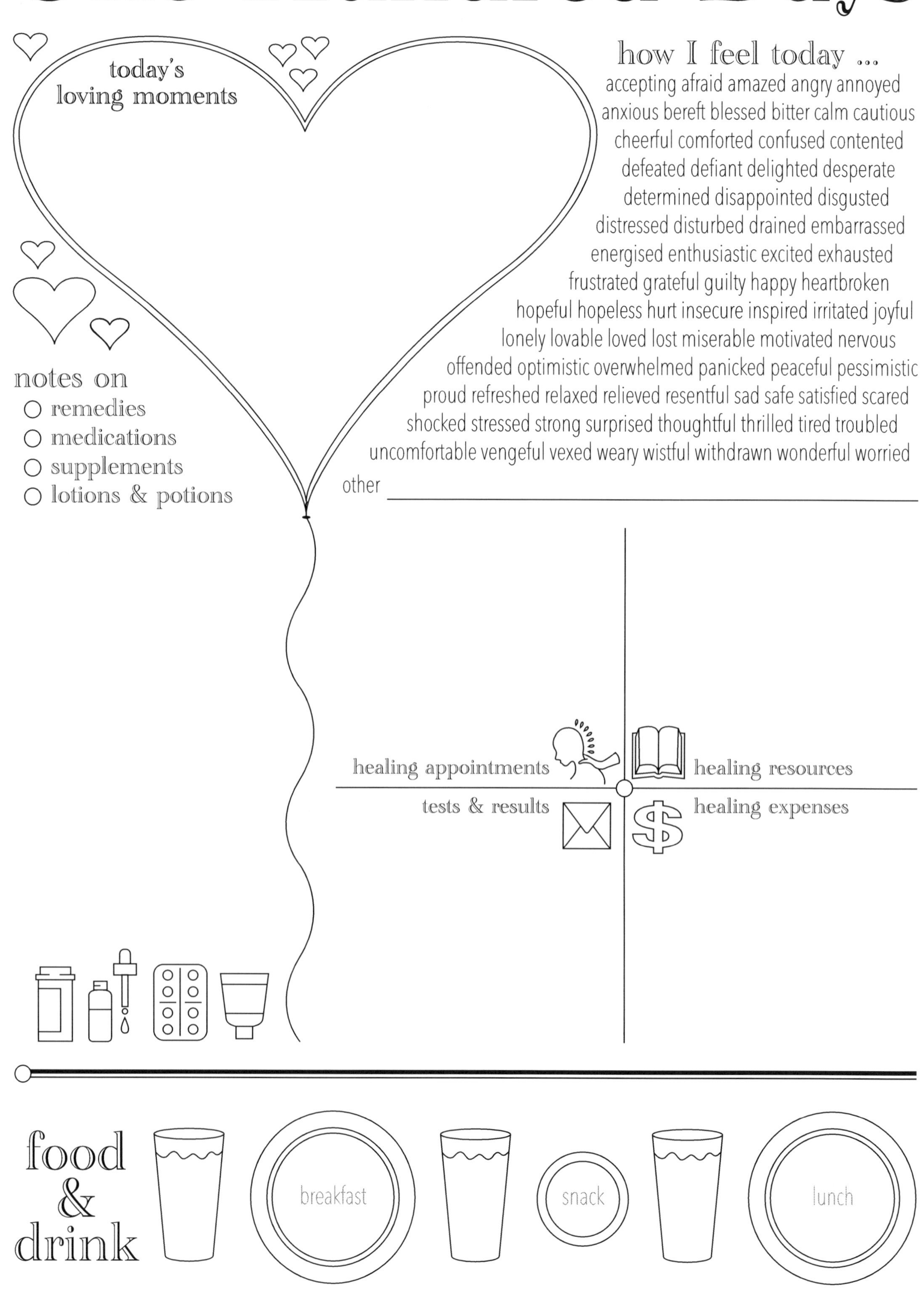

food & drink

# of Healing

physical activity

social activity

screen time

resting time

connections with nature

day 65

midnight

1am

2am

3am

4am

5am

6am

7am

8am

9am

10am

11am

midday

1pm

2pm

3pm

4pm

5pm

6pm

7pm

8pm

9pm

10pm

11pm

midnight

date:

One Hundred Days

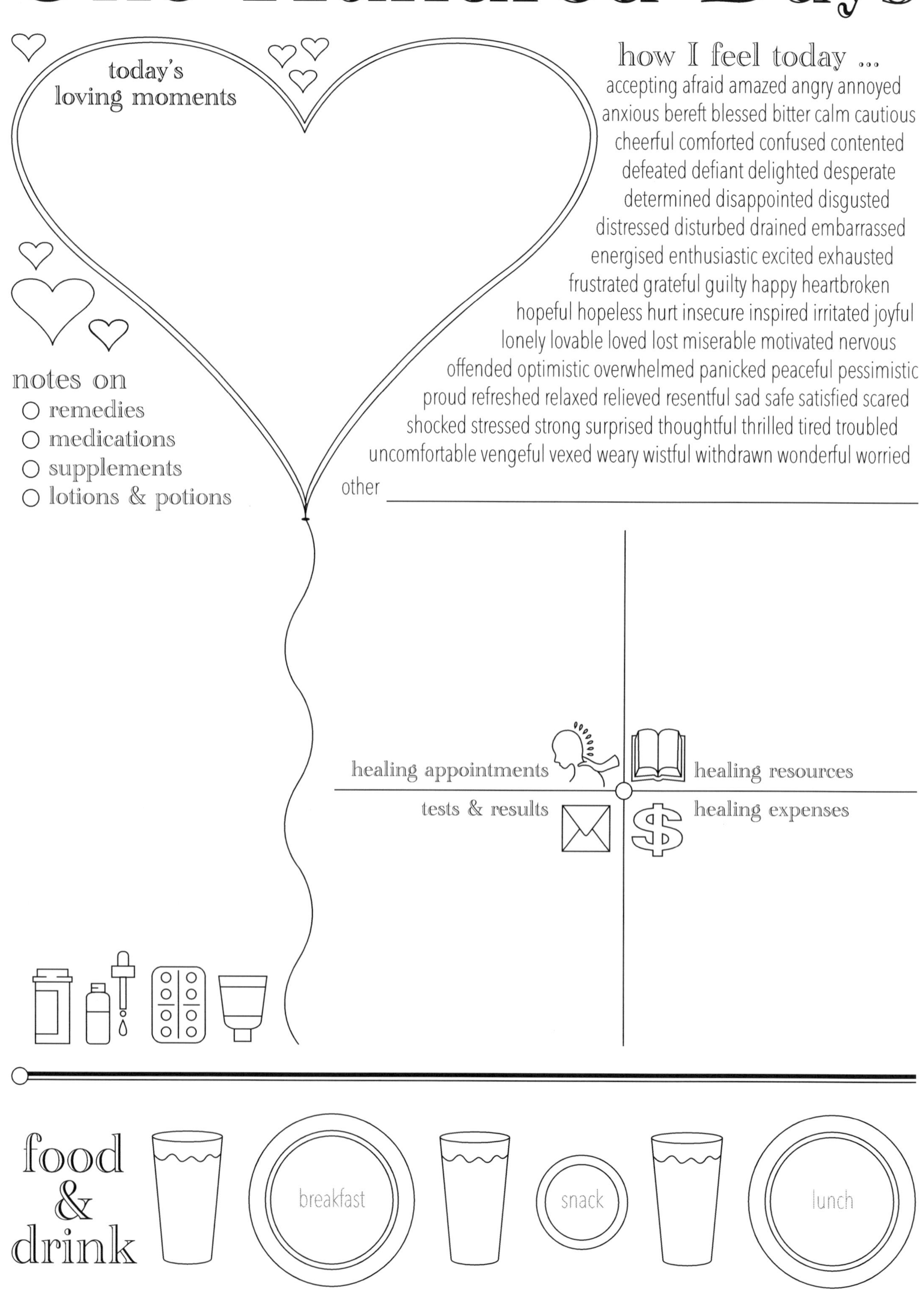

# of Healing

physical activity

social activity

screen time

resting time

connections with nature

wondering & wandering thoughts

snack

dinner

day 66

midnight

1am

2am

3am

4am

5am

6am

7am

8am

9am

10am

11am

midday

1pm

2pm

3pm

4pm

5pm

6pm

7pm

8pm

9pm

10pm

11pm

midnight

date:

One Hundred Days

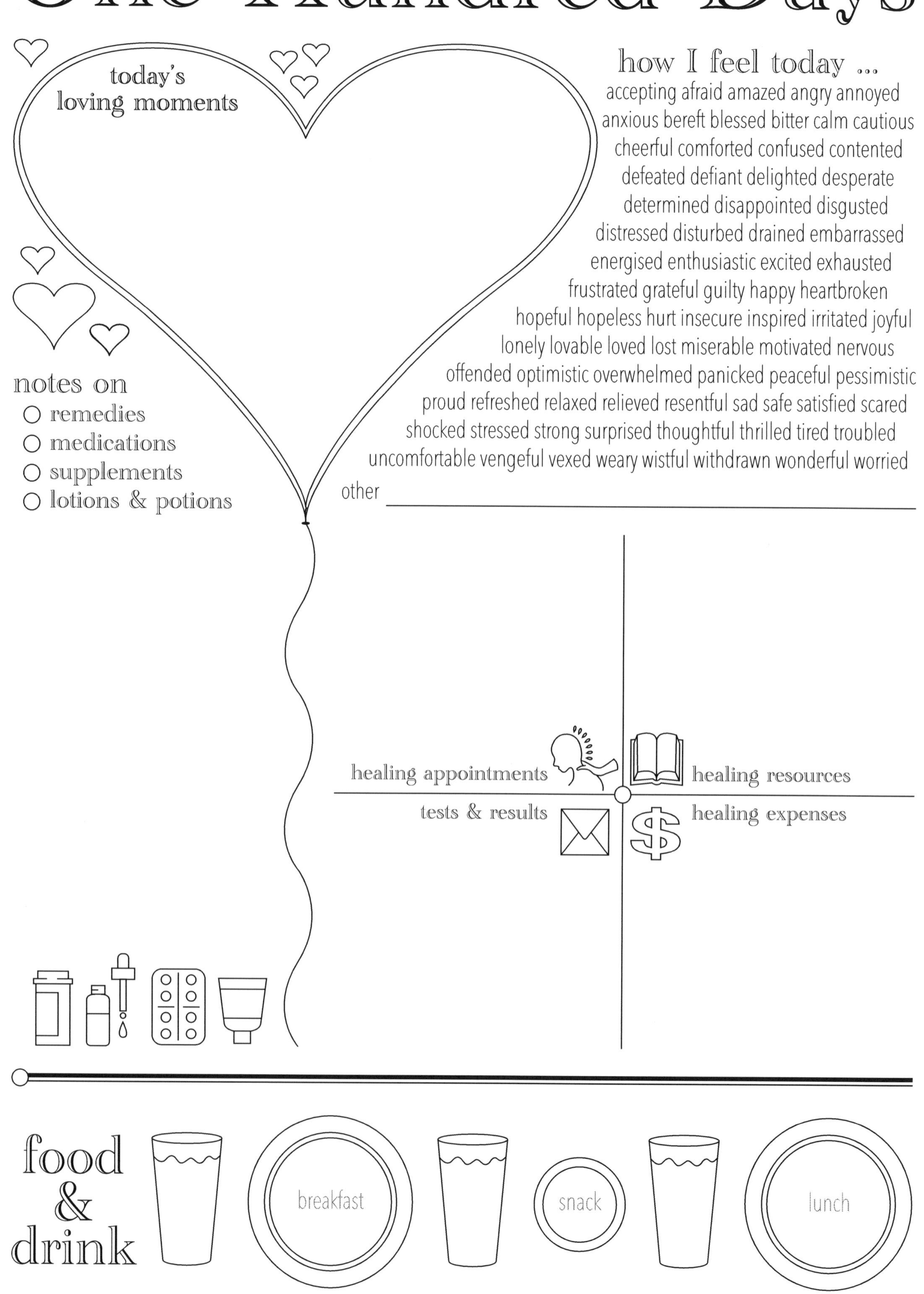

food & drink

breakfast

snack

lunch

# of Healing

physical activity

social activity

screen time

resting time

connections with nature

wondering & wandering thoughts

snack

dinner

day 67

midnight

1am

2am

3am

4am

5am

6am

7am

8am

9am

10am

11am

midday

1pm

2pm

3pm

4pm

5pm

6pm

7pm

8pm

9pm

10pm

11pm

midnight

date:

One Hundred Days

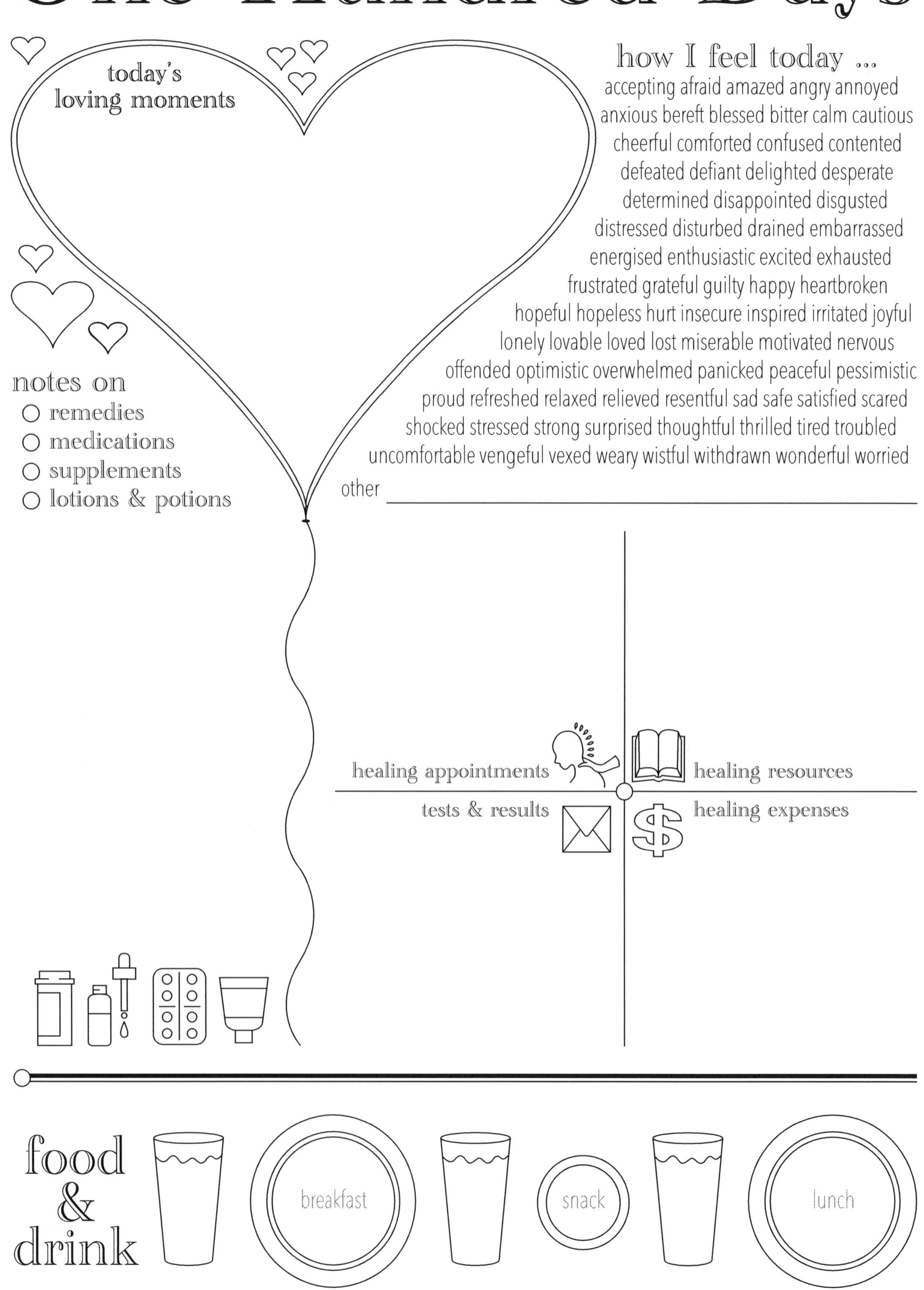

# of Healing

physical activity

social activity

screen time

resting time

connections with nature

wondering & wandering thoughts

snack

dinner

day 68

midnight

1am

2am

3am

4am

5am

6am

7am

8am

9am

10am

11am

midday

1pm

2pm

3pm

4pm

5pm

6pm

7pm

8pm

9pm

10pm

11pm

midnight

date:

One Hundred Days

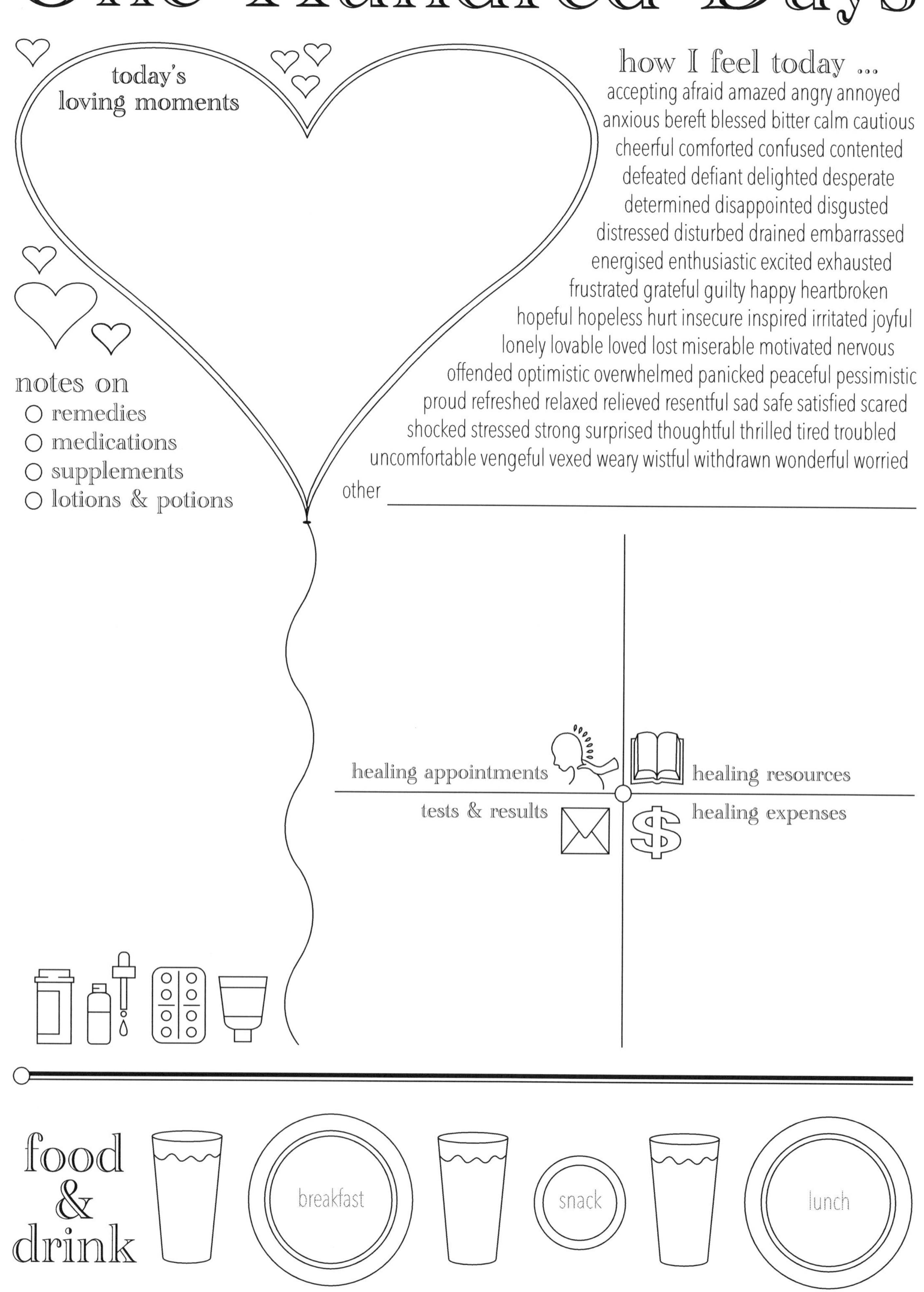

# of Healing

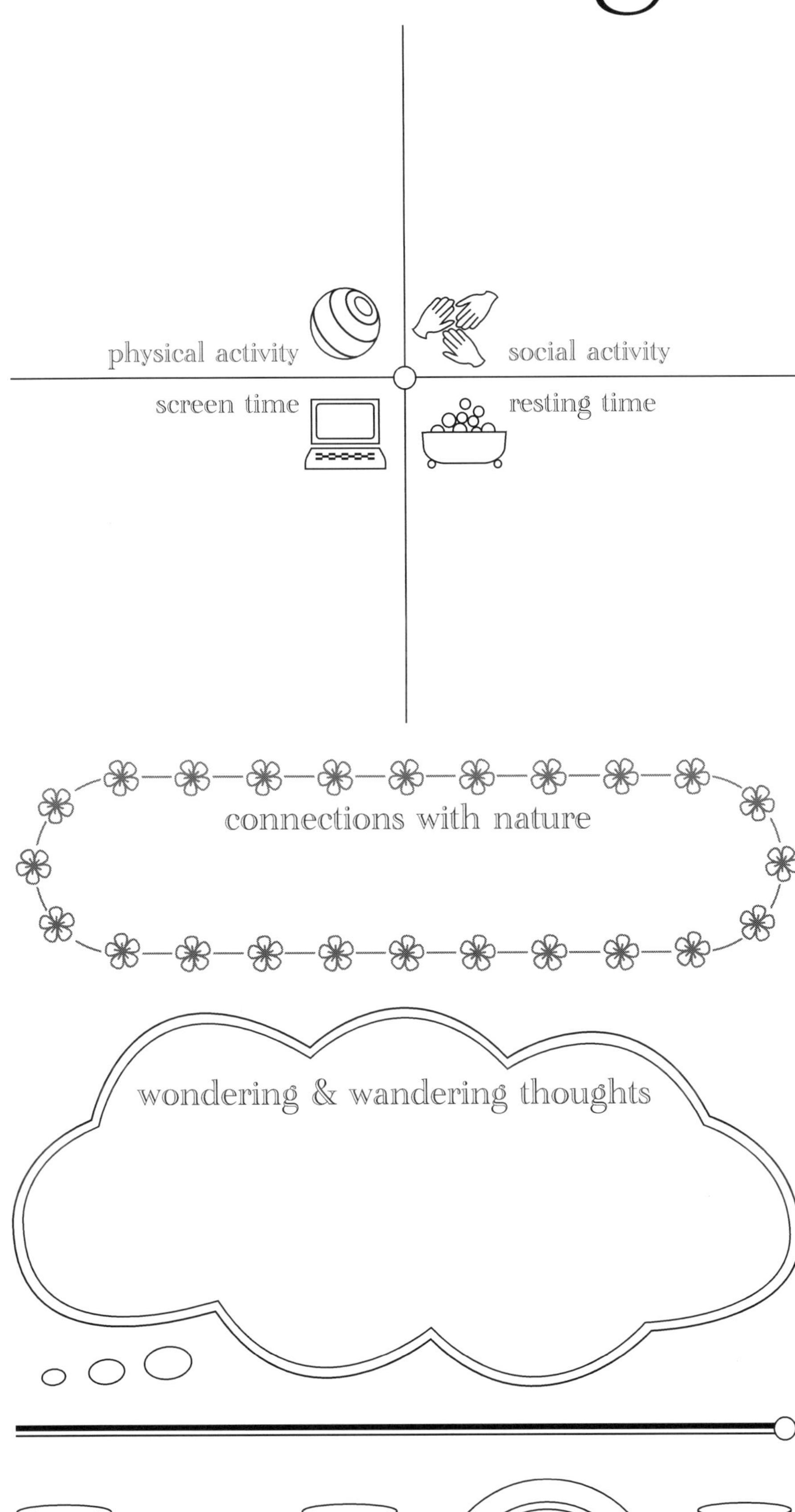

day 69

midnight

1am

2am

3am

4am

5am

6am

7am

8am

9am

10am

11am

midday

1pm

2pm

3pm

4pm

5pm

6pm

7pm

8pm

9pm

10pm

11pm

midnight

date:

One Hundred Days

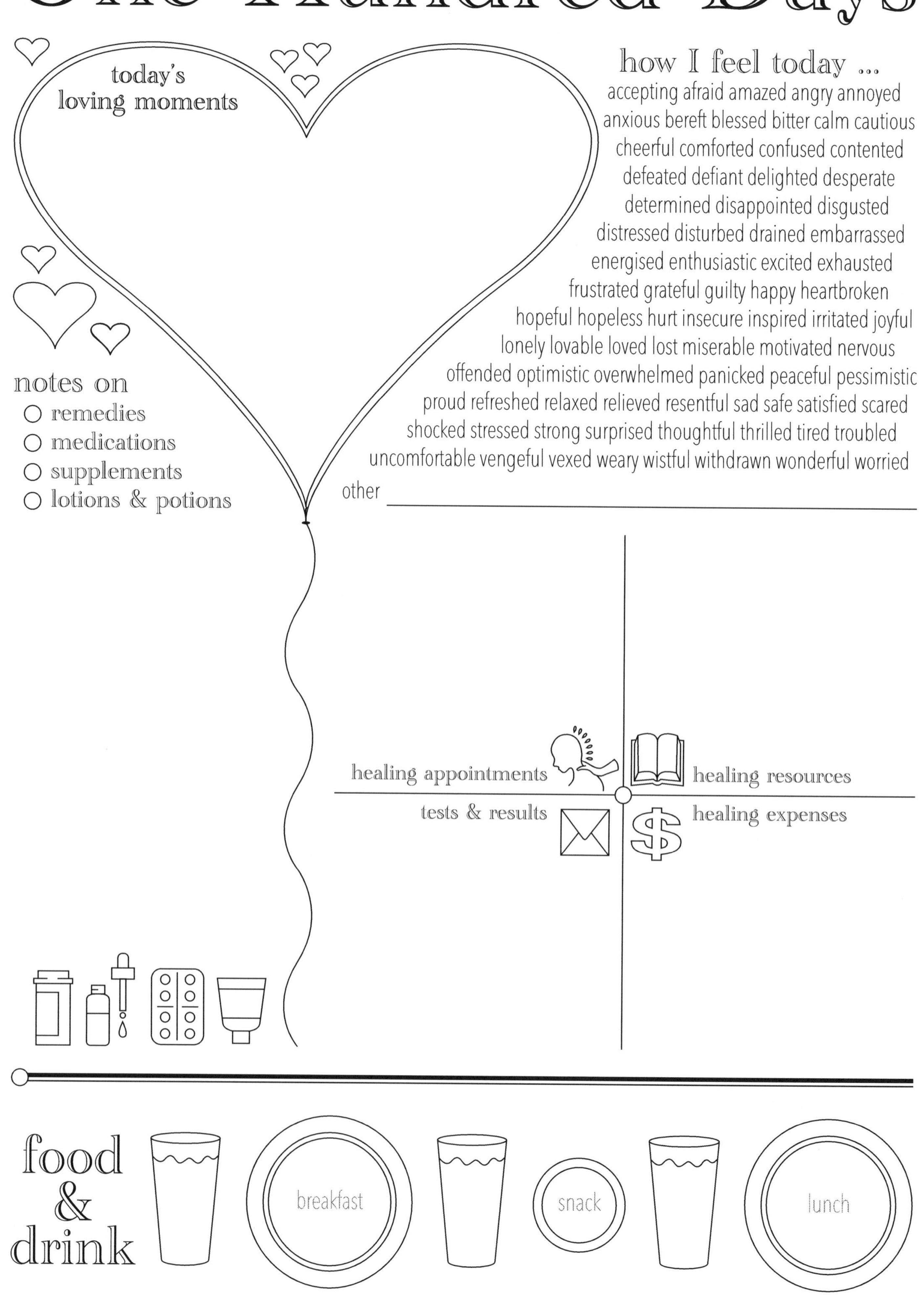

# of Healing

physical activity

social activity

screen time

resting time

connections with nature

wondering & wandering thoughts

snack

dinner

day 70

midnight

1am

2am

3am

4am

5am

6am

7am

8am

9am

10am

11am

midday

1pm

2pm

3pm

4pm

5pm

6pm

7pm

8pm

9pm

10pm

11pm

midnight

date:

One Hundred Days

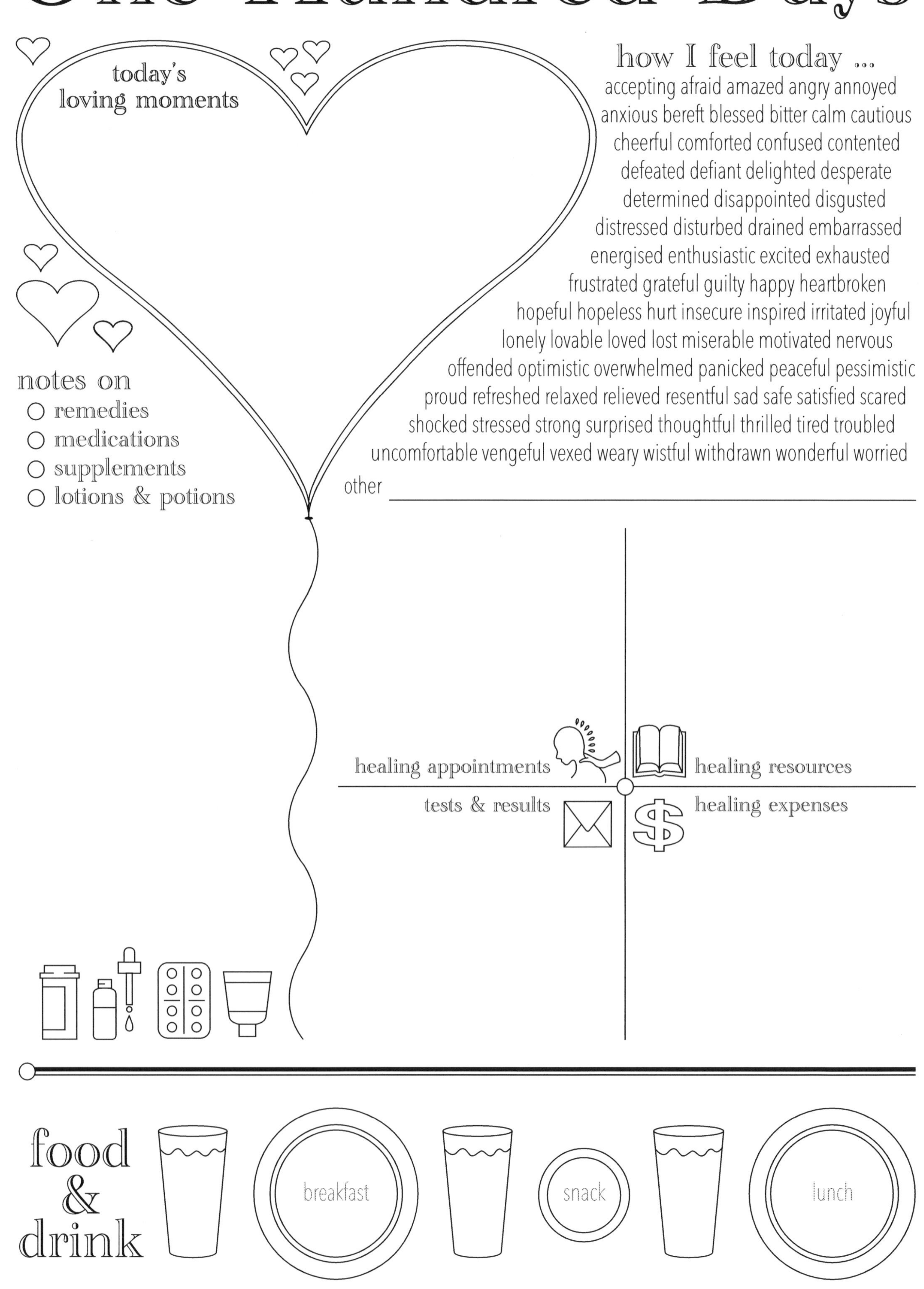

# of Healing

physical activity

social activity

screen time

resting time

connections with nature

wondering & wandering thoughts

snack

dinner

day 71

midnight

1am

2am

3am

4am

5am

6am

7am

8am

9am

10am

11am

midday

1pm

2pm

3pm

4pm

5pm

6pm

7pm

8pm

9pm

10pm

11pm

midnight

date:

One Hundred Days

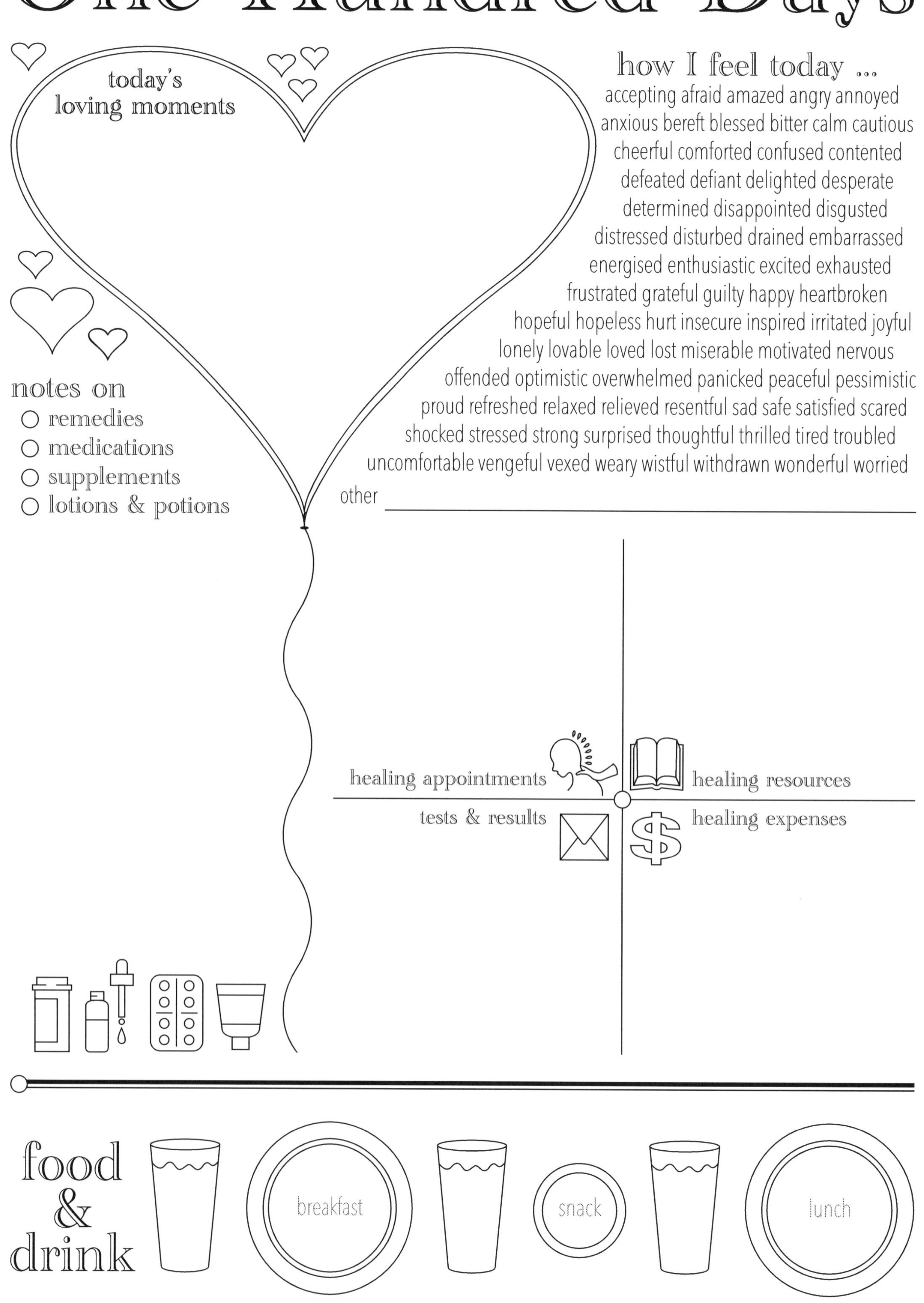

today's loving moments

how I feel today …

accepting afraid amazed angry annoyed anxious bereft blessed bitter calm cautious cheerful comforted confused contented defeated defiant delighted desperate determined disappointed disgusted distressed disturbed drained embarrassed energised enthusiastic excited exhausted frustrated grateful guilty happy heartbroken hopeful hopeless hurt insecure inspired irritated joyful lonely lovable loved lost miserable motivated nervous offended optimistic overwhelmed panicked peaceful pessimistic proud refreshed relaxed relieved resentful sad safe satisfied scared shocked stressed strong surprised thoughtful thrilled tired troubled uncomfortable vengeful vexed weary wistful withdrawn wonderful worried

other ______

notes on

- ○ remedies
- ○ medications
- ○ supplements
- ○ lotions & potions

healing appointments

healing resources

tests & results

healing expenses

food & drink

breakfast

snack

lunch

# of Healing

physical activity

social activity

screen time

resting time

connections with nature

wondering & wandering thoughts

snack

dinner

day 72

midnight

1am

2am

3am

4am

5am

6am

7am

8am

9am

10am

11am

midday

1pm

2pm

3pm

4pm

5pm

6pm

7pm

8pm

9pm

10pm

11pm

midnight

date:

One Hundred Days

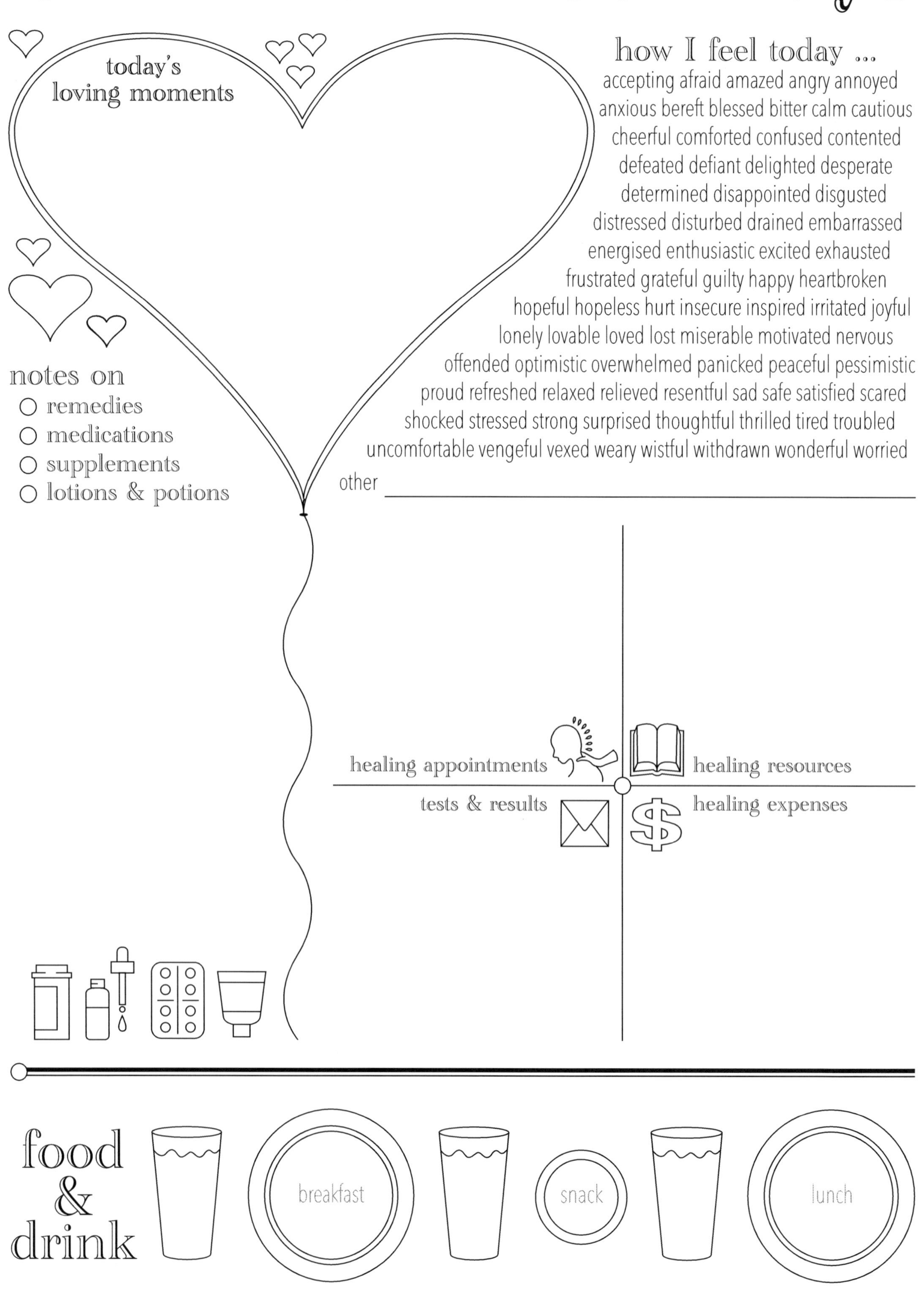

# of Healing

physical activity

social activity

screen time

resting time

connections with nature

wondering & wandering thoughts

snack

dinner

day 73

midnight

1am

2am

3am

4am

5am

6am

7am

8am

9am

10am

11am

midday

1pm

2pm

3pm

4pm

5pm

6pm

7pm

8pm

9pm

10pm

11pm

midnight

date:

One Hundred Days

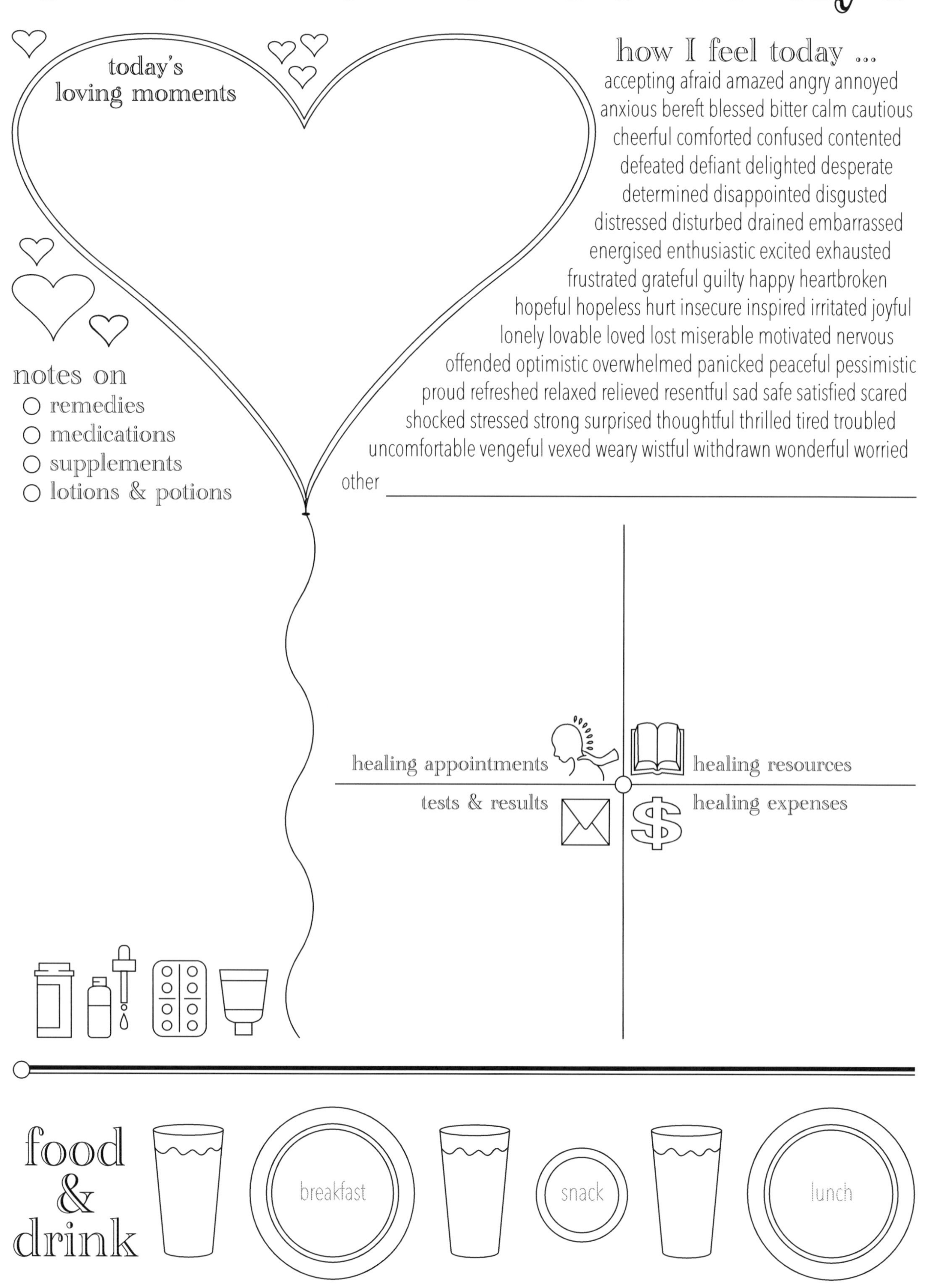

# of Healing

physical activity

social activity

screen time

resting time

connections with nature

wondering & wandering thoughts

snack

dinner

day 74

midnight

1am

2am

3am

4am

5am

6am

7am

8am

9am

10am

11am

midday

1pm

2pm

3pm

4pm

5pm

6pm

7pm

8pm

9pm

10pm

11pm

midnight

date:

One Hundred Days

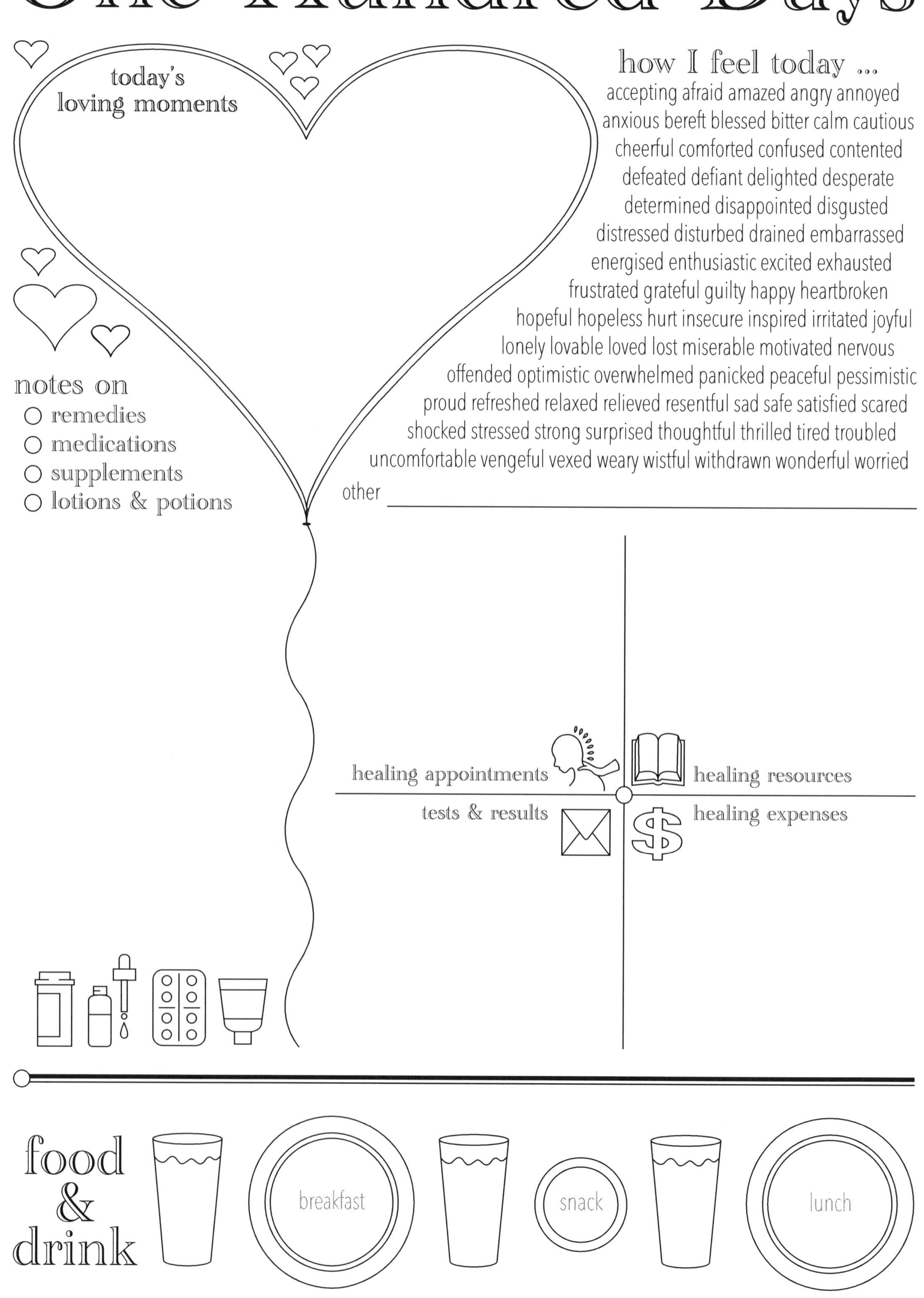

# of Healing

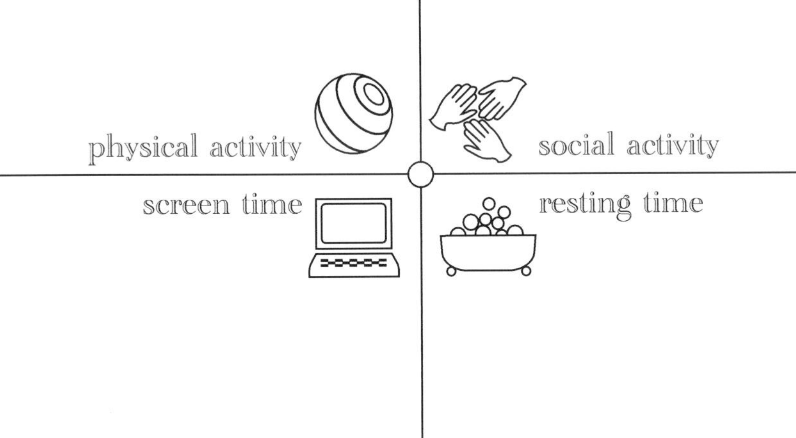

day 75

midnight

1am

2am

3am

4am

5am

6am

7am

8am

9am

10am

11am

midday

1pm

2pm

3pm

4pm

5pm

6pm

7pm

8pm

9pm

10pm

11pm

midnight

date:

One Hundred Days

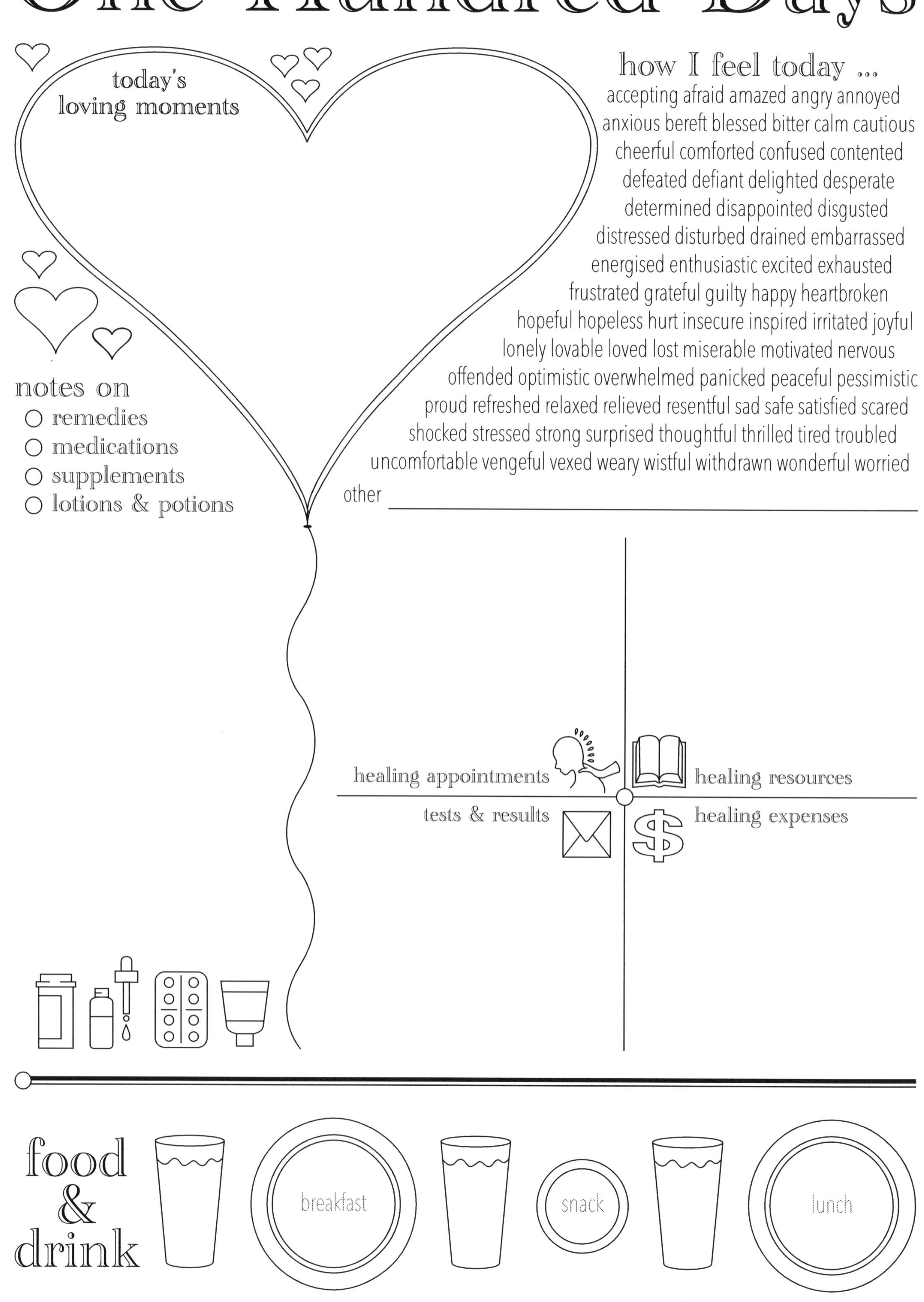

food & drink

breakfast

snack

lunch

# of Healing

physical activity

social activity

screen time

resting time

connections with nature

wondering & wandering thoughts

snack

dinner

day 76

midnight

1am

2am

3am

4am

5am

6am

7am

8am

9am

10am

11am

midday

1pm

2pm

3pm

4pm

5pm

6pm

7pm

8pm

9pm

10pm

11pm

midnight

date:

One Hundred Days

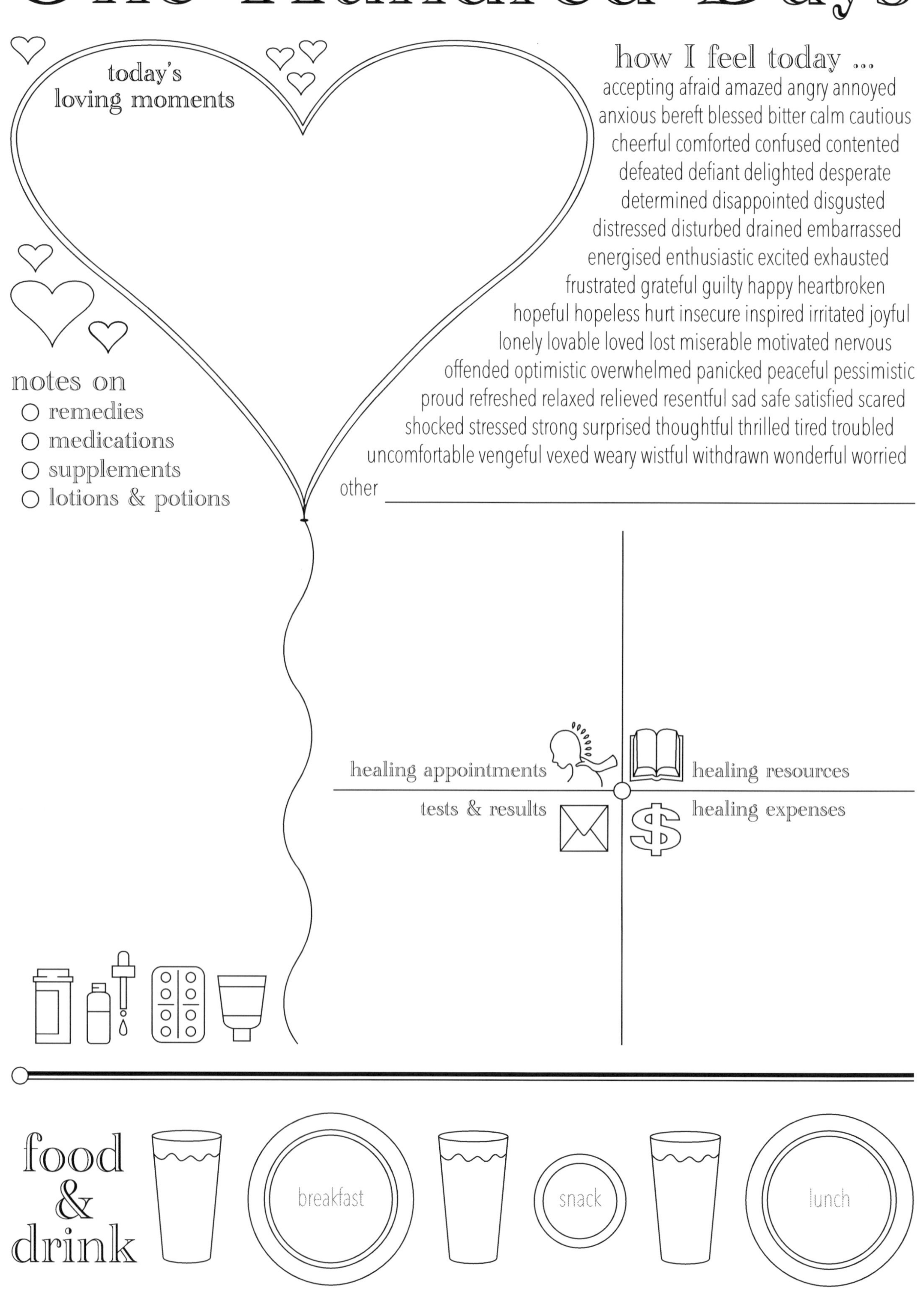

# of Healing

physical activity

social activity

screen time

resting time

connections with nature

wondering & wandering thoughts

snack

dinner

day 77

midnight

1am

2am

3am

4am

5am

6am

7am

8am

9am

10am

11am

midday

1pm

2pm

3pm

4pm

5pm

6pm

7pm

8pm

9pm

10pm

11pm

midnight

date:

One Hundred Days

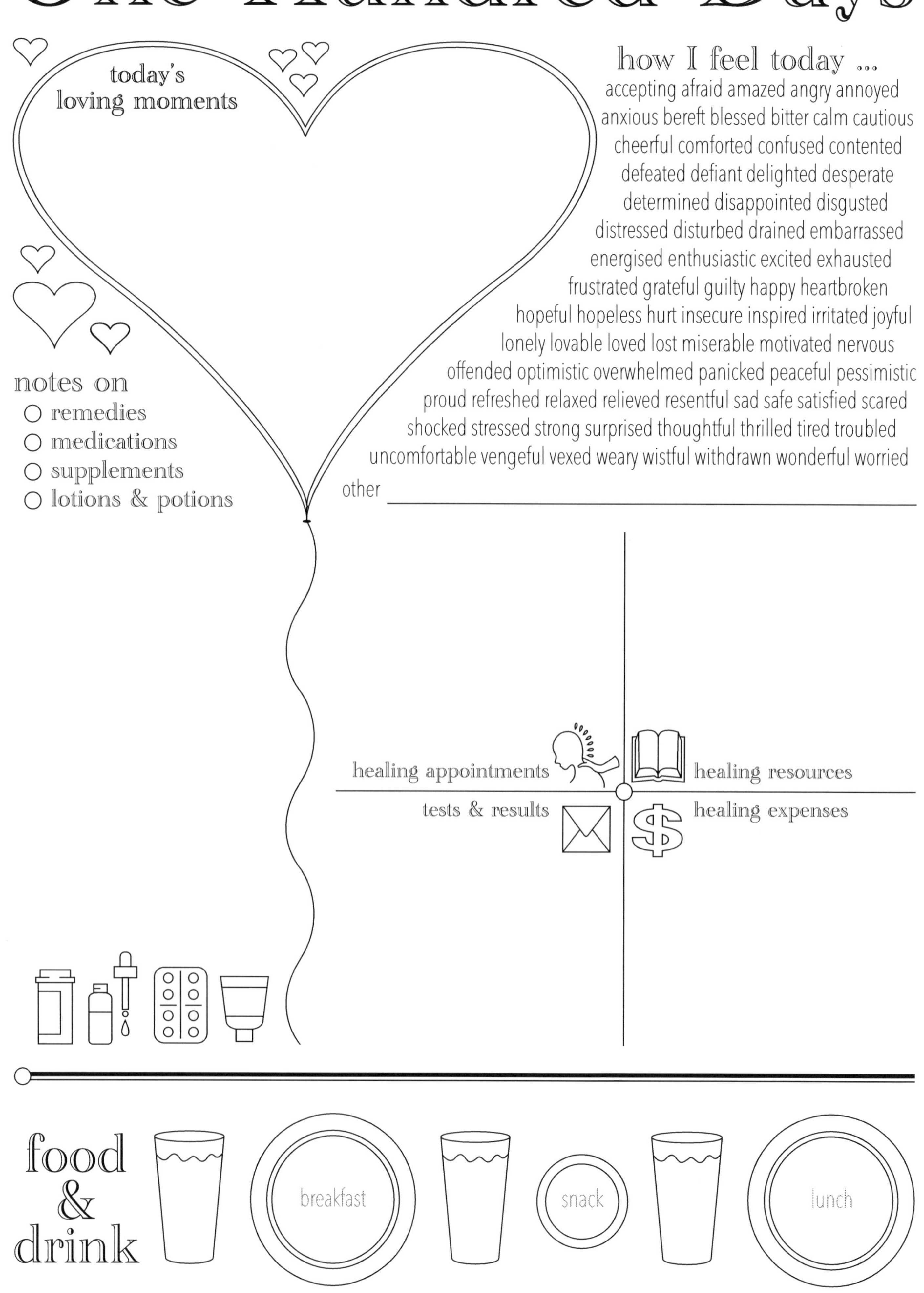

# of Healing

physical activity

social activity

screen time

resting time

connections with nature

wondering & wandering thoughts

snack

dinner

day 78

midnight

1am

2am

3am

4am

5am

6am

7am

8am

9am

10am

11am

midday

1pm

2pm

3pm

4pm

5pm

6pm

7pm

8pm

9pm

10pm

11pm

midnight

date:

One Hundred Days

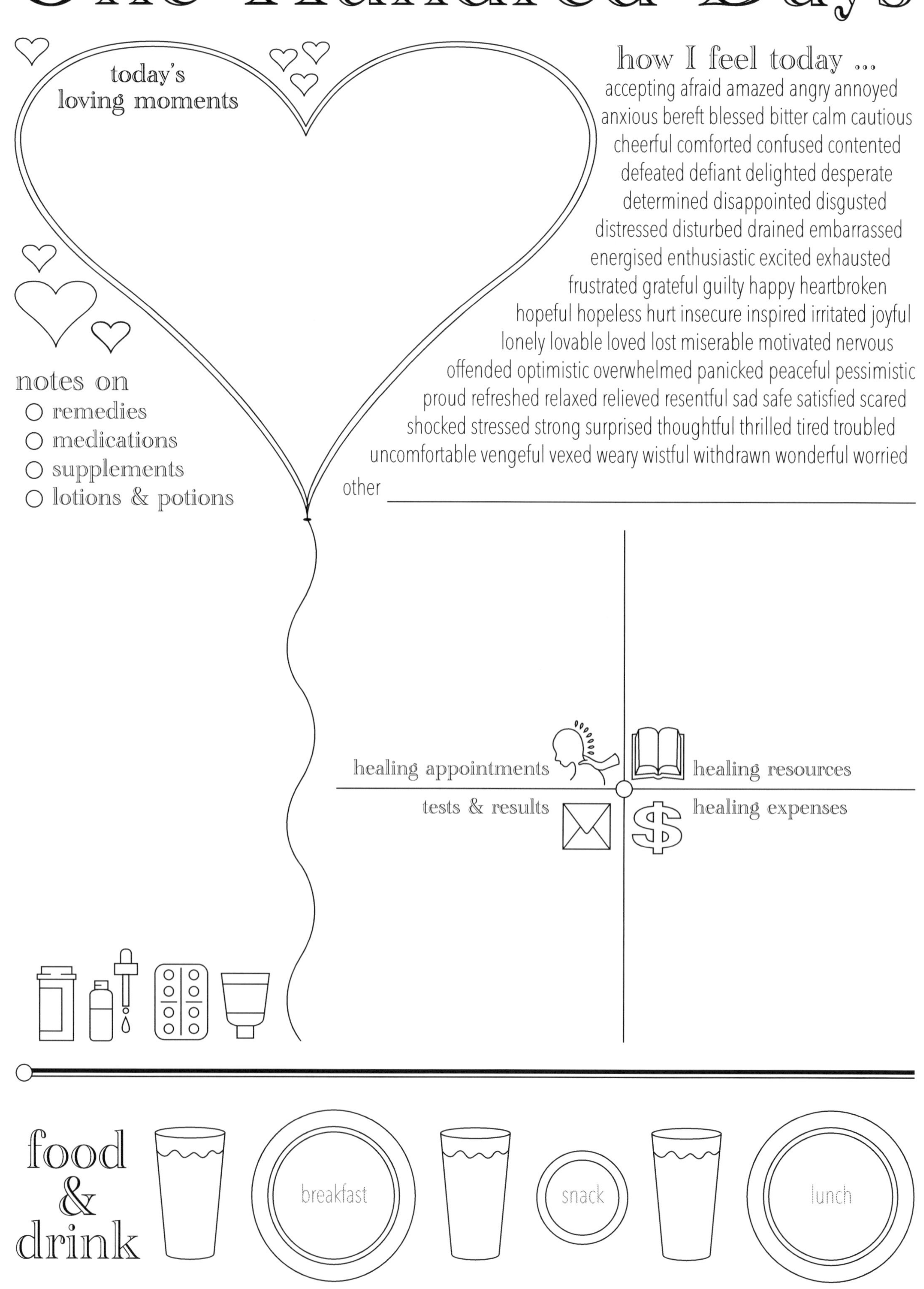

# of Healing

physical activity

social activity

screen time

resting time

connections with nature

wondering & wandering thoughts

snack

dinner

day 79

midnight

1am

2am

3am

4am

5am

6am

7am

8am

9am

10am

11am

midday

1pm

2pm

3pm

4pm

5pm

6pm

7pm

8pm

9pm

10pm

11pm

midnight

date:

One Hundred Days

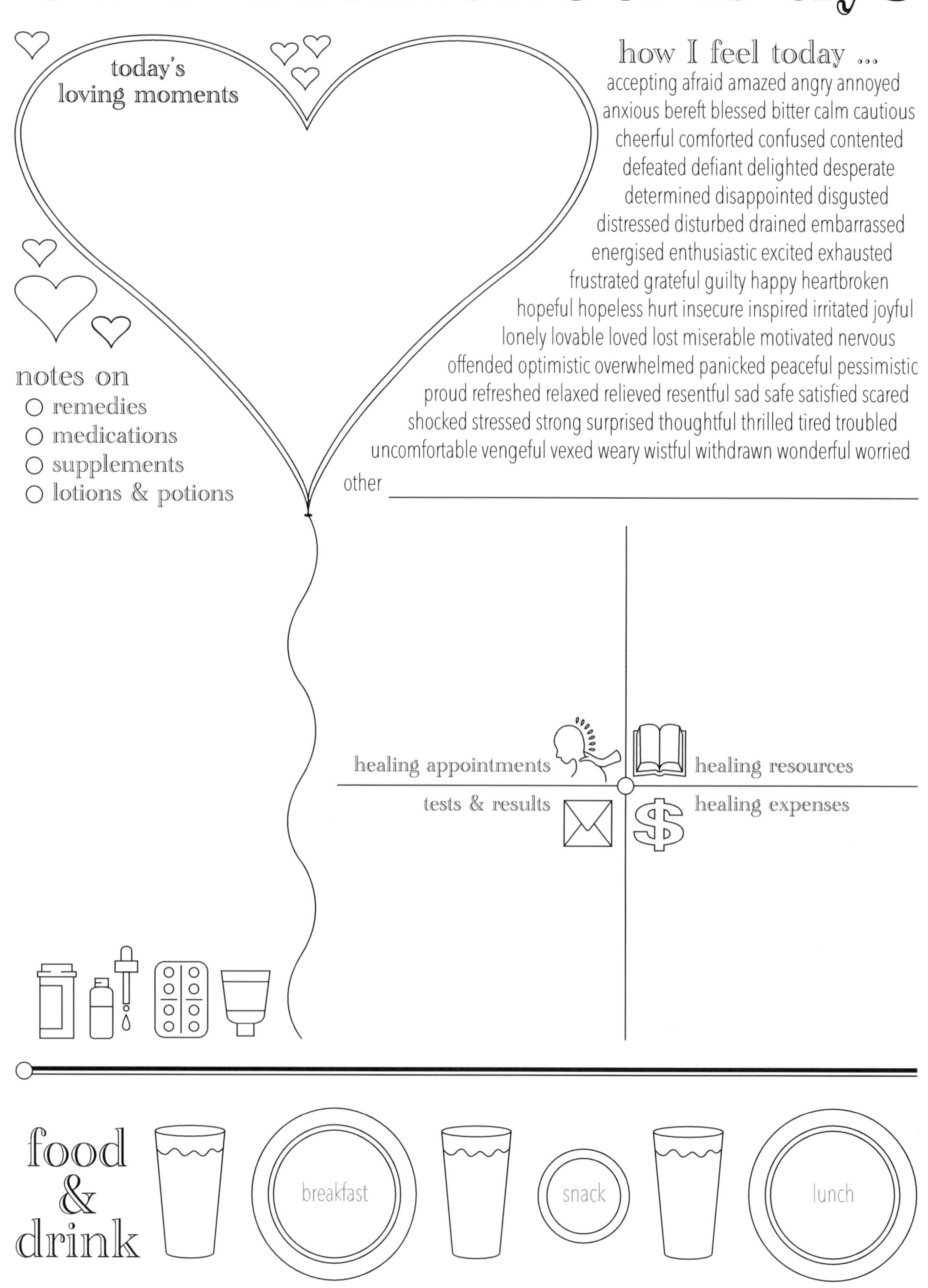

# of Healing

physical activity

social activity

screen time

resting time

connections with nature

wondering & wandering thoughts

snack

dinner

day 80

midnight
1am
2am
3am
4am
5am
6am
7am
8am
9am
10am
11am
midday
1pm
2pm
3pm
4pm
5pm
6pm
7pm
8pm
9pm
10pm
11pm
midnight

date:

One Hundred Days

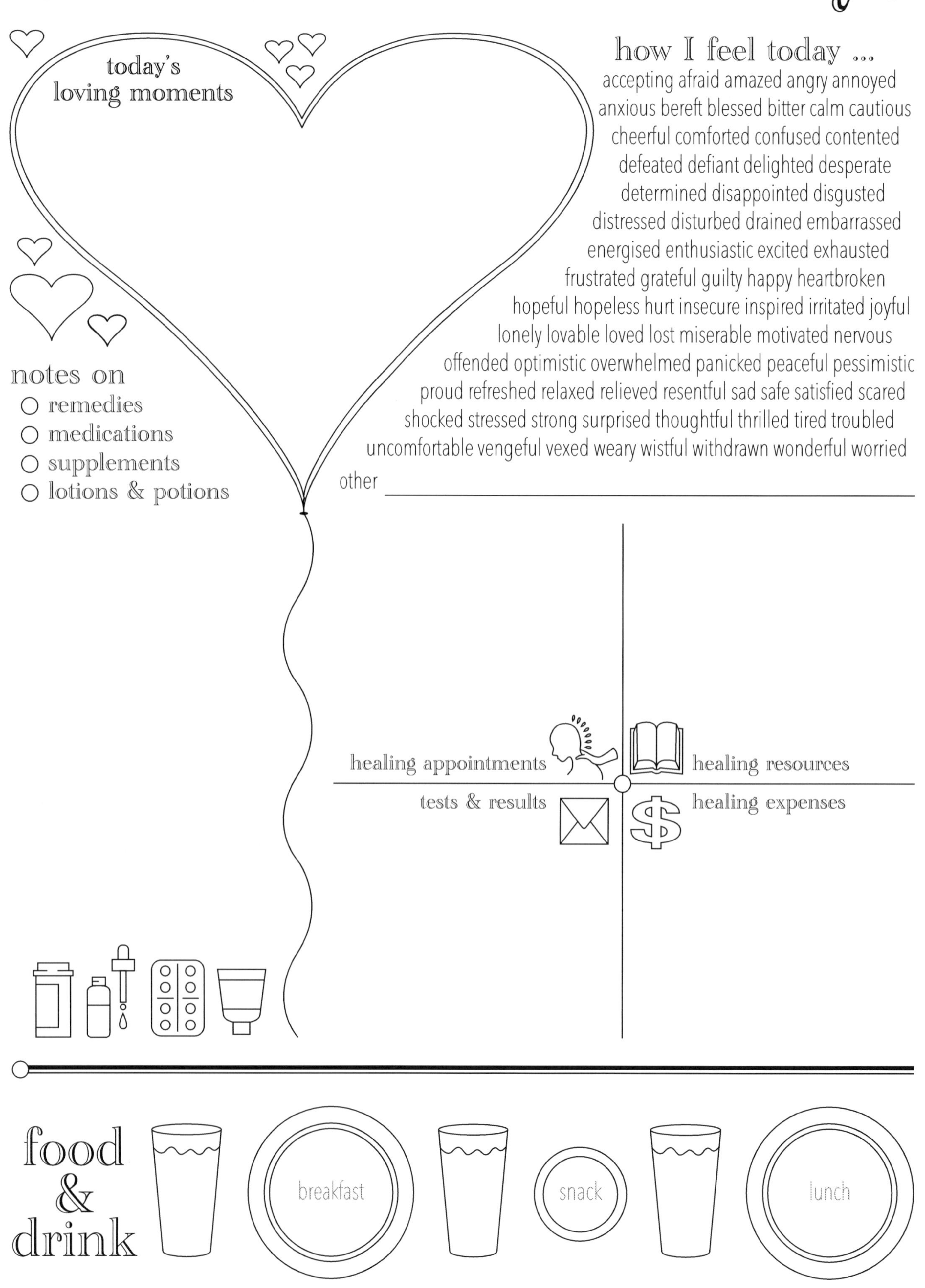

food & drink

breakfast

snack

lunch

# of Healing

physical activity

social activity

screen time

resting time

connections with nature

wondering & wandering thoughts

snack

dinner

day 81

midnight

1am

2am

3am

4am

5am

6am

7am

8am

9am

10am

11am

midday

1pm

2pm

3pm

4pm

5pm

6pm

7pm

8pm

9pm

10pm

11pm

midnight

date:

One Hundred Days

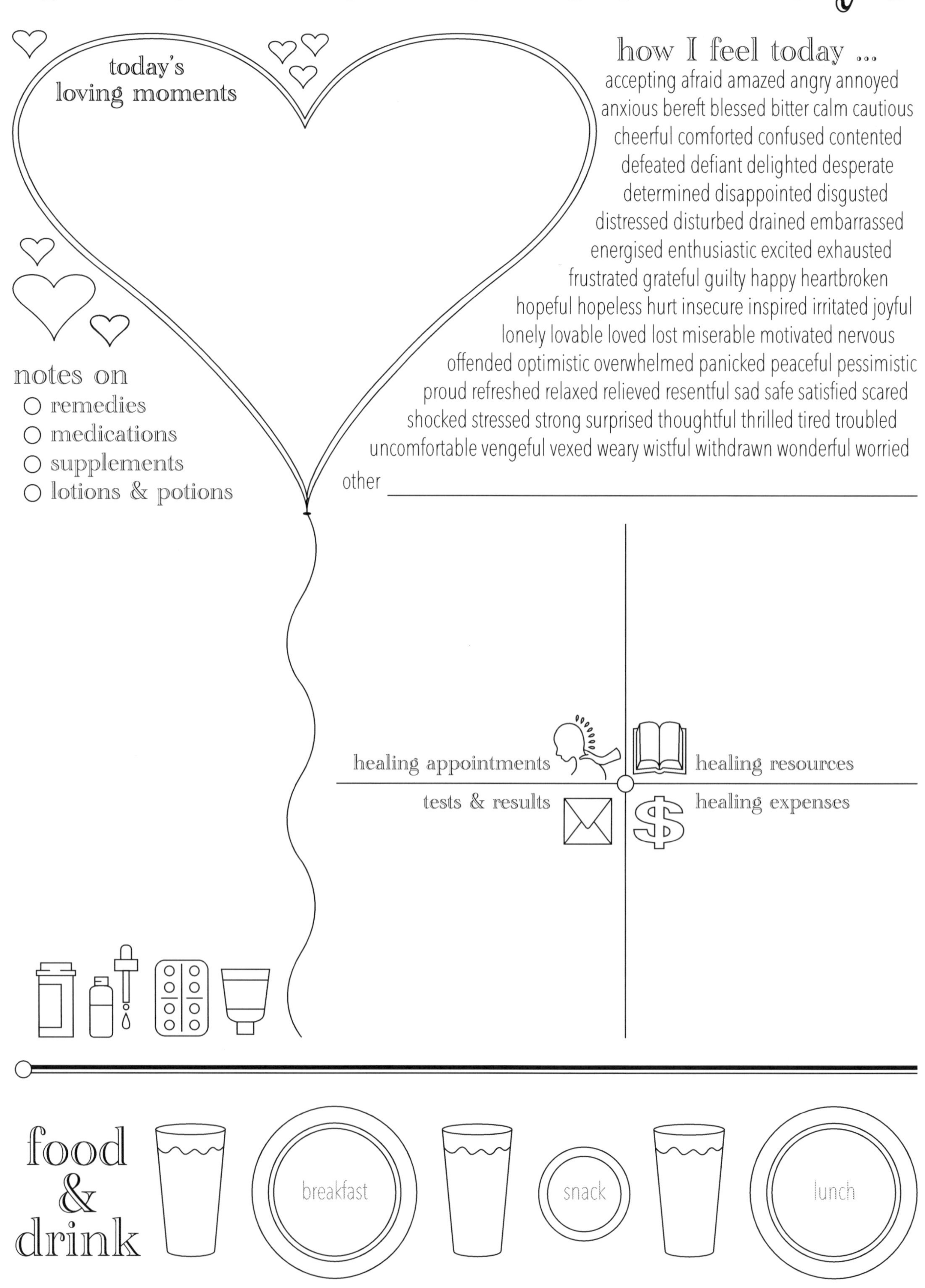

# of Healing

physical activity

social activity

screen time

resting time

connections with nature

wondering & wandering thoughts

snack

dinner

day 82

midnight

1am

2am

3am

4am

5am

6am

7am

8am

9am

10am

11am

midday

1pm

2pm

3pm

4pm

5pm

6pm

7pm

8pm

9pm

10pm

11pm

midnight

date:

One Hundred Days

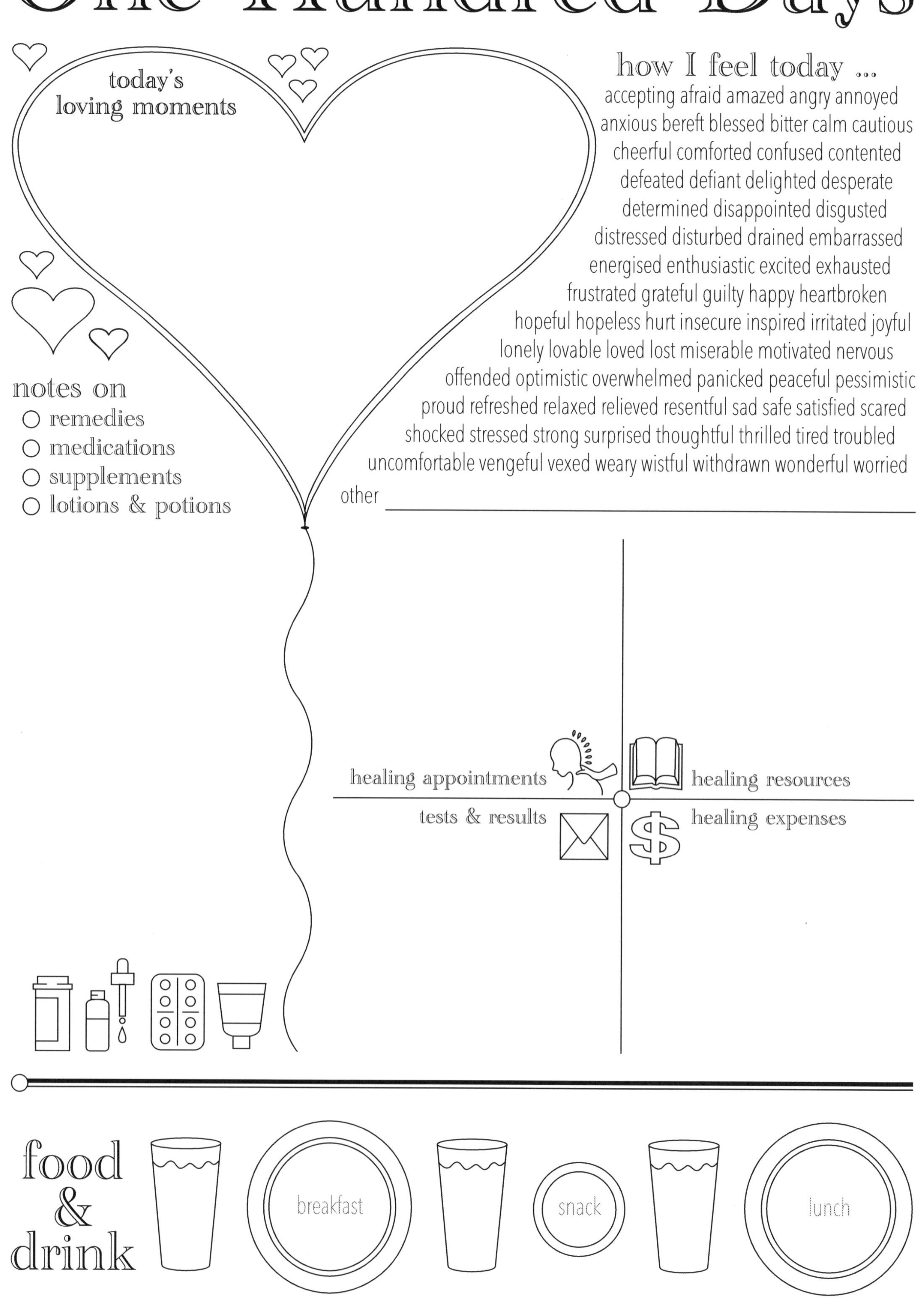

food & drink

breakfast

snack

lunch

# of Healing

physical activity

social activity

screen time

resting time

connections with nature

wondering & wandering thoughts

snack

dinner

day 83

midnight

1am

2am

3am

4am

5am

6am

7am

8am

9am

10am

11am

midday

1pm

2pm

3pm

4pm

5pm

6pm

7pm

8pm

9pm

10pm

11pm

midnight

date:

One Hundred Days

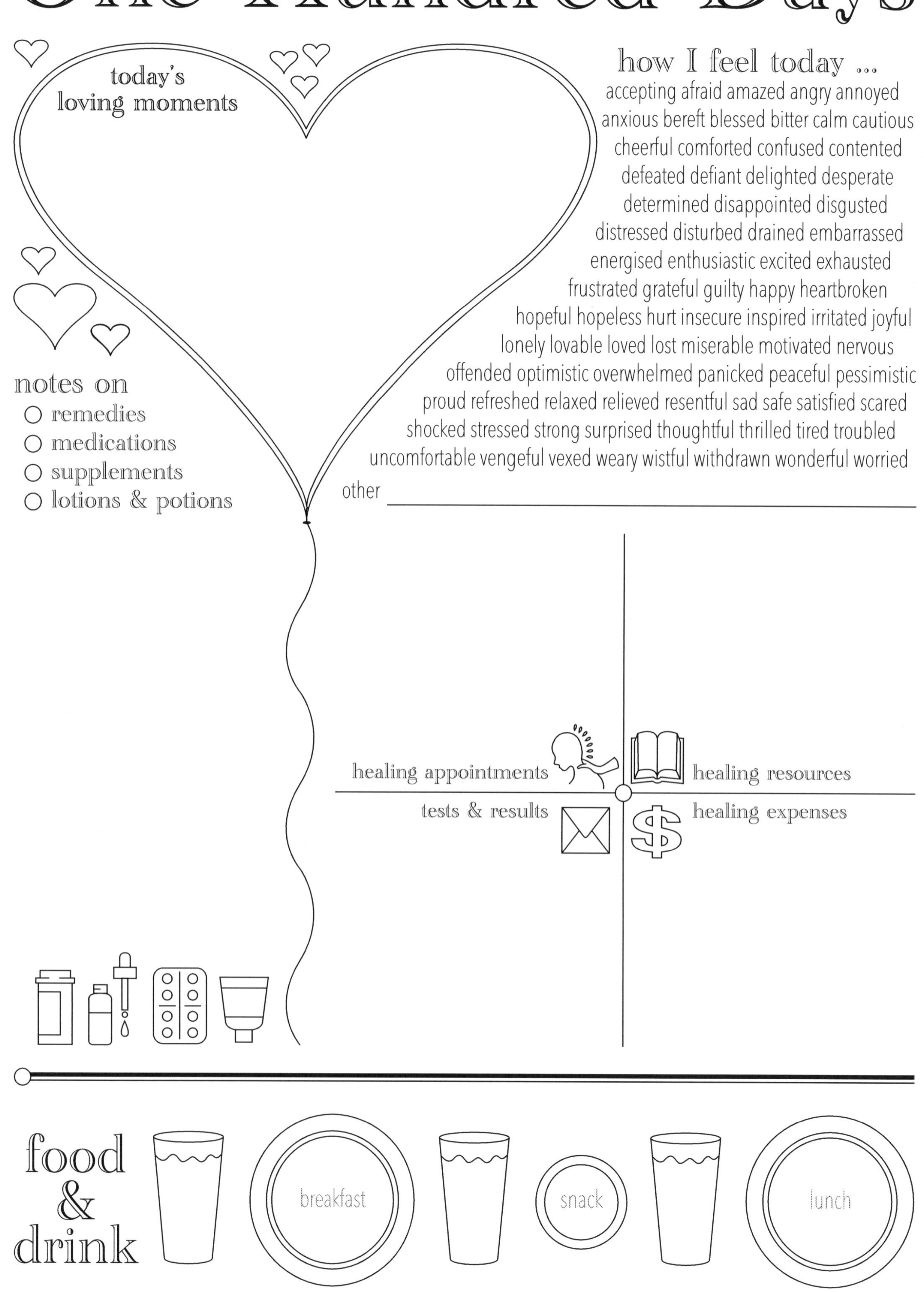

# of Healing

physical activity

social activity

screen time

resting time

connections with nature

wondering & wandering thoughts

snack

dinner

day 84

midnight

1am

2am

3am

4am

5am

6am

7am

8am

9am

10am

11am

midday

1pm

2pm

3pm

4pm

5pm

6pm

7pm

8pm

9pm

10pm

11pm

midnight

date:

One Hundred Days

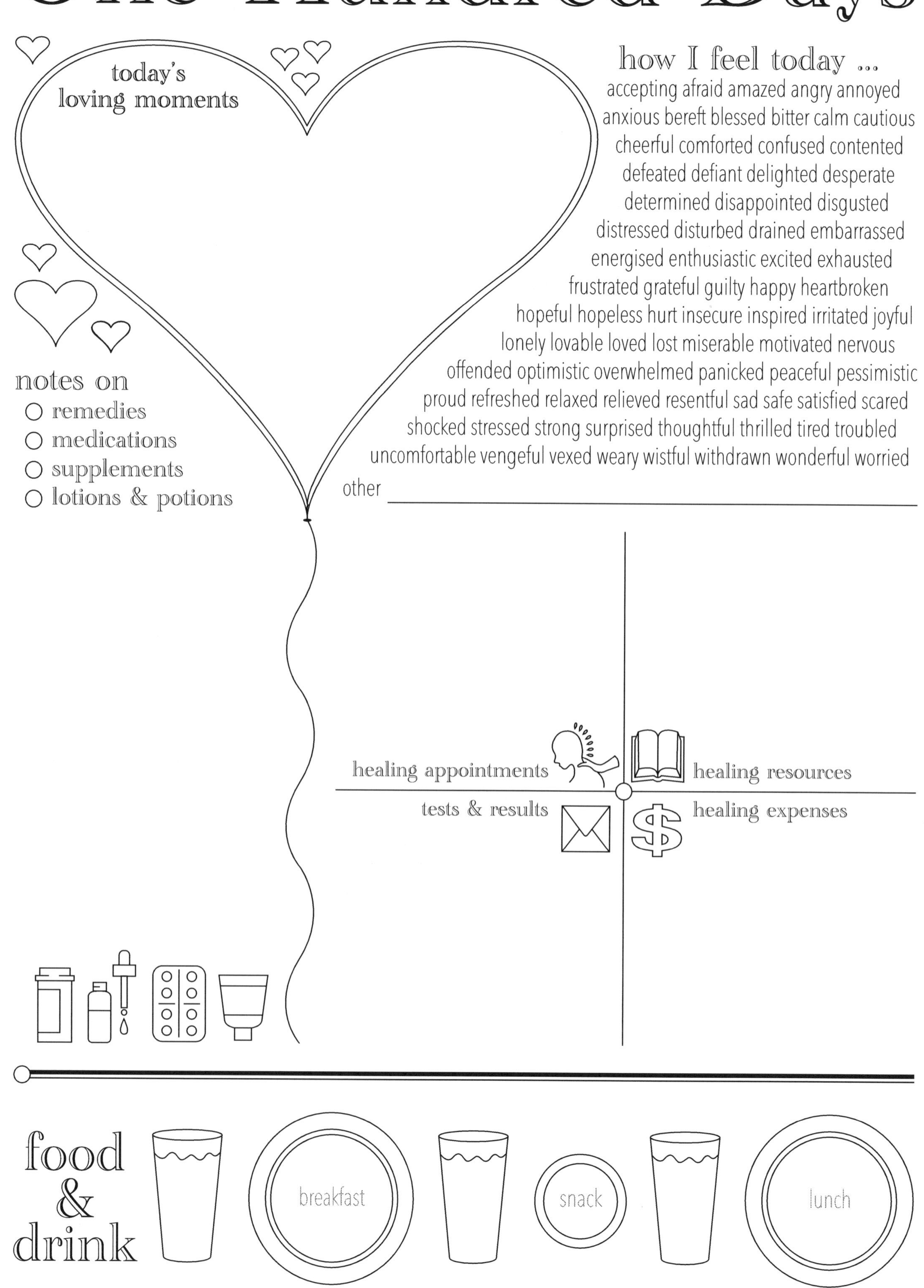

# of Healing

physical activity

social activity

screen time

resting time

connections with nature

wondering & wandering thoughts

snack

dinner

day 85

midnight

1am

2am

3am

4am

5am

6am

7am

8am

9am

10am

11am

midday

1pm

2pm

3pm

4pm

5pm

6pm

7pm

8pm

9pm

10pm

11pm

midnight

date:

One Hundred Days

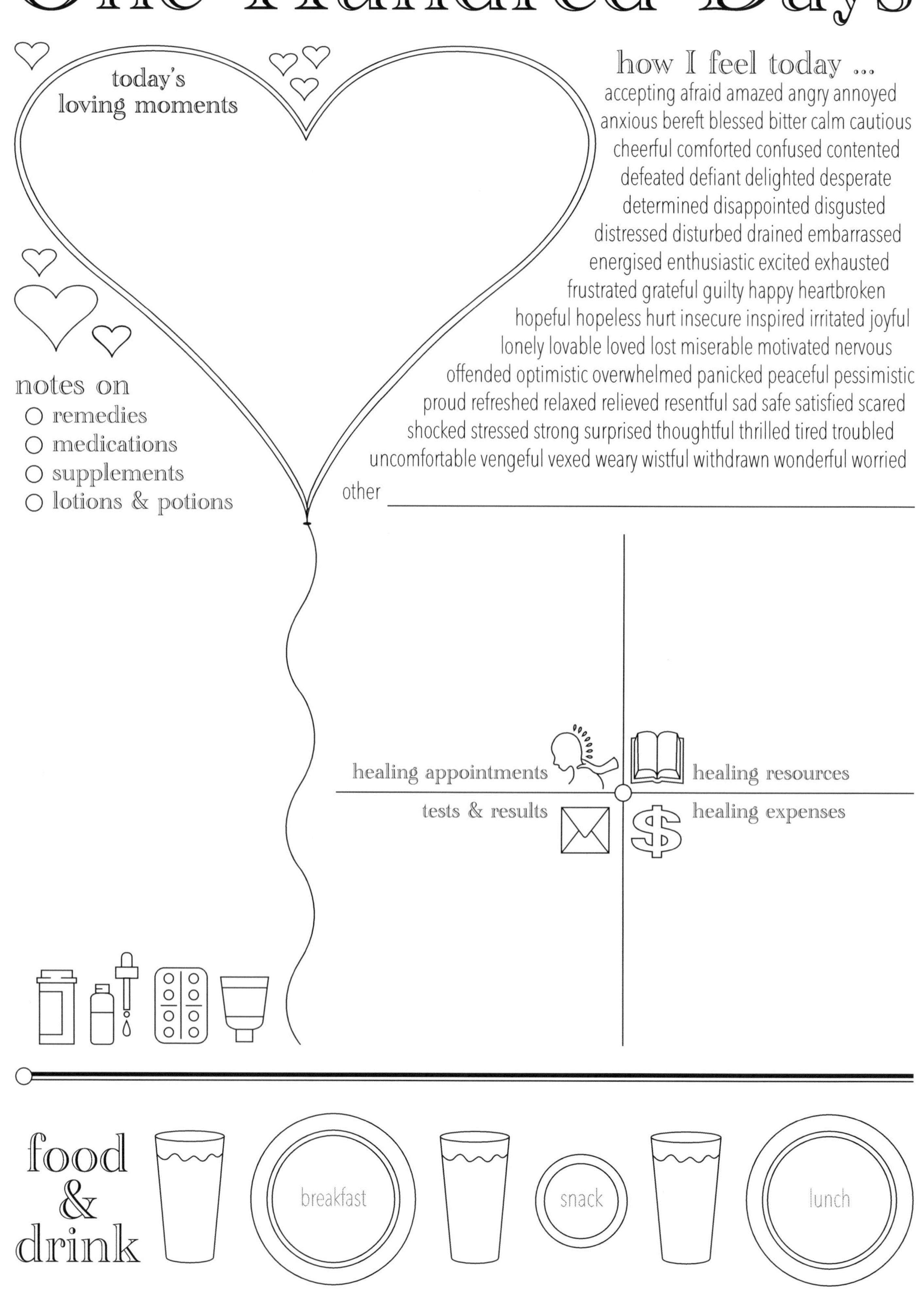

food & drink

breakfast

snack

lunch

# of Healing

physical activity

social activity

screen time

resting time

connections with nature

wondering & wandering thoughts

snack

dinner

day 86

midnight

1am

2am

3am

4am

5am

6am

7am

8am

9am

10am

11am

midday

1pm

2pm

3pm

4pm

5pm

6pm

7pm

8pm

9pm

10pm

11pm

midnight

date:

One Hundred Days

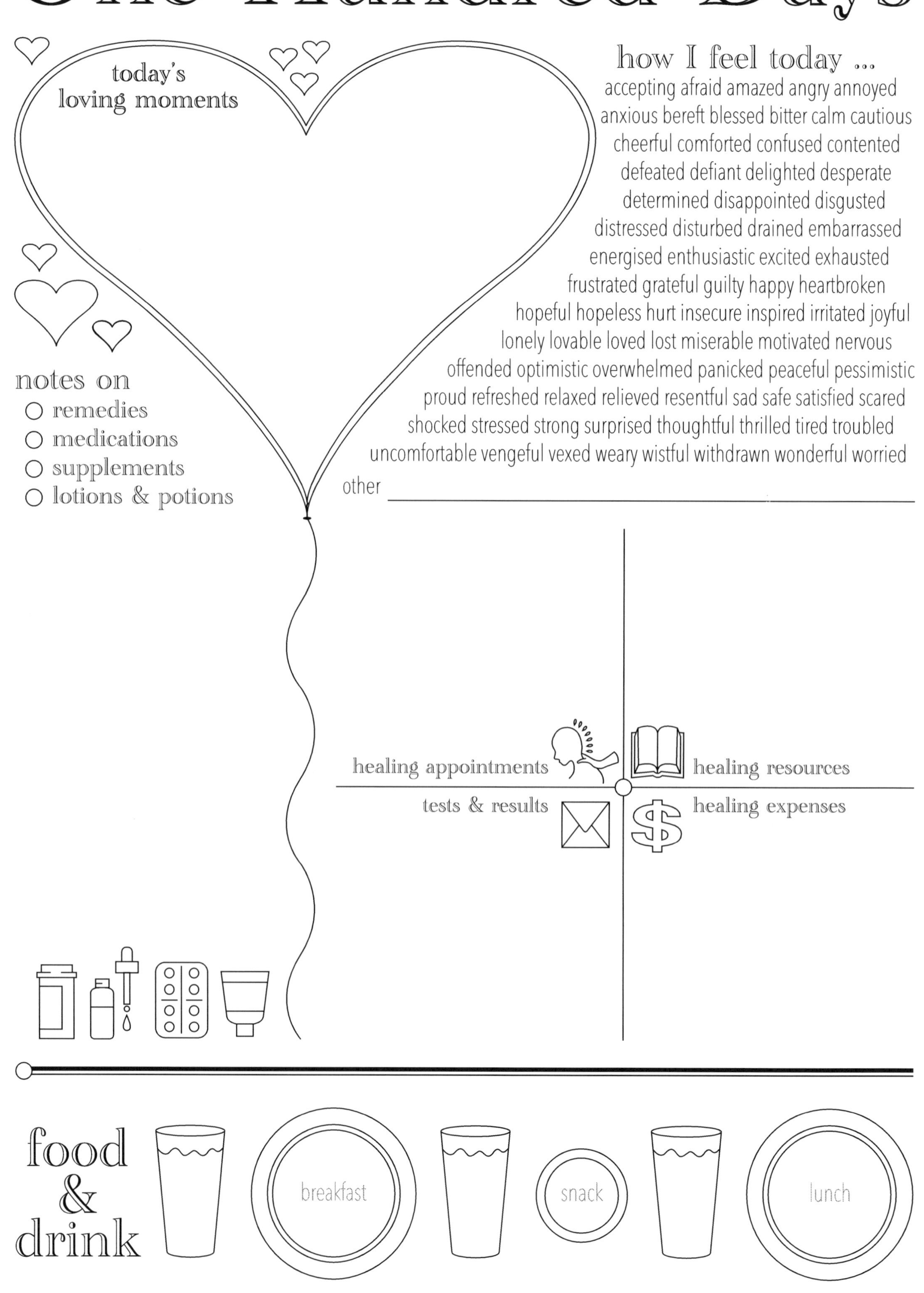

food & drink

breakfast

snack

lunch

# of Healing

physical activity

social activity

screen time

resting time

connections with nature

wondering & wandering thoughts

snack

dinner

day 87

midnight

1am

2am

3am

4am

5am

6am

7am

8am

9am

10am

11am

midday

1pm

2pm

3pm

4pm

5pm

6pm

7pm

8pm

9pm

10pm

11pm

midnight

date:

One Hundred Days

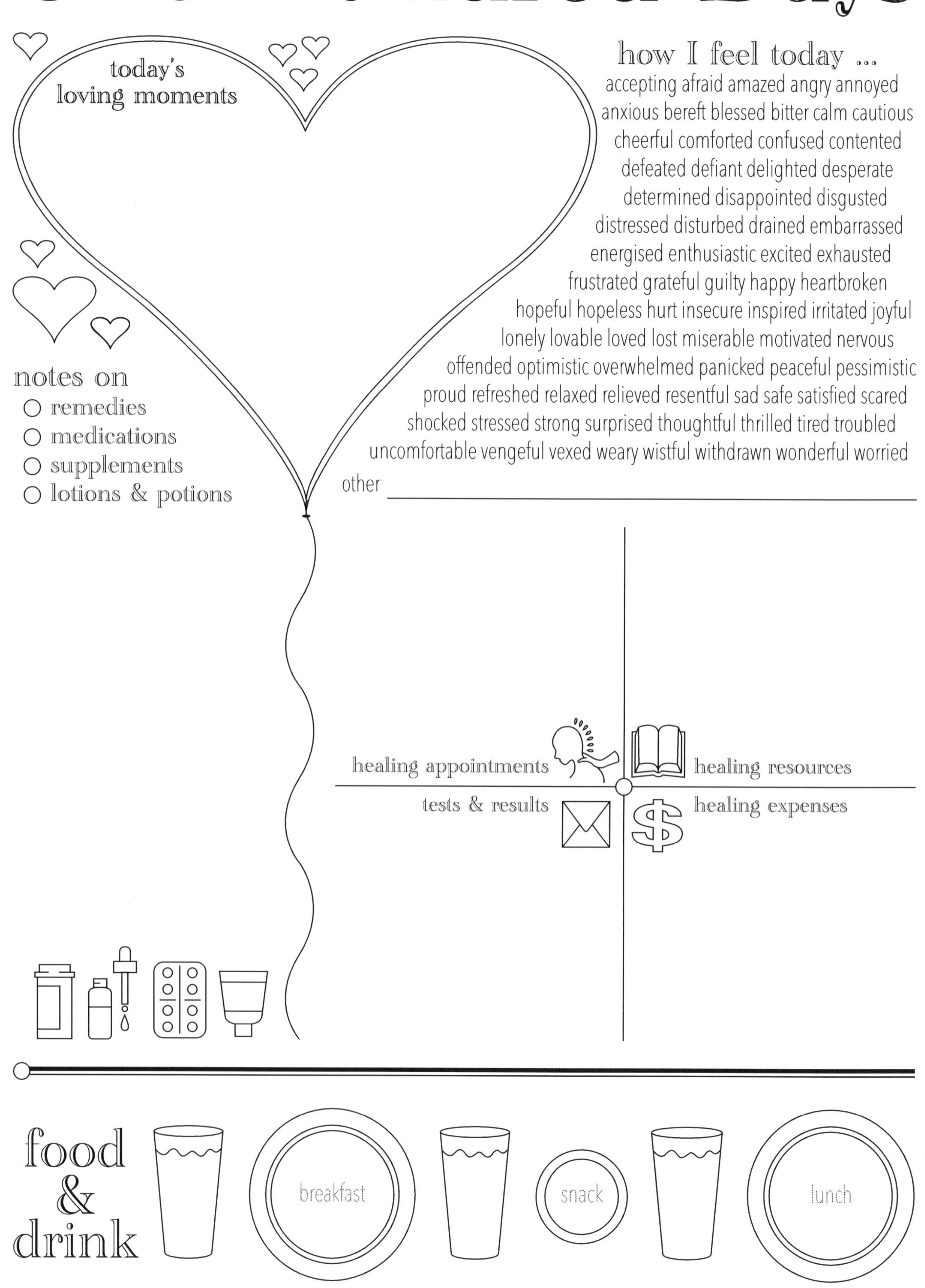

# of Healing

physical activity

social activity

screen time

resting time

connections with nature

wondering & wandering thoughts

snack

dinner

day 88

midnight

1am

2am

3am

4am

5am

6am

7am

8am

9am

10am

11am

midday

1pm

2pm

3pm

4pm

5pm

6pm

7pm

8pm

9pm

10pm

11pm

midnight

date:

One Hundred Days

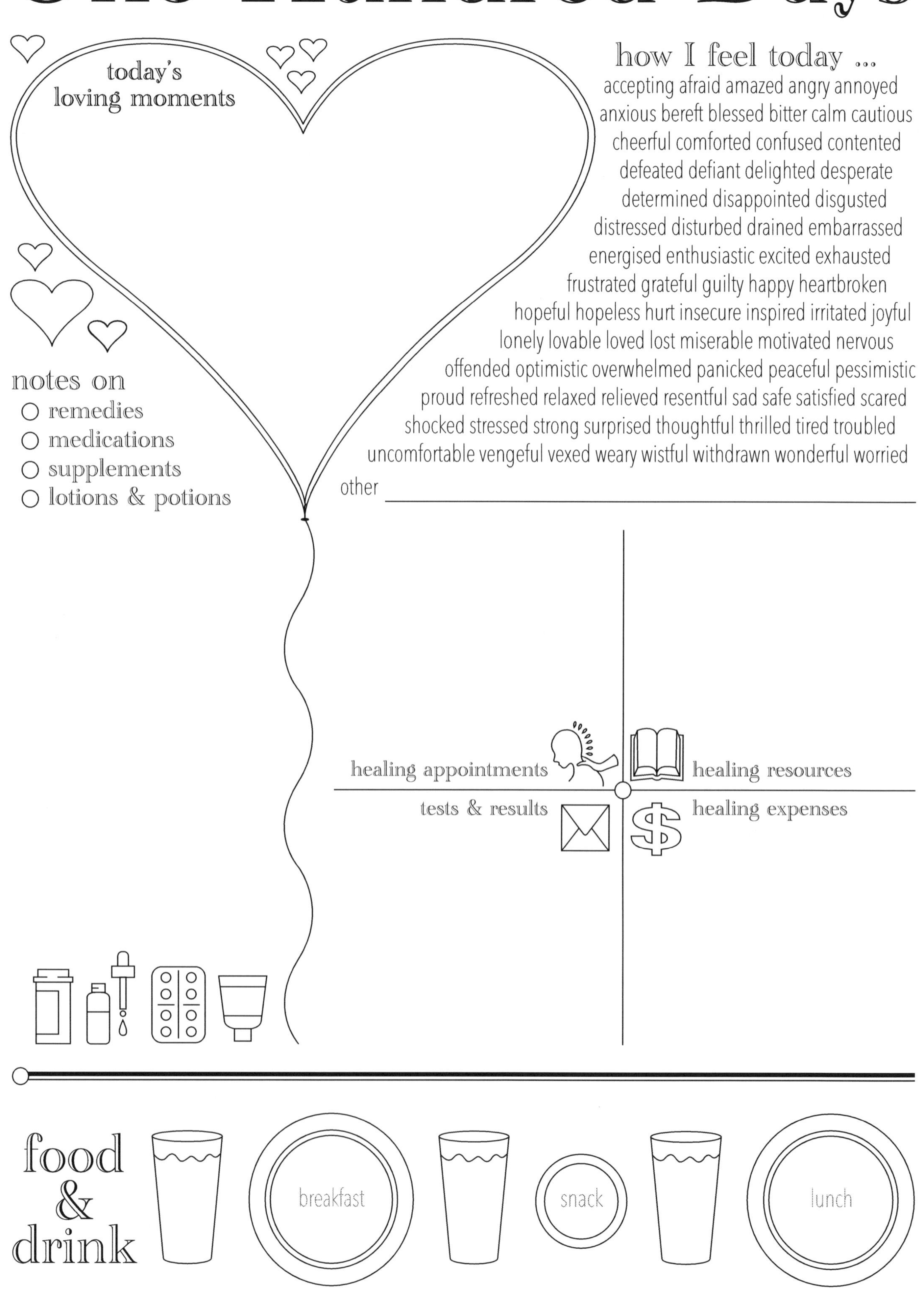

# of Healing

physical activity

social activity

screen time

resting time

connections with nature

wondering & wandering thoughts

snack

dinner

day 89

midnight

1am

2am

3am

4am

5am

6am

7am

8am

9am

10am

11am

midday

1pm

2pm

3pm

4pm

5pm

6pm

7pm

8pm

9pm

10pm

11pm

midnight

date:

One Hundred Days

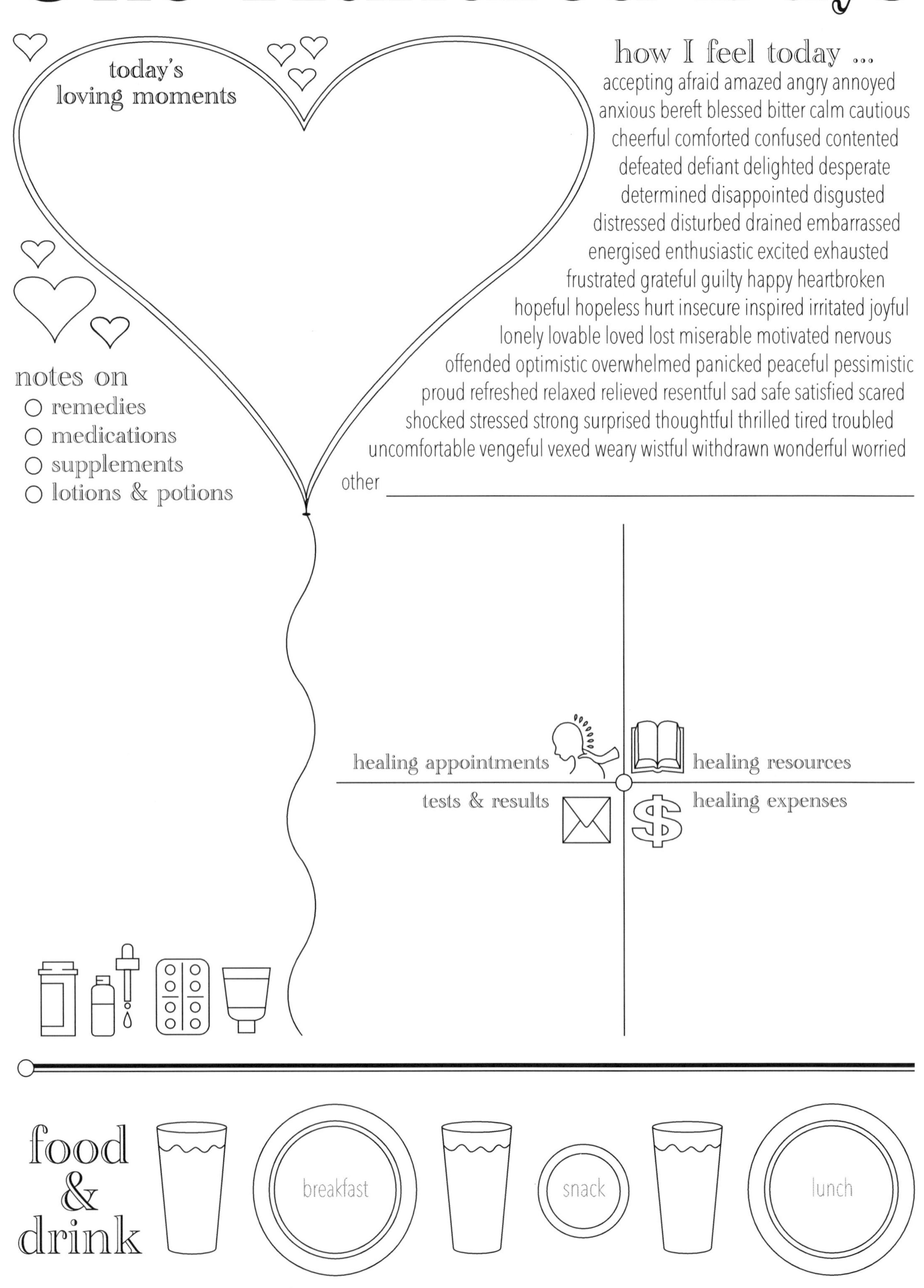

# of Healing

physical activity

social activity

screen time

resting time

connections with nature

wondering & wandering thoughts

snack

dinner

day 90

midnight

1am

2am

3am

4am

5am

6am

7am

8am

9am

10am

11am

midday

1pm

2pm

3pm

4pm

5pm

6pm

7pm

8pm

9pm

10pm

11pm

midnight

date:

One Hundred Days

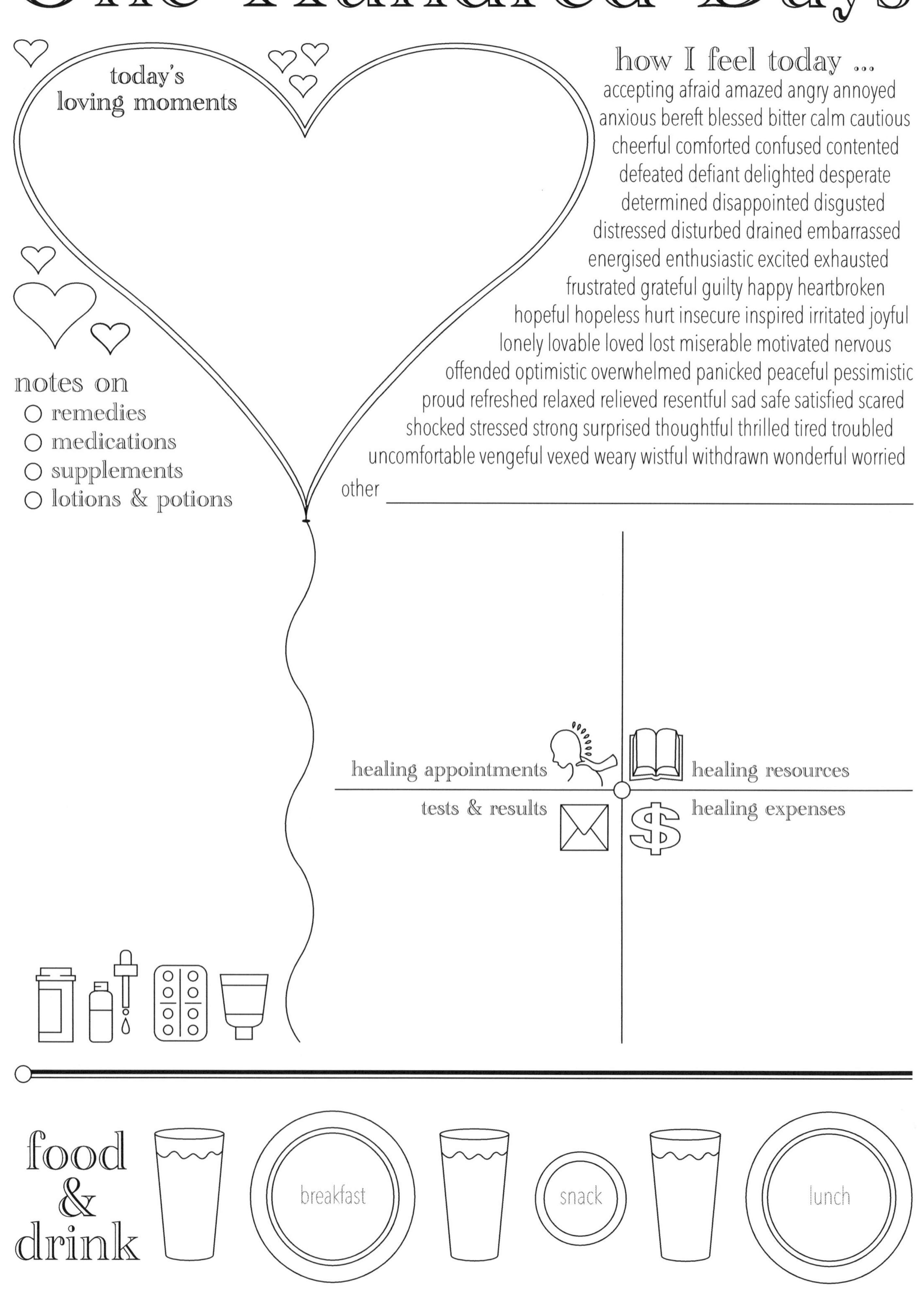

food & drink

breakfast

snack

lunch

# of Healing

physical activity

social activity

screen time

resting time

connections with nature

wondering & wandering thoughts

snack

dinner

day 91

midnight

1am

2am

3am

4am

5am

6am

7am

8am

9am

10am

11am

midday

1pm

2pm

3pm

4pm

5pm

6pm

7pm

8pm

9pm

10pm

11pm

midnight

date:

One Hundred Days

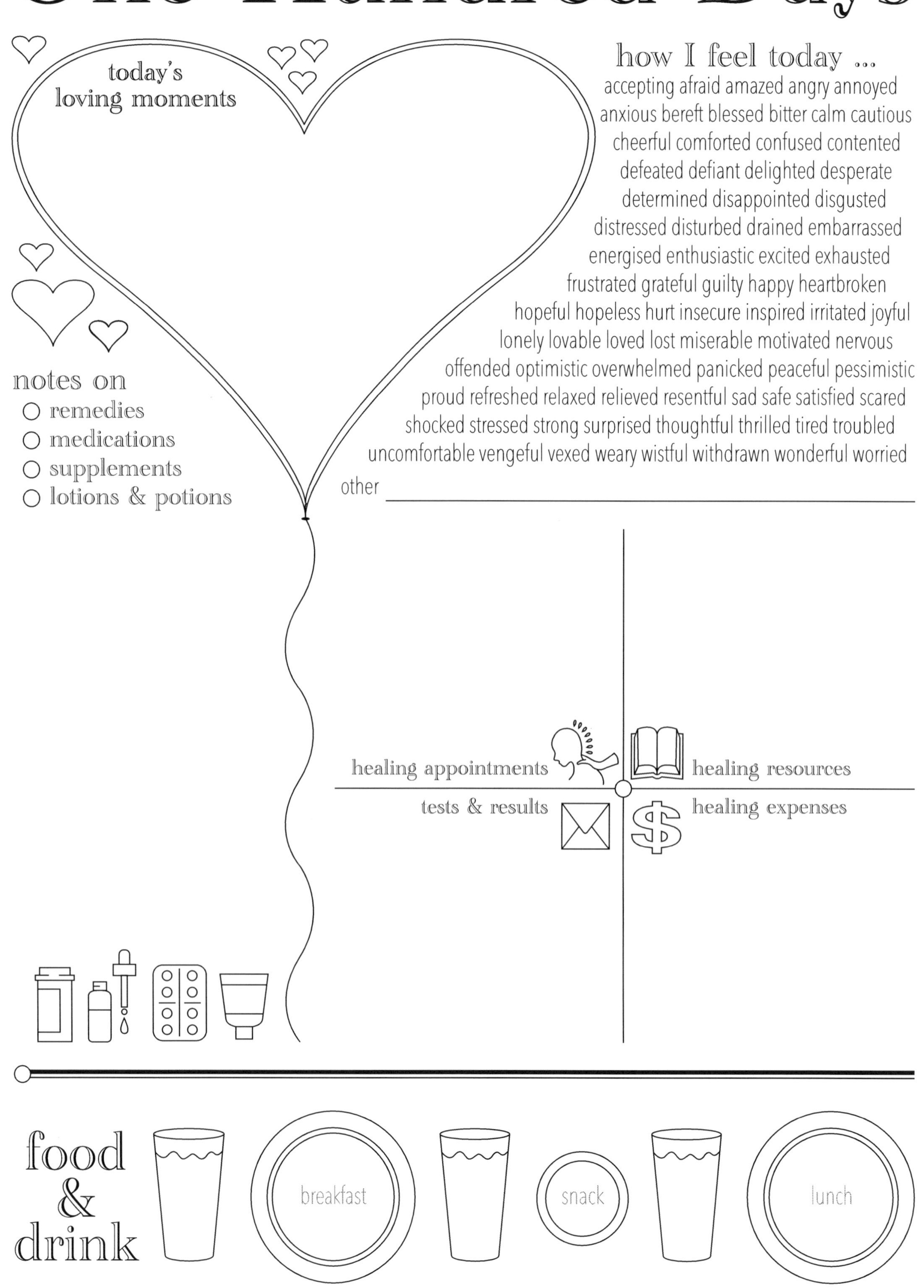

today's loving moments

how I feel today ...

accepting afraid amazed angry annoyed
anxious bereft blessed bitter calm cautious
cheerful comforted confused contented
defeated defiant delighted desperate
determined disappointed disgusted
distressed disturbed drained embarrassed
energised enthusiastic excited exhausted
frustrated grateful guilty happy heartbroken
hopeful hopeless hurt insecure inspired irritated joyful
lonely lovable loved lost miserable motivated nervous
offended optimistic overwhelmed panicked peaceful pessimistic
proud refreshed relaxed relieved resentful sad safe satisfied scared
shocked stressed strong surprised thoughtful thrilled tired troubled
uncomfortable vengeful vexed weary wistful withdrawn wonderful worried

other ______________________________

notes on

- ○ remedies
- ○ medications
- ○ supplements
- ○ lotions & potions

healing appointments

healing resources

tests & results

healing expenses

food & drink

breakfast

snack

lunch

# of Healing

physical activity

social activity

screen time

resting time

connections with nature

wondering & wandering thoughts

snack

dinner

day 92

midnight

1am

2am

3am

4am

5am

6am

7am

8am

9am

10am

11am

midday

1pm

2pm

3pm

4pm

5pm

6pm

7pm

8pm

9pm

10pm

11pm

midnight

date:

One Hundred Days

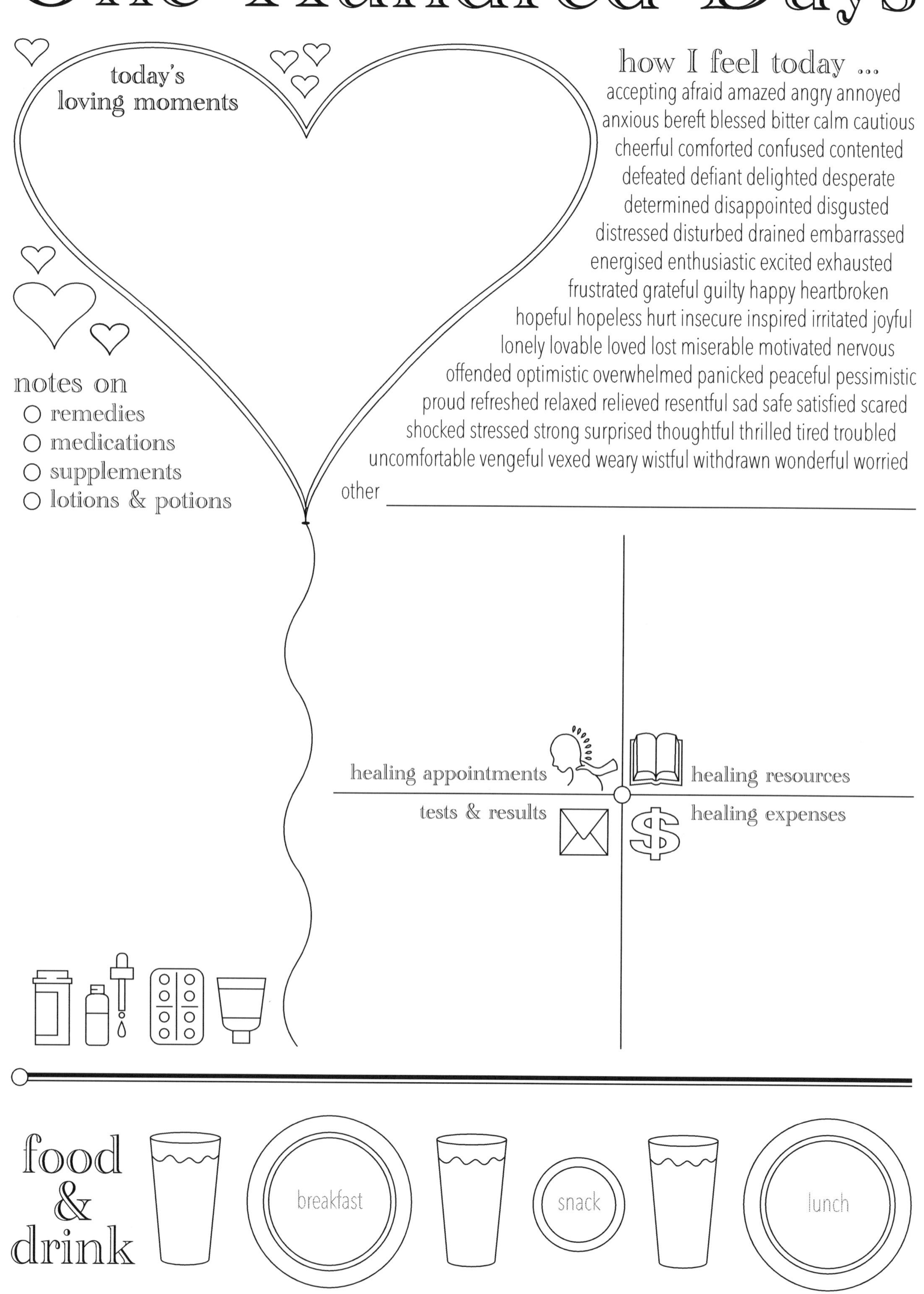

# of Healing

physical activity

social activity

screen time

resting time

connections with nature

wondering & wandering thoughts

snack

dinner

day 93

midnight

1am

2am

3am

4am

5am

6am

7am

8am

9am

10am

11am

midday

1pm

2pm

3pm

4pm

5pm

6pm

7pm

8pm

9pm

10pm

11pm

midnight

date:

One Hundred Days

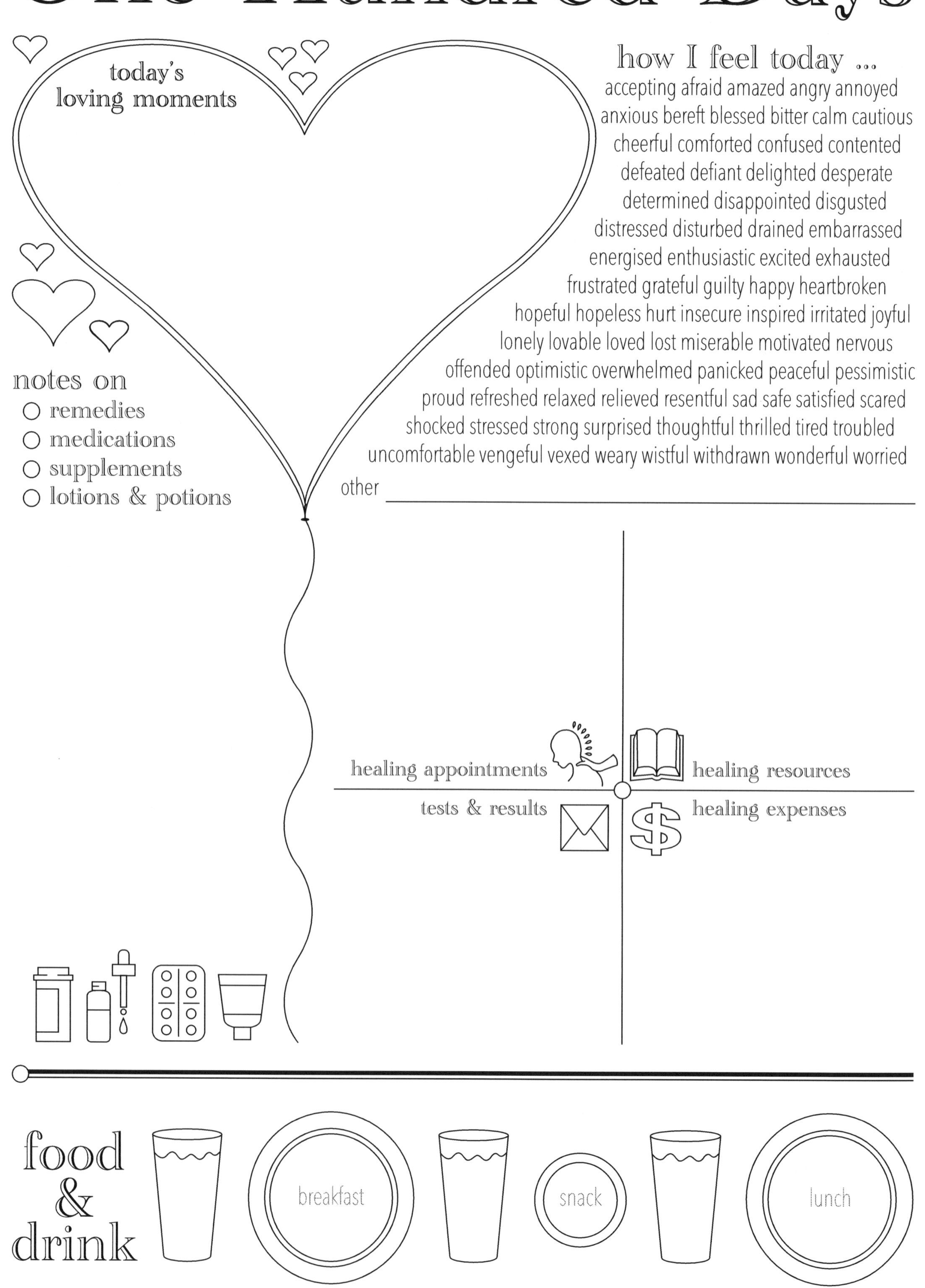

# of Healing

physical activity

social activity

screen time

resting time

connections with nature

wondering & wandering thoughts

snack

dinner

day 94

midnight

1am

2am

3am

4am

5am

6am

7am

8am

9am

10am

11am

midday

1pm

2pm

3pm

4pm

5pm

6pm

7pm

8pm

9pm

10pm

11pm

midnight

date:

One Hundred Days

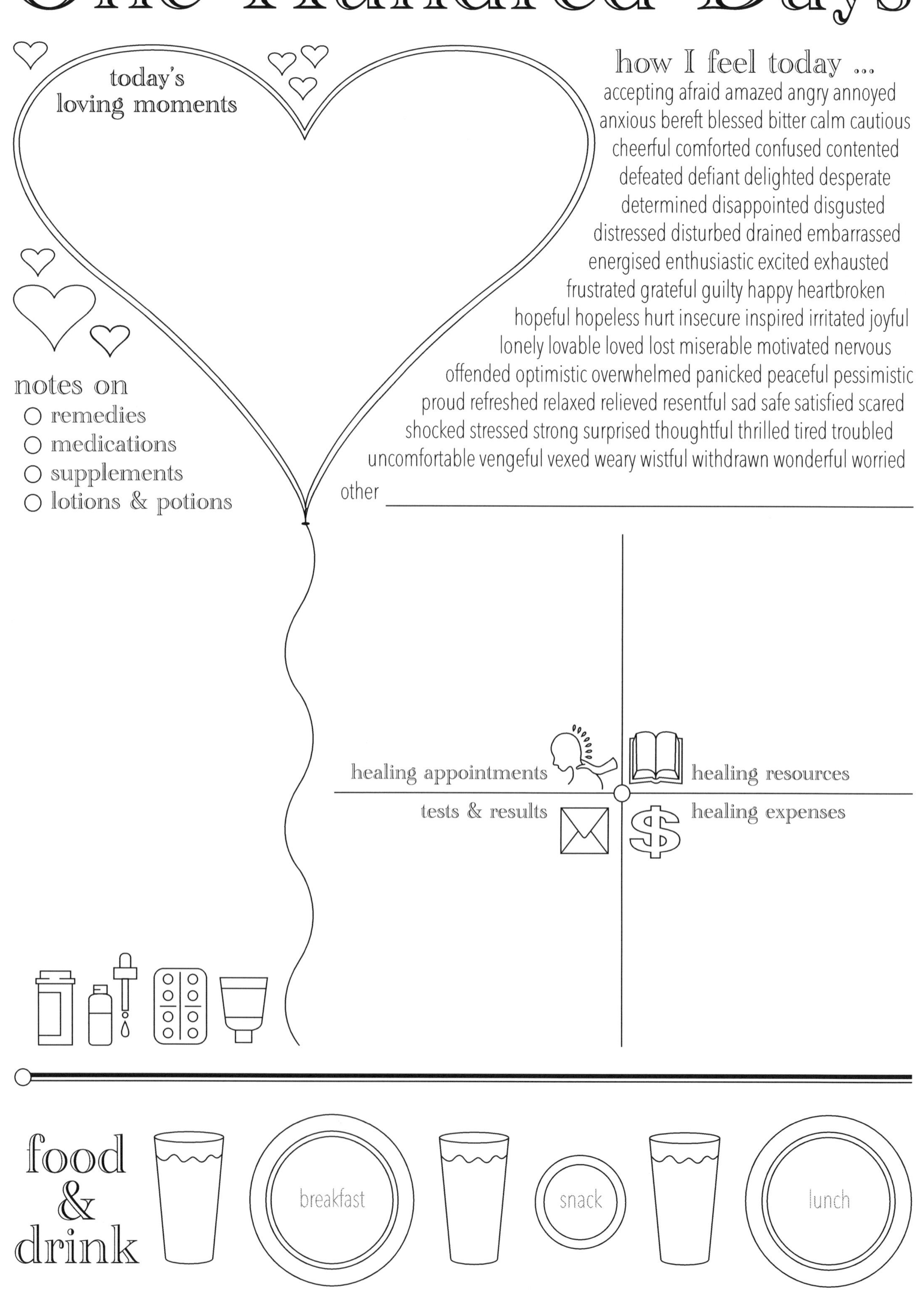

# of Healing

physical activity

social activity

screen time

resting time

connections with nature

wondering & wandering thoughts

snack

dinner

day 95

midnight

1am

2am

3am

4am

5am

6am

7am

8am

9am

10am

11am

midday

1pm

2pm

3pm

4pm

5pm

6pm

7pm

8pm

9pm

10pm

11pm

midnight

date:

One Hundred Days

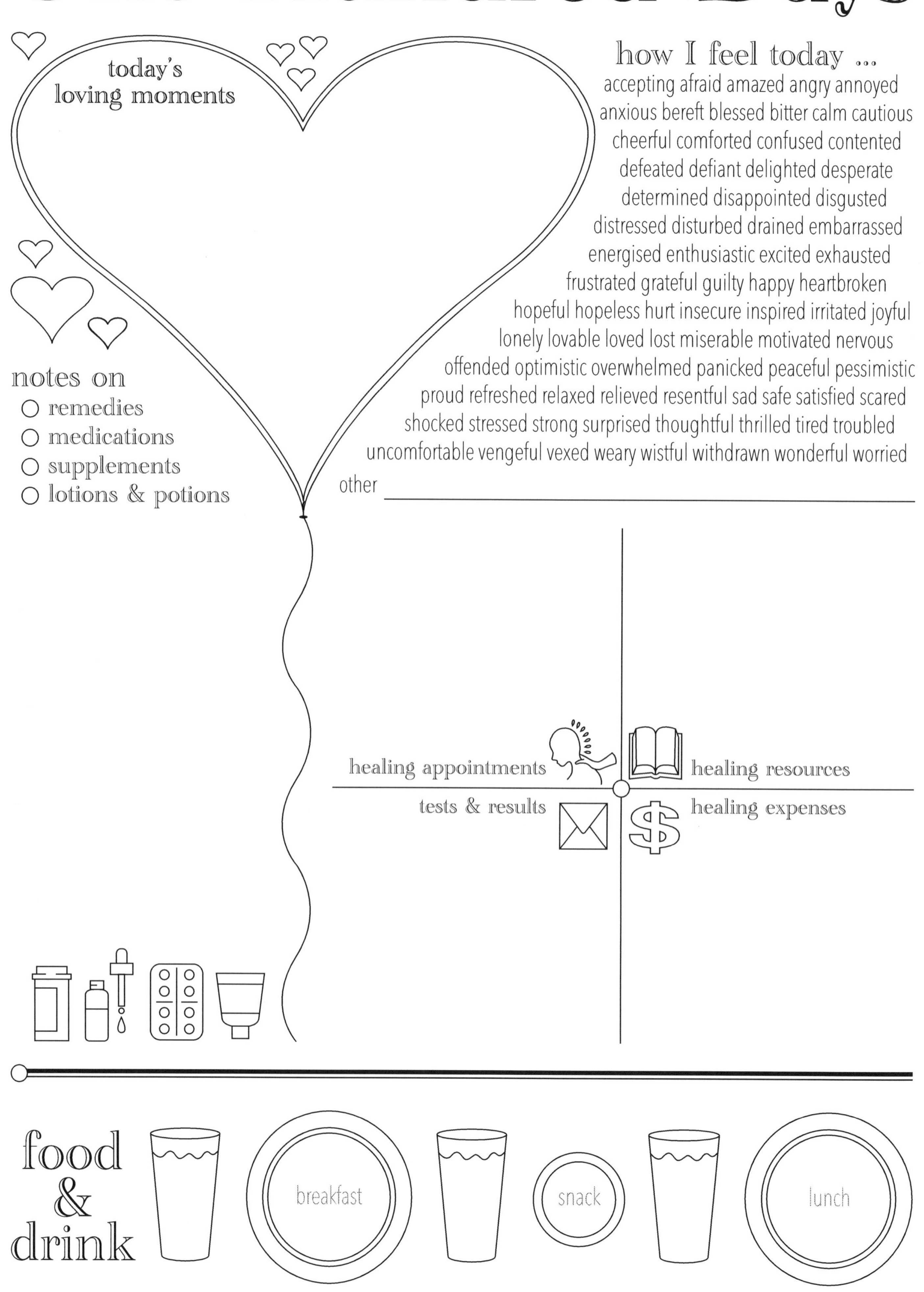

# of Healing

physical activity

social activity

screen time

resting time

connections with nature

wondering & wandering thoughts

snack

dinner

day 96

midnight

1am

2am

3am

4am

5am

6am

7am

8am

9am

10am

11am

midday

1pm

2pm

3pm

4pm

5pm

6pm

7pm

8pm

9pm

10pm

11pm

midnight

date:

One Hundred Days

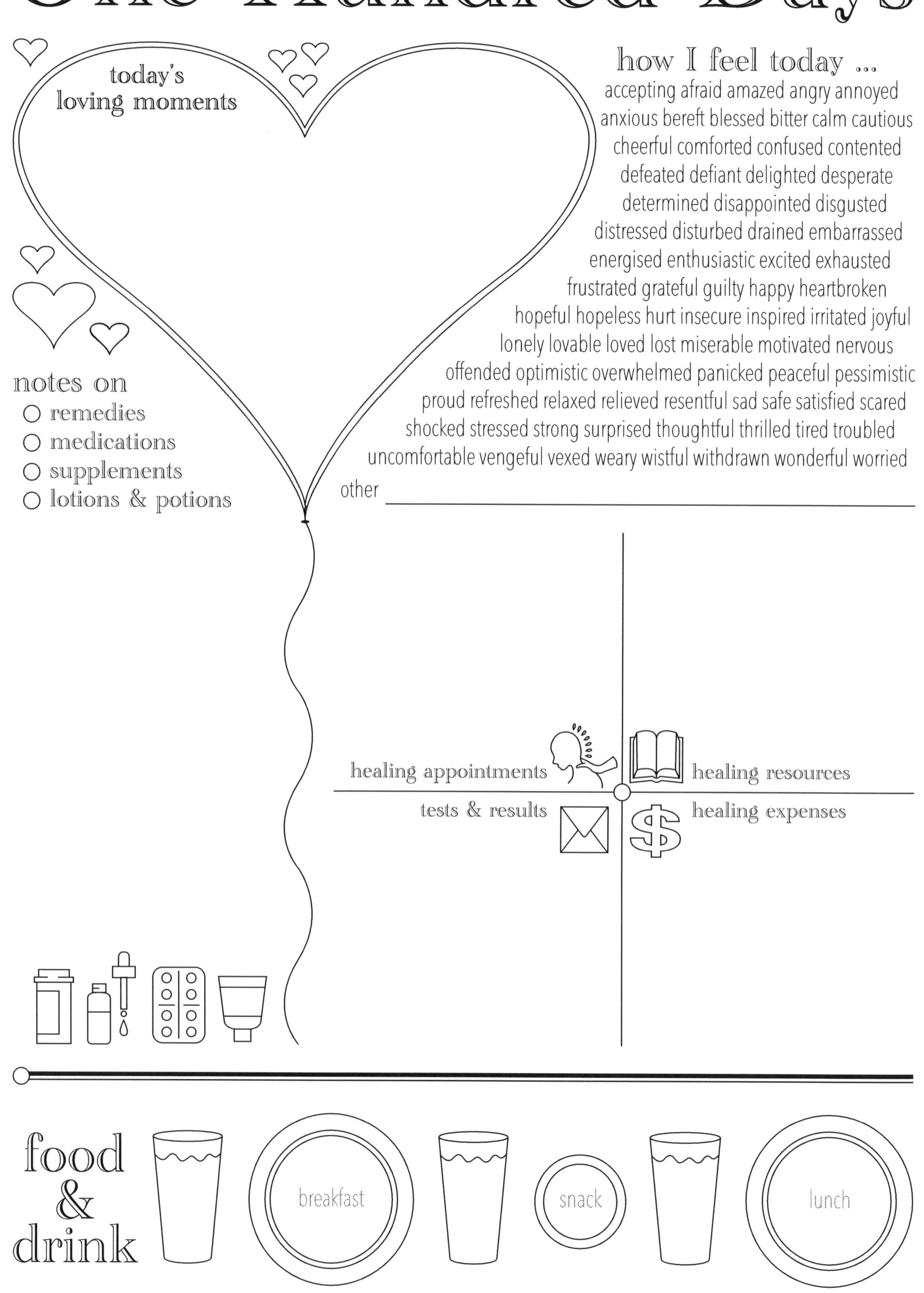

# of Healing

physical activity

social activity

screen time

resting time

connections with nature

wondering & wandering thoughts

snack

dinner

day 97

midnight

1am

2am

3am

4am

5am

6am

7am

8am

9am

10am

11am

midday

1pm

2pm

3pm

4pm

5pm

6pm

7pm

8pm

9pm

10pm

11pm

midnight

date:

One Hundred Days

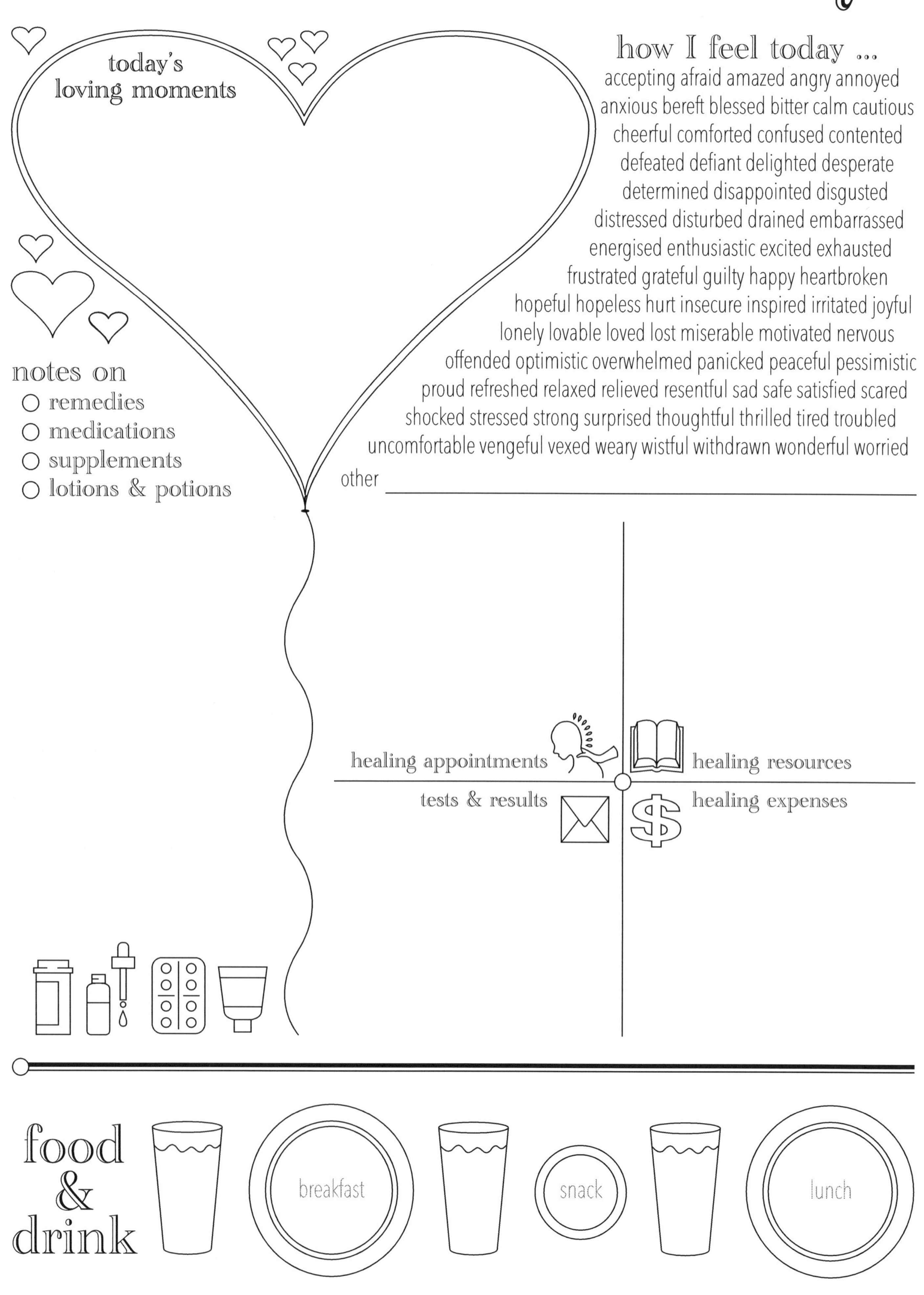

food & drink

breakfast

snack

lunch

# of Healing

physical activity

social activity

screen time

resting time

connections with nature

wondering & wandering thoughts

snack

dinner

day 98

midnight

1am

2am

3am

4am

5am

6am

7am

8am

9am

10am

11am

midday

1pm

2pm

3pm

4pm

5pm

6pm

7pm

8pm

9pm

10pm

11pm

midnight

date:

One Hundred Days

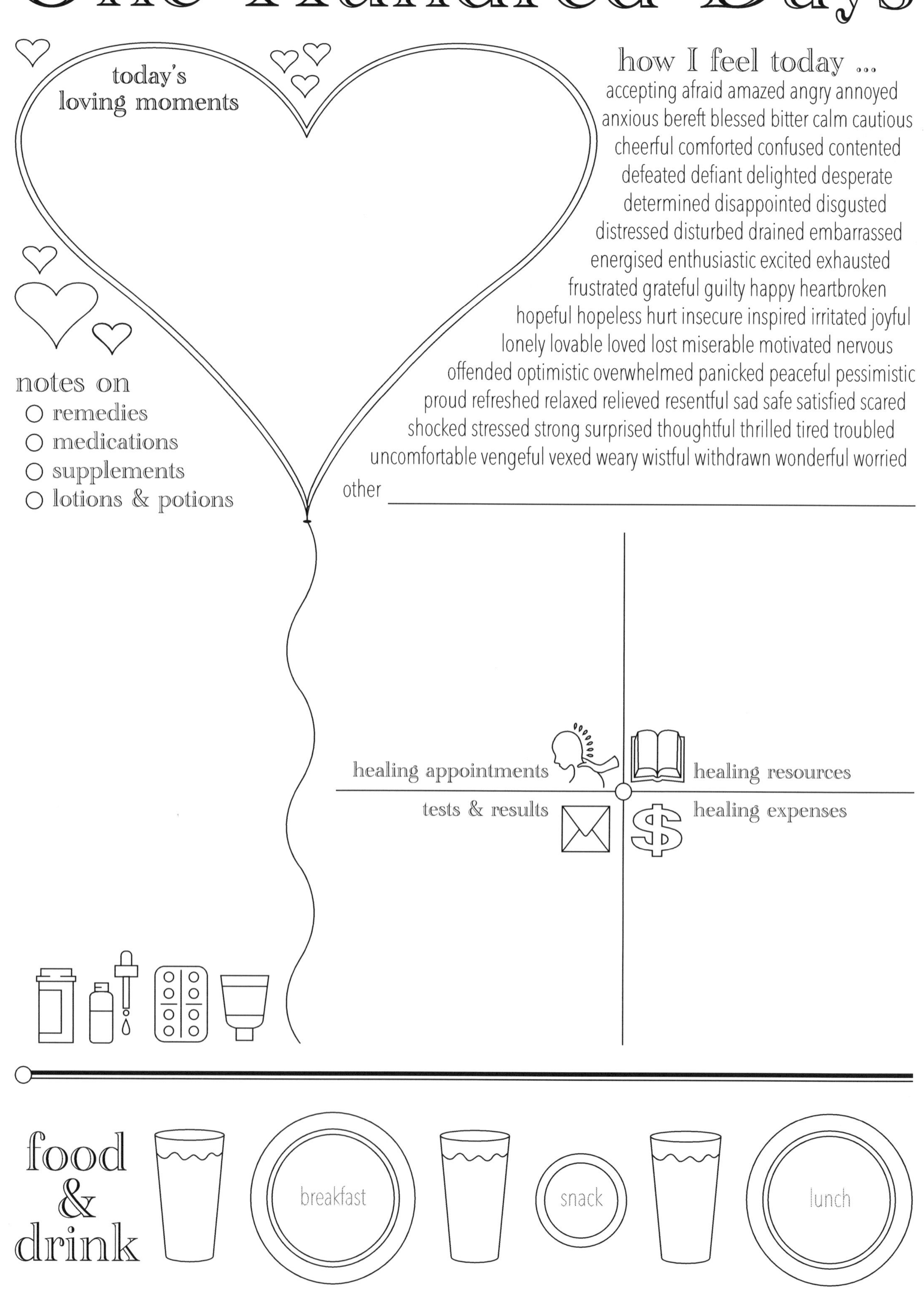

# of Healing

physical activity

social activity

screen time

resting time

connections with nature

wondering & wandering thoughts

snack

dinner

day 99

midnight

1am

2am

3am

4am

5am

6am

7am

8am

9am

10am

11am

midday

1pm

2pm

3pm

4pm

5pm

6pm

7pm

8pm

9pm

10pm

11pm

midnight

date:

One Hundred Days

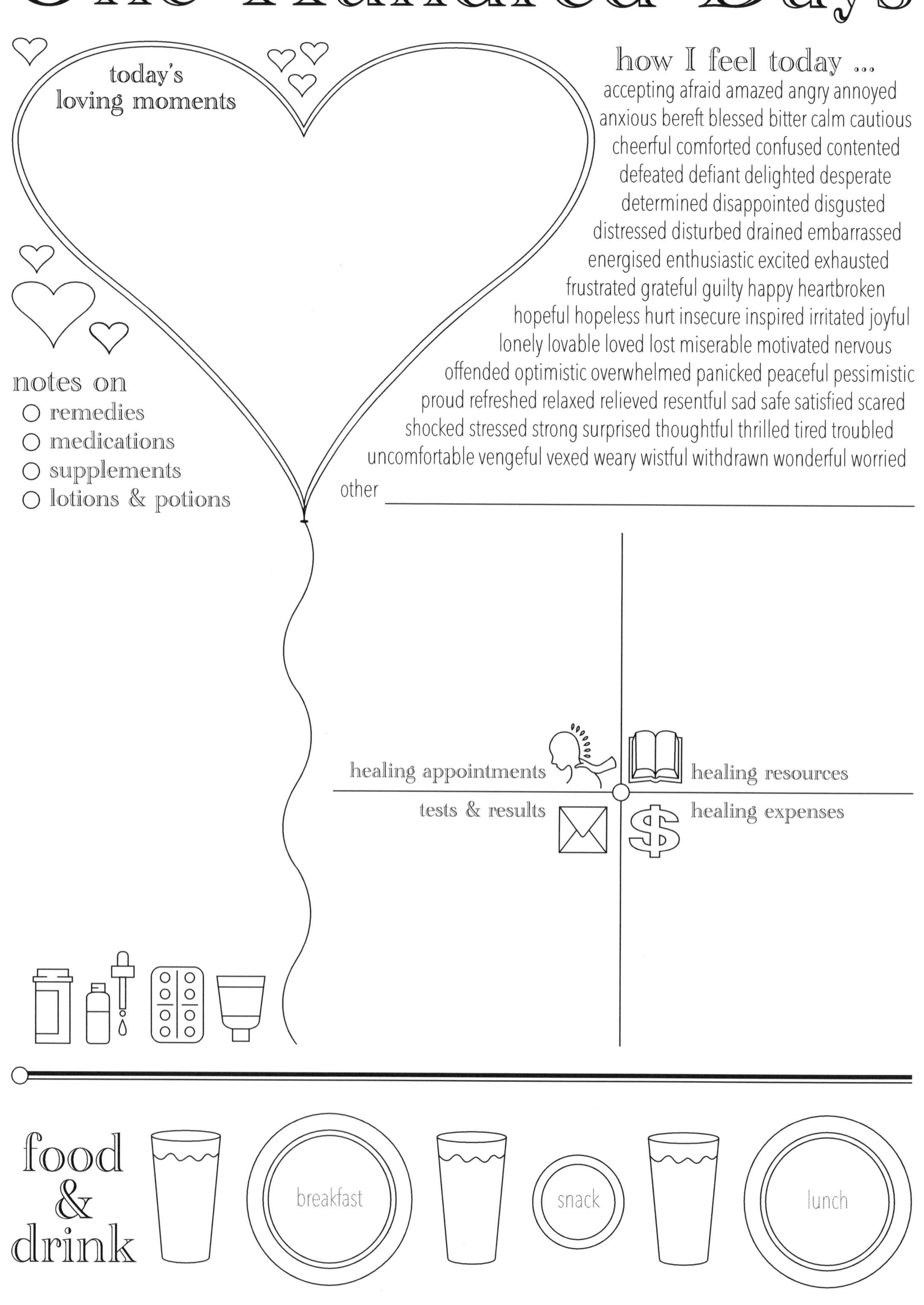

# of Healing

day 100

physical activity

social activity

screen time

resting time

connections with nature

wondering & wandering thoughts

snack

dinner

midnight

1am

2am

3am

4am

5am

6am

7am

8am

9am

10am

11am

midday

1pm

2pm

3pm

4pm

5pm

6pm

7pm

8pm

9pm

10pm

11pm

midnight

date:

Why I created this workbook

I happen to have experienced more than the average person's share of challenging, life-altering events.

I've had my life turned upside down on several occasions, usually without any warning or say in the upheaval that ensued. It's been an ongoing pattern for me, starting from childhood, and continuing well into adulthood, when I got married and divorced twice and had a number of other less than happy relationships. I have dealt with multiple serious, life-threatening physical health conditions starting from when I was a teen, yet have lived an incredibly active and joyful life, which included the wonderful adventure of making Japan my home for fifteen years. I became a dedicated volunteer during the decade after the 2011 tsunami, regularly spending months at a time living within a remote Japanese community that had been severely impacted. While I am yet to experience the inevitable death of a loved one, I have said goodbye to two beloved canine companions – and discovered that the grief of losing a pet goes on long, long after that moment when they take their last little breath in your arms.

Life changed every single time.

Despite all that, I have a huge smile and a naughty sense of humour. I have developed the ability to laugh at what life has thrown at me, and I love to spread joy. If I can make people smile through their own tears, if I can help someone's pain feel just that bit more manageable, then I can find meaning in my own difficulties.

For years I have written and spoken publicly about pain, abuse, trauma, recovery, and healing. I frequently hear from people who are utterly lost while dealing with their own challenges. Getting rid of an abusive partner, finally getting a diagnosis, or having major surgery is difficult enough – what happens afterwards is another thing altogether. You're not necessarily just rebuilding the day-to-day realities of your life – you might be rebuilding your career, your savings, your friendship circle, your confidence, your identity, perhaps even your faith in humanity. Our culture expects us to get back to work/exercise/family/routine as soon as possible after a life-altering event. We are expected to keep the money coming in and the bills paid. To just get on with it.

When "just getting on with it" was no longer an option for me, I learned about all sorts of different tools that could help me. I learned from healers who crossed my path, sometimes in unexpected places. I learned from both modern and traditional practitioners and philosophies. I learned from deep, intense conversations and casually spoken, sometimes flippant, words. And I learned from the people in the small town of Oshika, Japan, for whom life will never, ever be the same again.

When I was able to let go of the sorrowful desire to have things back the way they used to be, when I was ready to emerge from all the panic and pain, when I was willing to accept and adjust – that was when I could actually start creating a new life, bit by bit.

It took a lot of effort. Conscious effort. Every single day.

None of these tools are new. There are countless books, websites, videos, and professionals dedicated to all of them. But even engaging with those can feel overwhelming and be just too much effort when life has really knocked you down. I wanted to create something simple that gently addressed each of the tools that can be useful for those of us who need to heal. Those of us who are rebuilding our lives after trauma, perhaps not for the first time. Those of us who have been expected to "just get on with it" but for whom that's not working and may even be making things worse. Those of us who have been knocked down, can't get up, and actually aren't even sure that we want to. I want to help you lift your head up off the ground and face life again. I want to help you heal.

Please let this book be an excuse to focus on your healing. Please give yourself permission to heal.

What a beautiful thing it would be if we all gave ourselves permission to spend time actively healing. To make healing our absolute priority. To dedicate time, each and every day, to healing – maybe even the occasional whole day if we felt like it. Maybe consecutive days, maybe days here and there. Can you imagine what the world would be like if we all spent one hundred days healing?

I think the world needs us to do that right now.

Caroline Pover
March 3, 2023

Made in the USA
Columbia, SC
13 March 2023